understanding
journalism

Never have the media been so critically regarded as at the present time. Documenting many areas of debate and dispute between journalists, the media, public organizations and politicians, the author identifies why conflicts will continue. Covering topics from government bias to censorship, official secrets to freedom of information and animal rights to obscenity, this highly informative work is a valuable guide to all those involved in journalism and the media.

John Wilson is a freelance media consultant. He has wide journalistic experience in both radio and television and was formerly editorial policy controller for the BBC.

understanding journalism

a guide to issues

john wilson

london and new york

First published 1996
by Routledge
11 New Fetter Lane, London EC4P 4EE

Simultaneously published in the USA and Canada
by Routledge
29 West 35th Street, New York, NY 10001

Routledge is an International Thomson Publishing company

Typeset in Sabon by LaserScript, Mitcham, Surrey
Printed and bound in Great Britain by
Clays Ltd, St Ives PLC

British Library Cataloguing in Publication Data
A catalogue record for this book is available from the British Library

Library of Congress Cataloguing in Publication Data
A catalogue record for this book has been requested

ISBN 0–415–11598–1
ISBN 0–415–11599–X (pbk)

to my wife Anne
and to journalists everywhere,
including the bad ones,
who are endlessly stimulating

contents

preface

The idea was to pass on what had taken more than thirty years to acquire. The result is a critical celebration of journalism. Many of the insights from a life as reporter and editor were gained enjoyably, many others were struggled for, some were the outcome of disagreeable pressures, none the offspring of indifference or boredom, all the work of challenging experiences.

Writing the book was satisfying. Arranging the order of it was a problem. The topics are tackled one by one in essay form, each separate and identified, each written to be self-contained, able to be read without a need to refer elsewhere. Pages of continuous, flowing prose in traditional chapters were not an option because linking the wide variety of topics would have called for extreme artifice convincing to no one. A simple, easy alphabetical order had no sense of priority. So, after the introductory chapter, the topics are grouped. The identity of the groups is, to some extent, arbitrary, as are the decisions on which topics to include where. Some would have fit under several headings. A few are uneasy anywhere but deserve a place somewhere. Each group starts with either a general statement or a topic of importance. Other topics in the groups follow one another because they are connected. Where they occur alphabetically there was no good reason to put one before another.

However arranged and however approached, the pieces are meant to be easy to read and understand, of help to young people aspiring to journalism, to newcomers in the business, to interested observers and customers – the newspaper readers, television viewers and radio listeners – and perhaps even to those heavy with their own experiences of it.

John Wilson
1996

chapter one – the contest

Among the many things called into question during the Thatcher years in 1980s Britain was the tradition that government, whatever complaints it might have about television and radio programmes, did not accept editorial responsibility for broadcasting. Government and governing party, the Conservatives, initiated the attack on the tradition and right-wing national newspapers – the majority of national newspapers – encouraged it. The newspapers showed an abiding hostility to the BBC in a mixture of commercial interest and ideological conviction and they were intermittently critical also of other British broadcasters. The newspapers did not fully realise what they were doing. By the end of the 1980s they were themselves threatened by the very spirit of political criticism they had encouraged. They had helped make the idea of political interference in journalism acceptable.

The change was as subtle as it was significant. Before it, the established form of response to backbench members of parliament who criticised programmes was for the relevant minister to tell the House of Commons 'Programmes are a matter for the BBC.' The same response applied to complaints against independent television and independent radio. They were a matter for the Independent Broadcasting Authority (IBA), the regulator in those days. The tradition did not forbid government criticism of programmes. They were often so criticised and had been for as long as broadcasting had existed, but it was not the business of government to do anything about it. A few national crises had occasionally threatened the traditional approach, notably after the Egyptian leader, Colonel Nasser, nationalised the Suez canal in 1956 when the government in London considered taking over the BBC for airing critcisms of the British, French and Israeli invasion of Egypt.

The traditional attitude was to an extent a pretence because the official 'hands-off' policy was combined frequently with political pressures, often stealthy, sometimes overt. Harold Wilson, as prime minister of the Labour government during the late 1960s, tried to bring the BBC under control by appointing a former Conservative cabinet minister, Lord Hill, to chair the governors only to find Hill a vigorous defender of editorial independence, a quality he had needed while chairing the original independent television regulator, the Independent Television Authority. Many other instances of general and particular pressure by government have been attested to. The pretence was, however, important, not hollow. It said that whatever government might do it was no part of its official function to interfere with programmes any more than it was part of its official duty to interfere with newspapers.

The pretence wore thin under the prime ministership of Margaret Thatcher who had embarked on a mission for radical change to the thinking, the behaviour, the policies and the institutions of Britain. Broadcasting, in particular the BBC, was recalcitrant, badly organised, backward-looking, an encourager of the 'dependency culture' exemplified in the assumption that social problems were to be solved by government throwing money at them – an assumption kept alive, it was said, with the help of wet news programmes like *Today*, the BBC's flagship news and current affairs show at breakfast-time on Radio 4. Government complained bitterly in public and in private, and attacked the BBC about coverage of social policy, including public spending, about its treatment of the Falklands War in 1982, about its editorial attitude to the prolonged miners' strike of 1984–5, about its reporting of the American air raids on Libya launched from bases in Britain in 1986, about coverage of the troubles in Northern Ireland, about dramas based on real-life incidents, about violence, sex and swearing, and an endless list of other programme failings over the years. In addition, Thatcherites complained, the BBC did not earn its living in the market. It was bloated on a tax, the licence fee. It should be split up, made to take advertising and compete as best it could with the commercial newcomers of satellite and cable who paid their own way in the world.

When the government was not active in 'broadcaster bashing', Conservative party headquarters were and whoever took the lead, Conservative-friendly, right-wing newspapers joined in vehemently. Hardly a week went by without denunciations of the journalism and general programme making of the BBC. Independent television suffered less often, though at times severely. One of the most powerful government-cum-newspaper attacks was against Thames Television for an investigative programme, *Death on the Rock*, about the killing of three Northern Ireland terrorists in Gibraltar by British undercover security forces in 1988. Only months later that year, using powers not used for more than thirty years, government confirmed its willingness to interfere editorially in a direct act of censorship in the form of the Northern Ireland ban which stopped radio and television from broadcasting the voices of Irish terrorists and their supporters. As an additional restraint, government had already set up the Broadcasting Standards Council to oversee matters of taste and decency in programmes.

The zeal of a reformist government driven by party ideology combined with newspaper enthusiasm to de-stabilise British broadcasting. Deep editorial dislike travelled on the back of the commercial case for structural reform. In all the years of controversy stretching from the origins of the British Broadcasting Company in the early 1920s, broadcasting had never before been under an assault so sustained and so fundamental. Niceties of convention were abandoned. No longer was it 'a matter for the BBC' or 'a matter for the IBA'. It was abundantly clear that government and party, urged on by the acclaim of newspaper interests, required editorial reform.

The BBC survived the storm by reforming itself, slowly, painfully and with more editorial anguish among its journalists than editorial effect in its programmes. Independent television was shaken up by the Broadcasting Act of 1990, and the political hue and cry switched its attention to the national tabloid newspapers which obliged their critics by trampling on privacy like English soccer hooligans invading the pitch.

During the years of attrition, newspapers had attacked Granada or Thames, Independent Television News or the BBC, whoever was in the firing line that week, and because they believed their criticisms justified they did not recognise themselves to be in alliance with government against the editorial independence of broadcasting. In this, they were not behaving badly. They were behaving according to their nature. Part of their function is to expose and to criticise. In parallel with their right to criticise broadcasting, as any other part of national life, is a public interest need to do so. For their part, broadcasters failed to defend each other when they were under attack and they did not come to the rescue of newspapers when they were threatened with regulation and criminal sanctions. Those who thought about it were likely to conclude that as broadcasting is regulated, why should newspapers be totally excluded from any framework of control. In any case, radio and television are not allowed to take sides. So, the organisations that make up the news media acted independently, either to attack one another or to be indifferent to the plight of their fellows.

The idea of a free press in Britain, as accepted by its practitioners, calls heavily on the belief that news organisations must act independently, as well as freely, so that many voices are heard. Newspaper people are at best suspicious and often hostile to the idea of coming together under common editorial standards because they believe it would stifle individuality and variety of approach in news and views. They see it as a confinement even when the standards are commendable because in journalism the best of rules soon require exceptions, as recognised by the Press Council, predecessor of the Press Complaints Commission, which for years refused to draw up a code of practice.

The failings in the reality of newspaper behaviour frequently mock the decency of the theory. Part of the problem during the 1980s was that newspapers acting independently of each other moved together in the same direction because they were in league with the same political and commercial interests – and because, driven hard by the demands of competition, 'a good story' for one had to become a good story for them all. One of the best stories over the years was 'Beeb bashing', a story the BBC ineptly contributed to when it was under pressure by stumbling from one badly handled problem to the next. Tired of a story that had gone on for too long, recognising also that after Mrs Thatcher government took a more relaxed attitude to broadcasting, and sensing that the BBC, now in better control of itself, would survive strongly, newspapers turned to a bigger story, immorality bashing, seemingly endless revelations about private lives, mainly about sexual impropriety, financial impropriety and business greed. Government ministers, other politicians, other public figures and, most elevated of all, members of the Royal Family were victim to waves of disclosure and unabashed comment. Critics in parliament and in the country considered the press to be out of control and called for controls.

The problem reflects the permanent contradictions in which journalists are caught. They occupy a troubled position in a free society being an essential part of it, simultaneously as detached from it as they see fit, often working against what seem to be its best interests and being at odds with each other, with authority and with sections of the public about how they should serve it. Serious journalists can and do argue with conviction that the right to behave badly is fundamental to good journalism. They say journalists must question what large numbers of people would prefer to leave undisturbed. More than that: journalism is right to threaten cohesive values when there is occasion to question them; it is right to erode respect if it considers respect ill-deserved, to shake institutions on which society relies for stability if they are held to be lacking, to highlight intractable problems regardless of whether it makes the conduct of government more and more difficult, and to drag down individuals who are unworthy. Journalists of the most disrespectful school say that colleagues who aspire to respectability are more to be distrusted than journalists who, out of conviction or cussedness, refuse to observe conventional limitations on what should be written or said and how it should be written or said. But there are plenty of critics in newspaper journalism who accept that tabloid colleagues have gone too far. Few want laws aimed principally at journalists. A few more believe special laws are inevitable in the long term. More hope that self-regulation will work, a view strengthened in 1995 when the government declared against a privacy law. The broadcasters, by and large, stand aside because they are not so interested in 'sex and sleaze' but they know that a law on privacy, still a threat for the future, would affect their work as well as the work of newspaper journalists. It would harm serious investigative journalism almost as much as it would curb excessive intrusion.

The much talked about idea of a law to grant people a right to privacy, actionable in the civil courts and perhaps with criminal sanctions, is usually regarded as the most important of the suggestions for controlling journalists in Britain if they do not behave as their critics say they should. There are other ideas, normally put forward as additional restraints but which could apply alone. One would guarantee a right of reply to make sure the media put right what they got wrong, as exists in a number of European countries. Yet another, which ought to be the most disliked by newspaper editors because it is the most far-reaching and in truth the most important, would set up a statutory body for the print news media. In its most comprehensive, some would say vindictive version, it would set editorial standards and rules to be observed by all newspapers and periodicals, would oversee the training of journalists, would consider complaints and would have powers to punish – newspapers and magazines as well as individuals. Punishment would be by as large a fine as appropriate or, if necessary, by banning publication for a time. The strength of these ideas, seriously put forward and noisily resisted by newspapers who enjoy a greater reputation for independence than broadcasters do, demonstrates that the news media in Britain were rarely, if ever, more controversial than during the 1980s and 1990s.

The controversies over privacy and the use of intrusive technology like hidden listening devices and long lens photography obscured a contrary fact about the British media. Newspapers, television and radio in the UK operate in conditions of considerable restriction. Compared to the media in the

United States, they are seriously impeded. The rights of American journalists are constitutionally protected. Journalists in America benefit from the citizen's right of access to all but the most sensitive of officially held information under freedom of information laws. They face benign defamation law which makes it very hard for public figures to sue successfully. What the Americans know as 'prior restraint' – legal powers to stop publication or broadcast – is nearly impossible. Neither president nor congress has power to intervene in broadcasting. The concept of contempt of court is much lighter than in Britain, probably a deal lighter than is good for American justice. In the context of these freedoms, America's privacy law is a minor restraint most helpful to ordinary people whose improprieties are not worth disclosing.

Significantly, in their freer circumstances, American newspaper journalists are generally better behaved than British newspaper journalists. This is not to say their journalism is better. It says they offend less. Criticised they are but less often and less bitterly. They have more freedom to behave badly and they use it to behave better.

Some British journalists would be tempted by American benefits if they were offered a package of helpful reforms in return for a privacy law. As a prime instance, serious journalism and popular journalism would enjoy freedom of information. It would give them access to vast amounts of information held by Whitehall, by town halls and county halls, an incalculable contribution to insight about problems and policies. As it is now, in spite of tentative ministerial concessions, government in Britain is highly secretive, a protected process that puts the convenience of governing way above the need of the governed to know. The package would have to include a marked relaxation of British defamation law so that public figures would not be able to shelter behind problems of proving the truth. All journalists who have had anything to do with libel cases know that a number of people win damages for true allegations because they have not been proved to the satisfaction of the law. The reform package to improve the chances of good journalism in Britain would have to tackle the ease with which programmes and newspaper articles can be

7

stopped by court order, that is by injunctions. There are too many granted too readily. Contempt of court, also, is an all too sweeping restraint, the effects of which are not appreciated at all by the public and not much by politicians. It is noteworthy that contempt orders to restrict news coverage of cases before the courts are usually removed or reduced in scope when challenged by the media. But many are not challenged because the process is greatly time-consuming and can be expensive. Reform could curb the readiness of judges to restrict. For good measure, parliament could amend the Police and Criminal Evidence Act to make it more difficult for the police to acquire journalistic material for use in criminal investigations and prosecutions. On the uncontained power of government to restrict broadcasting as it did with the Northern Ireland ban, parliament could limit the use of the power to matters of the most serious national emergency – or could remove it altogether. It could make the Prevention of Terrorism Act less onerous in relation to journalists. It could, further, lift the power of veto over programmes given to political election candidates by the Representation of the People Act and could remove other restrictions in the Act on programme coverage of elections.

The list of desirable reforms might suggest that British journalism is a cowed creature when clearly it is not. It is bolder journalism, though not necessarily of better quality, than in France where there has been a general media law for many years. Journalists in other European countries benefit too from constitutional protections and from freedom of information without having better newspapers and better broadcasting. Public service broadcasting flourishes in Britain, in the commercial sector as well as in the BBC, to an extent enjoyed nowhere else and which has been eroded, in particular in the older Commonwealth countries where government lacked the will to fund it adequately. By comparison with the messy confusions of most of the countries of former communist Europe where numbers of journalists disregard standards of reliability or are bound in by politically motivated restrictions, Britain is a haven of media order and freedom. None the less, set against the mildest vision, its journalism labours under very considerable disadvantages.

The restrictions built up piecemeal over the years, not fashioned as a consistent whole, in many ways reflect canniness in the British character. Reporters who run up against reluctant informants recognise the preference in many British people for information to be private unless there is a powerful reason for it to be public. Although tabloid newspapers find a justification for their worst behaviour, public opinion is a restraint on journalism. The broadsheet newspapers and the local papers are sensitive to what their corner of the market tells them. They have to be if they are to reflect the interests of their readers who are their supporters. National broadcasting, though it cannot be all things to all people as many people would like it to be, appeals across the social spectrum in its news and current affairs in ways that take many more newspapers to satisfy. Just as the media are more controversial than ever, the public are more vigilant than ever. The media which holds authority to account is itself increasingly held to account – by its readers, its audiences and its contributors. They are more important as influences than the politicians. Newcomers to journalism and students of it might imagine that all journalists have to do is to make sure they 'get it right'. There are in fact many other problems and many acceptable answers. One of the worst things for a journalist is to stumble on them unawares and unprepared.

chapter two – regulators

too many and none

People in British broadcasting complain from time to time that they have to answer to too many regulators established by law. British newspapers, by contrast, do not have any regulators in law, and an essential feature of the voluntary Press Complaints Commission, the body that receives and examines complaints against newspapers, is that it is part of self-regulation. Its primary purpose is to stave off legal regulation by making self-regulation effective.

It can be argued that broadcasting in Britain has fewer regulators than the critics assert. For any body to be truly a regulator it must have a general or crucial authority over the activities of whatever it regulates. The Independent Television Commission (ITC) and the Radio Authority are certainly regulators. They are established by law, the Broadcasting Act, and exercise a general authority: they award the licences to broadcast to independent television, which generally means non-BBC television originating in Britain, and to independent radio, which generally means non-BBC radio originating in Britain; they oversee the system by setting terms consistent with the Act that the stations must observe; they assess performance; they consider complaints and they can impose sanctions. The board of governors of the BBC is a regulator in that it has to make sure the BBC, the first and still the biggest of the British broadcasting organisations, meets its obligations under the Charter and Licence, a matter of general authority. The Welsh Authority, S4C, is a regulator as well as a provider of a television service, the Welsh language service seen on Channel 4 in Wales. The Broadcasting Complaints Commission (BCC) and the Broadcasting Standards Council (BSC) – the two bodies usually objected to by the critics of excessive regulation – are set up by law, again the Broadcasting Act, but neither has general authority over any broadcaster. The BCC considers complaints from individuals and organisations that believe they have been treated unfairly, and the BSC considers matters of taste and decency generally on radio and television. Both have powers with regard to complaints: to require broadcasters to co-operate in the investigation of them and to publicise their adjudications. But their powers are not general or crucial. The BSC has a suggestion of general authority over broadcasting with its code on violence and taste and decency, issued at the behest of parliament and which broadcasters have to take into account in their programme decisions, a light requirement. However light their authority, the BSC and the BCC are officially regarded as regulators, an attitude adopted by government largely to satisfy European Union requirements on broadcasting policy. The two bodies are certainly watchdogs and they are among the bodies broadcasters have to answer to.

An understanding of the hostility of newspaper editors to any form of legally enforceable regulation is to be found in the layers of accountability confronting radio and television programme makers. Before or after the event, a producer may have to answer to an editor or head of department, a controller, a managing director, a board of directors, a board of governors or the licensing authority, and finally the BCC or the BSC, possibly both.

BBC governors

The governors of the BBC are notable outsiders sent by the political interest to restrain the broadcasting professionals in the public interest. To say they are close to the political interest, which they are, is not to say they behave in a party political way, which they do not. As decent people who have attained a higher profile than they had as a body two and more decades ago, their general failings are that they are chosen by government, that as with the Supreme Court in the United States they are liable to be packed in a like-minded way, and as a consequence, they do not represent a broad enough range of attitudes, far less a broad enough range of social experience. These limitations make their difficult function – to represent the interests of all of the public in their regulation of the BBC – more difficult. In spite of their determination to act independently, they are more likely to reflect the interests of the state, meaning the interests pressed upon them by the institutions of the country, official and unofficial, than the interests of ordinary people.

At the same time, most importantly, they are a shield against overt political interference, a fact which is either not accepted or is so taken for granted as to be seriously underestimated. If the governors did not exist, worse might be in their place.

They have an unenviable job. They have authority of sorts over a formidable array of services: BBC1 Television, BBC2 Television, BBC Worldwide Television, BBC World Service Radio, the domestic BBC radio networks known as Radios 1, 2, 3, 4 and 5 Live, BBC regional radio and television dedicated to Scotland, Wales and Northern Ireland, BBC regional television in England, over thirty BBC local radio stations in England and the Channel Islands, and a variety of commercial endeavours in BBC Worldwide. But they are not the day by day managers of the BBC and no one can reliably say where their overall, strategic responsibilities stop and those of the professional management begin. Unlike the Independent Television Commission, regulator of independent television, the governors of the BBC do not have a significant body of dedicated professional staff to serve them. They are not detached from the BBC as the ITC is detached from ITV. Though the governors are closer to their organisation, BBC programme makers do not often have to deal directly with them because their power lies mainly in the area of finance, corporate structure, broad programme policy and the most senior appointments. It is rare for a governor to intervene or to try to intervene directly in a programme matter as when the late Stuart Young, chairman of the board, suggested to the editor of *Today*, the breakfast news and current affairs programme on Radio 4, that Rabbi Lionel Blue, instant star of the religious spot, 'Thought for the Day', was not really suitable because he created an image many Jewish people did not care for. The suggestion was ignored.

The programme influence of the governors normally filters gently into the BBC's layers of editorial management so that it stops before it reaches the programme makers or pretends to be something else when it arrives. While they avoid explicit editorial directions, the governors have an influence on the editorial atmosphere of the BBC, more so now and since the 1980s than in earlier generations. At times of programme crisis, say when the government mounts a campaign against BBC coverage, the views of the governors will be made known. They may back the programme makers publicly, as they frequently do, making reservations known to the higher reaches of the BBC.

Now that the BBC has more formal corporate systems with aims, objectives, targets and reports to the board plus a policy on complaint and redress, the governors have a more formal role as the final arbiters on alleged failings. This, over the years, is bound to increase their editorial influence. But the governors are a long way from the bite shown now and again by the ITC.

Independent Television Commission

The Independent Television Commission (ITC) – licenser and regulator of the independent programme companies like London Weekend, Carlton and Granada – is well enough regarded by television people, as was the Independent Broadcasting Authority (IBA) before it and the Independent Television Authority (ITA) before that. The ITC has a reputation for independence to an extent that eludes the governors of the BBC. No one can say with confidence that this is fully justified, and one line of objection is that the ITC has presided over a decline in the quality and the ambitions of journalism in the independent television system. The argument asserts that ITV's tradition of popular, good quality television journalism has given way to tacky sensationalism, particularly in documentaries and features.

Justified or not, the ITC's reputation prospers in defiance of the same method of appointment that dogs the BBC board. Members of the ITC are chosen by government, part-timers from the 'great and the good' in the land, people not professionally involved in broadcasting but backed by full-time professional staff. It is worth noting that the most highly regarded BBC chairman of recent decades, Lord Hill of Luton, was appointed to that post after being chairman of the ITC's predecessor but one, the ITA. Lord Hill, a former Conservative government cabinet minister and intially famous as the BBC's avuncular 'Radio Doctor', was chosen by the prime minister, Harold Wilson, in the late 1960s to curb the wilfulness the BBC had developed under the permissive regime of director general, Hugh Greene. The move backfired because Lord Hill turned out to be a robust agent of editorial independence. Another leading politician who became IBA chairman, Lord Thomson, formerly George Thomson, cabinet minister in Labour governments and a European commissioner in Brussels, also acquired a strong reputation for independence.

Regard for the ITC stems partly from its semi-detached position in the independent television system. Like the IBA was, only more so, it is not part of the independent system in the same way as the BBC governors are part of the BBC, so the faults of commercial television do not visit the ITC as vigorously as the faults of the BBC visit its governing board.

Two newer factors contribute to the shine. The first is that under the 1990 Broadcasting Act, government and parliament reduced the powers of the ITC compared with the powers of the IBA while widening its responsibilities, for instance to cover cable programmes. It now has no authority over programmes before they are shown. It is not 'the broadcaster' as under the terms of the previous legislation. The ITC sets the terms of licences it awards, including licences for satellite services originating in the United Kingdom, monitors performance against those terms, passes judgement on performance, lays down a code for programmes, issues reprimands and if necessary imposes sanctions, including fines, on transgressors. But if mistakes are made, ITV and, in particular, the programme company, Yorkshire, Anglia or whatever, are held responsible, not the ITC. It is never now in the position of having to defend a programme decision it made itself because it is not involved in any.

The second reason for the fair reputation of the ITC is that the terms for allocating television licences, with overriding emphasis on highest bidder, leave the Commission with less room for judgement than before. In other words, politicians, not the ITC, can be blamed for the pressures on commercial television that destroy quality, and are so blamed by media commentators.

In spite of, perhaps because of, this aloof position, the ITC is significant in the lives of ITV programme makers. Its 'Programme Code', required by the Broadcasting Act, has to be observed. It provides guidance and, importantly, some rules, ranging unexceptionally across issues including impartiality, violence and sex on screen, taste and decency generally in programmes, secret recordings, privacy, terrorism, crime, family viewing policy and broadcasting during elections. The ITC receives complaints from viewers, adjudicating on them in the light of its code. It publicly rebukes programme makers when they offend. The hefty fine on Granada Television in December 1994 for persistent and unacceptable promotion of commercial products in a programme was a more powerful rebuke than the BBC governors have ever mustered against a BBC programme.

The Independent Television Commission is outspoken against television companies it considers have betrayed the promises in their bids for licences, again more outspoken more often than the BBC governors are about the Corporation's programme failings. The ITC was very severe in its strictures against the breakfast television company, GMTV, after its first year as successor to TV-AM, and unfriendly for a time towards the performance of Carlton, the company that ousted the well regarded Thames Television.

When Thames was heavily condemned by government in 1988 for *Death On The Rock*, its documentary exposé of the killing of Northern

15

Irish terrorists by British security forces in Gibraltar, the IBA emerged well from the controversy. The way to success for the regulator of ITV seems to be two-edged: it demonstrates independence from programme makers and programme companies as well as from government.

Radio Authority

The Radio Authority is best known for the licences it awards, occasionally for removing them from original holders as it did by a decision in 1993 with LBC, the news and news-talk station in London, the first of the independent stations in Britain. All of independent radio originating in the United Kingdom answers to the Radio Authority, the regulator empowered by the Broadcasting Act of 1990. Before that Act, commercial radio was overseen by the Radio Division of the IBA (Independent Broadcasting Authority). As with the Independent Television Commission, the BBC governors and the Welsh Authority, the members of the Radio Authority are appointed by government but as a body operate independently.

The Authority has overseen a significant expansion of independent, that is, non-BBC radio, from just over ninety stations in 1990 to 150 plus three national networks about five years later. Further expansion will come when a new stretch of frequencies becomes available.

The Authority advertises franchises, awards licences, sets agreed terms – for instance, on music policy – for each station, monitors performance, considers complaints, imposes a code it has devised as ordered by parliament, and takes action against errant stations, action ranging from rebukes, to fines and possible removal of a licence. Like the ITC and unlike the governors of the BBC, the Radio Authority does not bear any direct editorial responsibility for programmes. It is a 'regulator' not, in normal terms, a 'broadcaster'. It does not require any programmes or any programme decisions to be referred to it in advance of broadcast, nor does it have to answer for them. If it criticises or approves programmes or pro-

16

gramme schedules it does so after the event in response to complaints which are assessed on recordings supplied by the station. With more than 150 licensed charges in its care, the Authority's oversight is necessarily light. It depends heavily on comments from the public as thorough, routine monitoring to decide whether stations were living up to their 'promise of performance' would be forbiddingly onerous. To an extent, independent radio stations that do not live up to their promises have a good chance of 'getting away with it'.

The Radio Authority's code at the beginning of 1995 for what is heard on air has three parts. One deals with advertising and sponsorship. The other two are programme codes, one for violence, sex, children, religion and other sensitive matters, the second for 'news programmes and coverage of matters of political or industrial controversy or relating to current public policy'. Both programme codes are relevant to the journalism of independent radio. Both provide guidance and state a number of rules.

The code on violence and a range of other issues is unexceptional. It cautions against scenes that may be intolerably disturbing, that may be harmful or may be imitated. The issues it covers include terrorism (senior station management should consider, in advance, any programme that explores violence for political ends anywhere in the UK), medical subjects (avoid unnecessary distress by careful handling), secret recordings (they must be approved in advance by senior management), and interviews with criminals (must be justified by a public interest).

The codes encourage an impression that they are intended more for the good of the public than for the good of the journalism. For instance, a rule on interviews with members of the public says stations must be satisfied that words or actions by individuals in public places 'are sufficiently in the public domain to justify their broadcast without express permission being sought'. The tougher school of journalism would decry this on the grounds that what occurs publicly can be reported publicly and that the important consideration is whether the public should know about it, not whether the individual consents to it being made known. For the sake of the public, the Authority is bold on corrections. In the code on news programmes, it says 'Corrections of factual errors should be broadcast as soon as is sensibly possible after the original error', a straightforward policy which, if followed by the stations, puts them ahead of the rest of British radio and of television.

The code for news programmes deals also with impartiality, phone-ins, interviews, personal view programmes, library material, appearances by politicians and other political matters. It adopts a mechanistic approach to impartiality, an approach encouraged by the Broadcasting Act, the impartiality clauses of which were much influenced by right-wing members of the House of Lords who bothered obsessively about alleged leftist or anti-authority influences in radio and television. The 1995 code states a rule for national independent stations that 'Impartiality within a daily series must be achieved within a fortnight, within a weekly series within three weeks and within a monthly series within three months.'

Another rule in the code is that stations 'must keep a written record of the appearances of MPs and MEPs in programmes', an unexceptional requirement provided the unstated purpose of it does not have rigid editorial effects. One station may include few MPs, another many and both be justified. One political party may over a period be included in programmes many more times than another, a state of affairs that tends to agitate its rivals but which may be fully justified if, for instance, the better publicised party has gone through an internal turmoil with members arguing vigorously against each other. Much depends on how the code is interpreted. A decent document, as the Radio Authority's is, could dull the journalism if the rules are made to seem more forbidding than they really are.

Welsh Authority

Of the broadcasters and broadcasting regulators, the Welsh Authority – officially and in the language of heaven, Sianel Pedwar Cymru (Channel 4 Wales) – is the least known outside Wales. It is responsible for that concession to the Welsh language, the fourth television channel in Wales with which it shares its name, S4C, set up in response to a campaign of civil disobedience and a threat by a revered Welsh nationalist to starve himself to death if more was not done to serve the language through broadcasting. As with all the other regulators – the Independent Television Commission, Radio Authority, BBC board of governors, Broadcasting Complaints Commission and Broadcasting Standards Council – members of S4C are expected to operate independently after being appointed by government, appointments formally as in all other cases made by the relevant secretary of state, for years the home secretary, then later the national heritage secretary.

The Welsh Authority is more like the BBC board of governors than anything in the independent television system. It 'provides' and 'regulates' S4C just as the governors provide and regulate the BBC services. By contrast, the ITV regulator, the ITC, regulates but does not provide. For ITV channel three, the programme companies are the providers. And for the fourth channel outside Wales, the Channel Four Corporation is the provider, not the regulator. The two functions are closely related in the Welsh Authority. It runs S4C. Legally, it is the 'broadcaster'. It is intimately connected with programmes and programme schedules though unlike the BBC it has no programme-making staff. It commissions programmes for the schedules it draws up. At least ten hours a week of its programmes have to be supplied by the BBC – free of charge. Programmes from Channel 4 outside Wales are also free of charge.

The bulk of S4C's income comes through government. The amount is calculated annually as a percentage of the total revenues of independent television. Government regards itself as the conduit by which S4C receives money from independent television rather than as the funder, a distinction that cannot apply to the only other British broadcaster to receive its normal income from government, the international radio broadcaster, BBC World Service. S4C makes the lesser part of its money from advertising.

The Welsh channel is bound by the same rules of journalism as apply to ITV, as expressed in the Broadcasting Act of 1990 and as elaborated in the code drawn up by the ITC. News must be impartial and accurate. Public issues have to be dealt with impartially. Journalistic complications arise from the politics of Wales. Though not equal to the nationalist force in Scotland, the Welsh national party, Plaid Cymru, has to be recognised and treated fairly by all broadcasters. As in Scotland, the problem is complicated by the predominance of political programming coming from London but is eased in that programmes in Welsh can be judged to an extent in isolation from programmes in English. Very difficult decisions remain. They concern what representation nationalism merits on an impartial judgement, how many appearances the national party deserves, when, on what stories and at what length, decisions Solomon could not be trusted to make. They fall instead to the makers of S4C programmes – BBC Wales which provides the news as well as some current affairs, the ITV company for Wales, HTV, and independent producers.

Press Complaints Commission

The newspaper industry responded to political threats of statutory regulation and a law to punish intrusions of privacy by setting up the Press Complaints Commission and by enjoying itself to a greater extent than before in its accounts of the sexual adventures of public figures. The Commission, the code of practice it endorsed and its adjudications on complaints represented defensive self-regulation. Acres of copy on sexual shenanigans in high places was, in effect if not in design, the offensive. The offensive was at first much the more successful of the two. While it created the belief that intervention by the politicians against the press would disreputably benefit their own kind, the PCC floundered in controversies over intrusion.

The Commission was set up in 1991. It grew out of dissatisfaction with the Press Council which during the late 1980s had seemed inadequate to the fight ahead and which for years had resisted calls to devise a code of practice, though late in the day it had conceded on that issue. The setting up of the Complaints Commission, with eighteen months to prove itself and self-regulation effective, was recommended by the Calcutt Committee appointed by government and chaired by David Calcutt, a lawyer. Newspapers accepted that self regulation had to be strengthened, the best signal of determination, so it was calculated, being the setting up of a new, stronger body. Inaction by the newspapers would have caused action by the politicians.

Self regulation meant the Commission was voluntary, not created by law as are the watchdogs and other regulators of broadcasting. The Commission was to be funded by contributions from the industry, again voluntary and organised by another new voluntary body, the Press Standards Board of Finance. The code of practice too would be self-imposed. The Commission would have no powers, only an ability to investigate, to approve or to condemn what newspapers had done and to publicise its decisions. Newspapers complained against would publish Commission adjudications into those complaints which was much as before because nearly all of the adjudications by the old Press Council had been published. Public figures of some stature and not connected to newspapers were appointed to the Commission as were a number of newspaper editors. They and their first chairman, Lord McGregor of Durris, were quickly mired in difficulties. Lord McGregor, a man of integrity, an academic who had chaired the Royal Commission on the Press from 1975 to 1977 and who understood more about press freedom than most, was criticised as hapless by backbench politicians and other critics hungry for restraints on what they saw as a press out of control. For a time it looked very much as though the government would follow recommendations by the Calcutt Committee which called for legal restrictions, notably to make intrusion on privacy actionable in law. But the more it was considered the more remote it seemed to become.

Newspaper strategy appeared to be working. The Press Complaints Commission continued to do its job as best it could. The political criticisms of it and of its chairman were in truth more a reflection of the intractability of the issues in a small handful of high profile cases than of the overall efforts of the Commission. The vast majority of complaints against

21

newspapers were dealt with quietly. Their outcomes satisfied readers who complained and editors complained against. In its advocacy of self-regulation, the Commission also argues that all complaints represent a minute proportion of the many thousands of stories published.

At the beginning of 1995, a new chairman took over at the Commission – Lord Wakeham, former secretary of state in the Thatcher governments, well liked and widely regarded as an astute political fixer, injured by the IRA Brighton bomb in 1984 that almost assassinated the cabinet and which killed his wife. The man chosen to sit in judgement on newspapers was immediately newsworthy, the subject of a great deal of newspaper coverage in a high profile controversy, nothing to do with his PCC position but brought about by a lucrative job he took in the City. The media were full of questions about the extent to which people like Lord Wakeham recently in government should exploit their public service experience for their own advantage.

On Wakeham's arrival, the Commission had fifteen members, nine from outside the newspaper industry. They included a privacy commissioner, Professor Robert Pinker of the London School of Economics, to investigate cases of alleged intrusion on privacy. The members of the Commission had included Peter Preston, editor of the left-of-centre, daily broadsheet newspaper, the *Guardian*. He resigned during a noisy row with politicians over the faking of a fax by the paper in its campaign to nail a government minister on the question of who paid for an expensive weekend the minister had in Paris, though the 'cod fax' of Preston's description could have been justified under the newspaper code of practice. A declared offence against the code was no bar to membership of the Commission for Brian Hitchen, editor of the Conservative-supporting, popular-style but struggling *Sunday Express*. The Commission had condemned Hitchen for comments in his newspaper column when he was editor of the down-market tabloid *Daily Star*: he had described homosexuals as 'poofters'.

Lord Wakeham caused a stir at the Commission not long after he arrived when he pressed for the appointment, as a member, of Sir Bernard Ingham, best known as Margaret Thatcher's irascible press secretary during the 1980s when she was prime minister. Wakeham's effort was thwarted. But he later proclaimed an increased number of lay members on the body that makes the appointments to the PCC, evidence, he said, of the Commission's greater independence from newspapers. He gained credit too with a success over privacy when the international media boss, Rupert Murdoch of News Corporation, severely reprimanded the editor of one of his British papers, the *News of the World*. The reprimand was for intrusion on the privacy of Lady Spencer, sister-in-law of the Princess of Wales, when she was being treated for an eating disorder. The Commission had condemned the paper and Lord Wakeham had written to Murdoch about it. Wakeham accrued yet more credit when the government said it would not introduce a privacy law. It called instead for the newspaper code to be tightened and for the PCC to operate a newspaper fund for victims of intrusion.

The self-regulation argument goes on, the heat depending on how the national newspapers have recently behaved. They see statutory regulation as an attack on press freedom. Their critics, especially in parliament, want a commission empowered in law, publicly appointed – which usually means appointed by government – and responsible for more than the investigation of complaints, for it to have powers to fine and perhaps to suspend newspapers that flout decent standards. The powers, say the critics, should hurt. The argument is fundamental and constitutionally important. The case against newspaper regulation says the voluntary Press Complaints Commission, for all its faults, represents the ineffable principle that parliament and government must keep a clear distance between themselves and the newspapers if freedom of the press is to mean what it says.

Broadcasting Complaints Commission

The BCC is not popular with broadcasters. Some of the criticisms of it have been justified although, since representations during the late 1980s and after, and a change at the top, the Commission has rid itself of some of the more arguable aspects of its processes. It sits in judgement on programme makers, a body of significance to them and to the public, and likely to become more significant when, as government intends, it is merged with the Broadcasting Standards Council.

Unlike the Press Complaints Commission for newspapers, the Broadcasting Complaints Commission is established in law. It gains its powers from the Broadcasting Acts. The Act of 1990 states its purposes, powers and general composition clearly. It is funded by the broadcasting organisations who have no choice in the matter. The original complaints commission was set up by the BBC, in response to demand, with the name 'Programmes Complaints Commission'.

Broadly, the BCC's function is to receive, to consider and to adjudicate on complaints from the public about the way they have been treated by programmes on radio and television. Complaint can be made by individuals or groups, including organisations, provided they are the people directly affected by the treatment or they are authorised to act for the people affected.

The complaint must strictly be that the treatment was an infringement of privacy or that it was unjust or unfair in some other way. General, impersonal complaints about, say, schedule changes, will not be looked into – 'entertained' as the Commission puts it – no matter how heart-felt they are. To be considered a qualifying complaint, a schedule change would have to involve personal unfairness, which would be very unusual. And complaints about sex on the screen or bad language or violence fall to the Broadcasting Standards Council. In other words, the Complaints Commission exists to consider whether programmes have badly treated people who either appear in them or whose interests are directly affected by the substance of the programme.

There is legalistic argument about the validity of certain complaints. It arises because the Act speaks of treatment 'in programmes', not 'by programmes'. Although the 'unjust or unfair' treatment must be 'in' a programme, this leaves open the possibility that material left out could make the programme unfair. Another aspect argued about is whether material gathered for a programme but not used can constitute an unwarranted infringement of privacy 'in a programme'. Even more obscurely, it is wondered whether unsuccessful attempts to gather material could amount to unwarranted infringement. People who complain see these as technicalities. Programme makers sometimes try to hide behind them.

An area of lively dispute is whether the Commission considers complaints from people whose interest is not direct enough. A good example of this was a complaint from the mayor of Milford Haven that a programme was unfair when it said prices at eateries in the town had been increased for the holiday season. A complaint from restaurateurs or a hot-dog vendor would clearly have been appropriate, and the mayor's involvement would have been unremarkable had the programme said the public loos were disgusting. As it was, the Commission held that because the mayor and council were concerned with the town's tourism, they had a direct interest in whether comments about the price of meals were unfair. To broadcasters, this sounded like a tenuous interest being allowed to pretend it was 'sufficiently direct'.

A big disagreement between the Complaints Commission and the BBC about direct interest occurred in September 1994 over a *Panorama* programme on single mothers, *Babies on Benefit*. The Commission had looked into and sided with complaints from a pressure group, the National Council For One Parent Families. The BBC protested, rejected the criticisms and launched a legal challenge. It gave as grounds for the challenge at law that the Complaints Commission had exceeded its remit. It should not have considered the complaints because the National Council did not figure in the programme in any way and did not represent anyone who did. The High Court ruled in the BBC's favour.

The Complaints Commission is in a hole on this general question: broadcasters protest and threaten legal action if they consider the Commission has overstretched its terms of reference, and then if a complaint is not considered because it is thought to be outside the remit, the complainant is liable to protest and to threaten legal action.

The amount of time programme makers

have to give to answering complaints to the BCC is a serious problem. The Commission has reduced some of the worst verbosity of complainants but producers might still have to work their way through many pages, many points and many supporting documents. There is no escape. The law requires the work to be done.

The Commission can order the relevant radio or television station to broadcast a summary of its decision, called an adjudication, on a complaint. It can also order the summary to be published, this usually in programme listings magazines. Summaries ordered to be made public are now usually those in which the complaint is upheld. The wording of the summary is agreed with the broadcasters and the complainant. It is broadcast at about the time of day of the offending programme.

As many complaints are complex, involving sometimes numerous objections, there is always a high chance that at least one aspect will be upheld. If programme makers responding to a complaint do not answer every point raised, they might lose by default.

Critics in broadcasting have argued that the BCC, generous, they say, to complainers, is in danger of inhibiting debate on difficult issues of public importance. Inevitably, there have been some questionable adjudications but there is no evidence of programme makers being inhibited by the prospect of a BCC ruling. It is a mild system with no sharp teeth and no power of prior influence, far less prior restraint, more an irritant than an obstruction when it is unreasonable.

Broadcasting Standards Council

The BSC is concerned with sex, violence, and taste and decency generally, including bad language, on television and on radio. Like the Broadcasting Complaints Commission and unlike the Press Complaints Commission, it is set up by statute. The Broadcasting Act of 1990 lays out its terms, though it was set up before then, partly as a Thatcherite gesture to the lobby that blames television for declined social standards. It

26

is officially regarded as a regulator as are the BCC, the ITC, the Radio Authority, the Welsh Authority and the BBC governors. As with the others, its members are chosen by government and act independently. Its costs are paid for directly by government.

The Broadcasting Standards Council can initiate investigations into programmes or programme issues within its remit. It does not have to wait, as the Broadcasting Complaints Commission does, for a complaint to be received. It can, in effect, complain to itself, though it usually does not have cause to do so because people are ready enough to complain.

The remit of the BSC is generally much wider than that of the other broadcasting watchdog. Unlike the BCC, it has a duty to monitor programmes so that it can report on the standards for which it is responsible. In another difference from the BCC, it commissions research into and studies of relevant issues. Most importantly, and again unlike the BCC, it draws up a code against which the work of the broadcasters is judged. In the terms of the Broadcasting Act, this code gives guidance in connection with the portrayal of violence and the portrayal of sexual conduct in programmes and on standards of taste and decency generally for programmes.

The Council decides how its findings on complaints should be made public. It can require them to be broadcast or published in newspapers, or both. It orders only a few of its decisions to be made public in those ways. But it gains publicity anyway because the newspapers always pick up a story or two from its regularly published bulletins, sex, swearing and violence being endlessly newsworthy.

The BSC has an easier job than the BCC because it is largely concerned with offended feelings and qualitative judgements, not with the frequent rigmarole of fact and allegation that attends complaints about unfairness. Programmes complained about to the BSC also have an easier time in responding because all they need is a convincing analysis rather than a meticulous point by point rebuttal. Programmes are much more likely to confess a fault to the BSC than to the BCC, slipping in a bit of mitigation, of course. These differences of approach on the two types of complaint may survive when the two bodies are merged.

chapter three – editorial values

news

News journalism has a bad reputation in Britain, worse than in some other advanced countries, and, in contradiction, news programmes are more viewed and listened to and more newspapers more avidly read by larger numbers of people than in many advanced countries. It suggests that news is widely regarded as a grubby necessity. The people who supply it are suspect, not to be trusted, and their product is to be treated sceptically in the knowledge that some of it will be downright wrong, some of it mildly misleading and some of it disgracefully intrusive. Together the newshounds pursue newsworthy people without respect for privacy and position.

The hard school of journalism says it is exactly as it should be. Respectable journalism fails to do all of the job. If journalism is to make society face its ills wherever they are, it will have no friends. In particular, it will be disliked by people in power because it expects them to answer issues decided by the media, not solely those agreed on the political agenda. The attitude is summed up in the comment 'The proper relationship between a journalist and a politician is the same as the relationship between a dog and a lamp-post.'

No one believes, though, that news and journalism are simply a service to democracy. They are products, commercially judged even when, as with the BBC, they are paid for by a tax, not by money earned in the market place. News is a way of making money just as selling bread is a way of making money. News is also in some hands a way of exercising power. The social importance of news remains. In industrial society which may be called scientific society, news is, for all its failings, a major branch of the information business, not an option, a basic necessity. Western civilisation needs good flows of information like it needs good flows of air to breath.

editing

Editing begins as soon as a journalist sees and hears of something newsworthy. The process of selection, elimination and presentation starts almost instantly. No reporter reports everything known, nor in the order it occurred. To that extent, the reporter edits. The sub-editor edits some more, as does the lay-out sub or the video-editor. The process continues until the page is published or the programme broadcast. As a result, even when all involved in the chain are greatly skilled and not mischievous, what is made public often departs significantly from reality without anyone in the process realising it. Uncertainty is expressed as an ambiguity, and ambiguity transmutes into falsehood, usually inadvertently, occasionally wilfully. People who have been involved in a newsworthy event, actively or as witnesses, recognise the problem when they say the news story is seriously wrong.

Journalists generally underestimate the extent of the process of falsification. Many news stories contain important errors of fact or emphasis and the journalistic process is to blame for less than all of it. Other contributory factors include inadequate information from sources when the journalist is not an eye-witness. But journalistic failure nearly always makes the unreliability worse.

agenda-setting

The concept of agenda-setting is one of the most over-blown in discussion of the media. It is at its most inflated when theorists, journalists or politicians assert, as at times they do, that the media *decide* what topics the nation should discuss and how important they are. It was a power often claimed in the BBC by people working for *Today*, the breakfast-time all news and current affairs show on Radio 4, a programme that met competition from breakfast television by strengthening its reputation for being what anyone who is anyone listens to and seeks to be interviewed on, a role confirmed by the notables waiting their turn to be interrupted in the studio or climbing, sometimes in a dressing gown, into the radio car, the mobile studio parked at their homes. *Today*'s record urged prime minister Thatcher to be a regular if editorially agitated listener who at least once had a call made to the programme to say she would like to be interviewed, which she was. Two decades earlier when Harold Wilson's government had a majority so small it would fit into a taxi-cab, he would occasionally call the BBC's breakfast radio news from Ten Downing Street to correct a story or to suggest that the script refer to him in the first mention as prime minister rather than plain Mr Wilson. But these political 'interventions' acknowledge media influence, not media power to set, meaning fix, the agenda. Equally, when political concern about agenda-setting is at its height during main elections in Britain and many other countries, the United States included, it is an exaggeration that newspapers and broadcasting, television especially, dictate what issues voters should consider most important and how they should see them. Surveys of public opinion at election times show that voters develop for themselves agendas different from news priorities.

The idea of agenda-setting is, at best, a hackneyed half-truth. In open societies, no one organisation, no one group or category of people, journalistic or political, far less one programme or newspaper, fixes an agenda for the nation. The very idea of a set list of topics somehow observed is faulty. It implies that every-one attends to the same list. It suggests that the

30

people of the country all attend to the items in the list in the same order. It seems to suppose that the importance they give to each topic is dictated in defiance of personal inclinations and concerns. Analysed so, the concept is clearly inadequate.

The issues attended to by a country of interested, wilful and variously informed people and the different ways they attend to them are the result of complex influences, some aimed at the citizen voter from a distance by programmes, newspapers, politicians, and others, some particular to the person and in a combination exclusive to the individual. The supposed agenda-setters are in truth not able fully to fix their own agenda, let alone the multitude of agendas eventually adopted by the multitude of readers, viewers and listeners. What rivals and the forces of nature do change the news agenda. What a news programme calls its 'running order', the list of reports, features and interviews to be included, is seldom broadcast as intended. Items crash before take-off. Reports are dropped because others are too long. Stories give way to better latecomers. Journalism enjoys the unexpected, the story no one knew was going to happen, what the agenda of a business meeting would call 'AOB'. On a good day in journalism, 'Any Other Business' leaps excitedly to the top of the programme, knocking out many other items on the agenda, and consumes most of the front page of the newspaper so that the earlier intended 'lead' goes down page abbreviated and other stories become 'news briefs' with more coverage inside. And in the fastness of their homes and their places of work, some people uncritically absorb impressions from journalists who had too little time to consider what they were doing, others rebel in their minds against what they believe the news made too much fuss of, and others distracted by their own problems are indifferent.

public interest

A plea of 'in the public interest' is a favourite defence for journalists under attack. It is at the heart of the argument about the extent to which prying reporters and cameras should be allowed to invade personal privacy. Journalists plead the public interest when they are accused of disclosing official secrets, usually on the grounds that the secret protected a scandal. Journalists condemned for using 'stolen documents', which means documents leaked to them, say the public ought to know what the documents contain. Stories that wreck or threaten to wreck secret talks by premature disclosure are similarly defended. Grand theory says journalism is a function fundamentally in the public interest.

The defence is often used fancifully, asserted more than argued, though everyone seems agreed that the public interest does not mean whatever interests the public. It refers to serious matters in which the public have or ought to have a legitimate interest, better still a legitimate concern. What is 'serious' and what is 'legitimate' are the points of dispute. Attempts are made to describe the areas of concern covered by 'the public interest' in the context of journalism. A neat version is included in the newspapers' code of practice ratified by the Press Complaints Commission. The code, drawn up by newspapers and periodicals at the height of the debate about privacy, specifies journalistic acts which are not acceptable unless they are justified in the public interest. One is intrusion into private life without the consent of the individual, including the use of cameras with long lenses for pictures of people on private property when passers-by cannot easily see them unaided. Another is the use of hidden listening devices. Others are misrepresentation and subterfuge to get information and pictures, persistent attempts to talk to people or to take pictures of them when they have refused, staying on private property after being asked to leave, and payments to people involved in crime or current criminal court cases.

To help journalists decide when these unacceptable acts become acceptable in the public interest, the code gives a definition of the public interest by describing its purposes. The public interest is being served if the efforts of the journalist detect or expose crime or a serious misdemeanour. It is also being served if the story would help protect public health and safety. And, with an editorial eye on public figures who live by images that are often partial and by fine-sounding statements that may be in conflict with their private lives, the journalist is serving the public interest if the story would prevent people at large 'from being misled by some statement or action of an individual or organisation'. The code recognises that the public interest could be larger than the list it gives. Accordingly, if editors responding to complaints believe particular stories serve the public interest in other ways, they put their arguments case by case.

The public interest argument is clearly reputable. Sincere journalists believe in it genuinely. It is damaged but not negated by journalists who use it disingenuously. It may, however, be too comprehensive for its own good. Inventive use of it justifies the worst journalistic behaviour – a danger acknowledged by Lord Wakeham, chairman of the Press Complaints Commission, when in 1995 in the controversy over intrusions on privacy he said the Commission would not tolerate 'spurious' use of the public interest defence.

independence

Journalism is suspect if its editorial judgements are not made freely and independently by individual journalists 'on the ground', by editorial teams or by trusted editors. Journalists in countries newly emerged from authoritarian control in the former communist eastern Europe are passionate about the independence of individual journalists. After decades of restriction, they are inclined to see any restrictive editorial act by a 'grey suit', a boss, as a disgraceful interference – and a 'boss' is any supervisor who does not normally make detailed editorial decisions. The attitude is shared by exasperated journalists in systems long used to freedom when they are overruled by the chief sub, senior producer or editor. Dissatisfaction of this kind visits all news teams at some time because no sensible journalistic organisation anywhere in the world accepts that what is decided by the people who normally make the decisions must be allowed to stand. In the normal course, nearly all decisions are made at low level, by the reporters who gather the news, by the subs who prepare it for the page, or the producers who finalise it for the programme. Most editorial machines could not work in any other way: decisions are normally made and applied at the lowest competent level. The norm has, however, to give way at times to editors and other senior editorial people who have the authority to intervene. They usually have to answer for what the paper or the programme has done and they are not prepared to sanction whatever answer those below them think appropriate.

Editors of newspapers fight vigorously for their right to edit. They often seek assurances from proprietors and controlling interests that they will not be interfered with. At the same time, they assert their responsibilities downwards, over their editorial staff. Sometimes, their independence from owners is doubted. Doubts of this kind are often made and equally often denied about editors of newspapers owned by Rupert Murdoch, the Australian-born, naturalised-American creator of the multinational media giant, News Corporation. They were made also, and denied, about the *Observer*, the Sunday paper, when it was in the empire of Tiny Rowland, for many years boss of the conglomerate, Lonrho. Robert Maxwell, as owner of the *Daily Mirror* and much more, behaved in a way that encouraged everyone to believe he was the editorial driving force who made whichever decisions he chose.

Whatever terms and assurances they win, even the most independent newspaper editors are not free to do whatever they wish. They have to operate within the established position of their paper. The editor of the staunchly Tory broadsheet, the *Daily Telegraph*, for instance, probably has as much editorial independence as many others without being free to dedicate the paper against the wishes of the owner to long-term support of the Labour party or to take its news and feature columns significantly downmarket to appeal to large numbers of people in the unskilled, low-wage and benefit-supported socio-economic groups that fill the depressed urban wastelands on the outskirts of struggling British cities. For those newspaper editors with assurances of independence, the theory is that owners choose them to do the kind of job known to be required by the established editorial approach of the paper and leave them to it until confidence evaporates at which time the editors are sacked. The theory accords reasonably with the reality, provided it is understood that even the best owners nudge their editor now and again.

Serious doubts about the independence and integrity of newspaper journalism arise in other ways. Direct interference by advertisers is loudly denied; stealthy editorial influence is suspected. In financial journalism, alert readers become suspicious in the weeks approaching the beginning of the financial year in April when PEPS (Personal Equity Plans) are heavily advertised – investors being allowed one each financial year – if the advertisements are accompanied by friendly editorial copy that proclaims the attractions of PEPS after a spell in which they did badly. The same suspicion occurs over the property pages of local newspapers. Estate agents put a great deal of money into local paper advertising and sceptical readers discount as a sop to the advertisers hopeful editorial copy that hypes an aspect of the property market, often that sales are about to emerge from the doldrums.

The problems and the structure in broadcasting are less clear. A newspaper editor could scrutinise all important editorial columns, and in some newspapers, every editorial word, before publication. Higher bosses in broadcasting organisations could not possibly vet all speech programmes before broadcast. Even if they could, they would still have the problem of how to supervise live programmes that are not scripted. The director general of the BBC used to be referred to as 'editor-in-chief', a title that could not mean much and a responsibility that could be discharged only exceptionally at critical moments in a small number of editorial issues. The reality of being editor-in-chief is not available either to managing directors of independent radio stations, regional television MDs and channel controllers. None is able to exercise the degree of editorial oversight to justify the description 'editor'. At best, they are called in on special problems which ordinary programme makers prefer to be as few as possible. Editorial authority devolves, of necessity, to programme editors and producers, the ordinary toilers in the newsrooms, at the programme editorial desks and in the cutting rooms.

The speed with which television and, more so, radio can move from receiving the news to broadcasting it, combined with the frequency of news broadcasts, requires instant editorial decisions, and this, though not a guarantee of independence, means that people at programme level have to be allowed to get on with it. The opportunity for anyone else to intervene against them is very small. And being very small for managing directors and their channel controllers, it is even smaller, less than minuscule, for members of governing bodies and any other appointees who are sometimes said to interfere in the editorial process.

Newspapers and some political critics on the left like to portray broadcasting as controlled, unduly influenced by government appointed agents or by ultimate dependence on political decision, except, that is, when television outrages the critics, in which case the docile creature is a beast out of control. The picture is a caricature. The publicly declared terms of the regulatory framework, in which British broadcasting operates and which do not apply to newspapers, do not prevent and need not deter television and radio from tackling any issue and do not direct their editorial efforts in any direction. In all essentials, newspapers and broadcasting are equally influenceable and equally resistant. They are both liable to be leaned on, subjected to political pressure, special pleading that comes in confidence down the telephone or at the private dinner table. Newspaper editors are courted ardently by prime ministers and others in the cabinet to an effect that cannot be calculated, while broadcasting bosses are inveighed against and called to account, again to an effect not calculable.

The caricature of control says that if the Conservative party chairman calls a broadcasting boss about an eve-of-election exposé of dubious dealings by a Conservative-controlled local council, the programme will be postponed, as was a *Panorama* on that subject on BBC1 in 1994. The truth is stealthier. Such calls are certainly made but political pressure alone does not stop programmes. Even the politically prompted decision by the BBC governors in 1985 to stop the programme *Real Lives: At the Edge of the Union* – a portrait of two Northern Ireland activists, one republican, one loyalist, with views as far apart as possible – cannot confidently be designated a bald concession to political pressure and, almost certainly, was not. Pressure from the home secretary spurred the governors to consider the programme in advance but their wrong-headed decisions, first to view it before broadcast and then to stop it, seemed based on genuinely held objections. Pressures may confuse genuine editorial doubts and, conceivably, influence the final assessment because a suspect programme that causes political flak is much harder to defend than a thoroughly well-founded programme that causes political flak. Such possibilities usually remain conjectural, impossible to prove in particular cases, because it is impossible to know the secrets in the heads of the people who made the decision. There are, at the same time, many instances of political pressure being put aside and many representations that never find their way to the people who make the editorial decisions.

The truth about the effect of political pressure on newspapers is also stealthy. But the relationships between national newspaper owners, newspaper editors and politicians are often more wilful and even less transparent than the relationship between broadcasting chiefs and politicians. Hard as it is to believe that a major newspaper would forgo a story of government scandal or would seriously restrain it because the editor dined at Downing Street, has a knighthood, or is friendly with a cabinet minister, somewhere along the line, at some time, an editorial favour is done. As in broadcasting, it is not blatant. The effect through cabinet minister, newspaper proprietor and newspaper editor is surreptitious. Sometimes it is illusory.

In spite of connections that give rise to doubts, British journalism has as much independence as it needs. So long as a wide variety of editorial outlets exists, so long as they have the will to expose and so long as journalists are prepared to dig painstakingly for the facts, the journalism can do anything the editorial brief calls for. Three factors stand in the way if the will is weak. One is indeed the quiet influence that works confidentially through contacts, which editors can allow to affect them, which exists in all societies and which cannot be abolished. Another is the grip British officialdom has on information which effectively hides truth. The third is the inhibiting power of the British system of justice to provide ready court orders to stop suspect publication, a shield for public figures when strong suspicions cannot be aired because they cannot be proved minutely.

powerful interests

It is easy to say that editorial decisions should be made only on the basis of proper journalistic imperatives and that blandishments, pressures and threats should be resisted. The problem is that as some pressures – euphemistically called representations – make fair points, conceding to a fair point can seem like a craven concession while to resist a point for the sake of it can be a short cut to unreliability and unfairness. As pressure is concerned often with judgement, less often a matter of simple fact, there is always room for dispute, one journalist seeing the point as unreasonable, another seeing it as fair.

The problem is psychologically most acute when dealing with powerful interests. And it is not rare. Every day, journalists are being pressed 'to put it right'. At times, they are genuinely being asked to put right a mistake of fact or an omission of importance. At other times, they are asked to excise or downplay a significant and uncomfortable truth. Demands come openly and surreptitiously from many powerful centres – government departments, political party headquarters, MPs, local councillors, company bosses, the police, health service authorities, advertisers who put money into all the commercially funded media and who threaten at times to stop it. Weak journalists change a story because somebody who matters demands it. Strong journalists change a story because they are convinced it deserves to be changed – and it does not matter where the demand for change comes from. The only acceptable way is for the journalists to decide. It means isolating the point made, considering it fairly regardless of whether the source is important or ordinary, accepting the point if it seems reasonable, rejecting it if it is not – and putting up with scepticism or wrath as the case may be.

Ordinary journalists may not be in a position to resist when an approach is made stealthily. An important advertiser who fears damage from a candid story or a favoured MP with a gripe will go direct to the highest editor and, as this danger exists most strongly in local than in national media, may be rewarded with a change to the story made as stealthily as the approach or with a crude, shameless editorial cut – or, on a good day for journalism, with a refusal to interfere with justified copy.

impartiality

Impartiality is demanded of regulated British broadcasting but not of British newspapers which are not regulated. Audiences, generally much more politically mixed, especially for national programmes, than newspaper readerships, are sensitive to partiality. Promised an impartial approach, they expect it, at times so sensitively that they challenge good sense. In the early part of the British general election campaign in 1992, the BBC had hundreds of complaints against the blue background of the studio set for the *Nine O'Clock News* on television, a programme which reported a great deal of election news. Callers said blue favoured the Conservative party because it is the party colour. According to one, 'The blue background cannot be considered impartial.' The colour of the set was changed.

For the BBC, 'due impartiality' was for years enshrined in a constitutional annex attached to its Charter and Licence, and for independent radio and television, the same phrase is used in the Broadcasting Act of 1990. The full statements were not identical. The commercial sector was and is required by the law to present news and, generally, to treat controversial public issues with due impartiality, whereas the BBC, through its governors, traditionally promised to behave with due impartiality on controversial matters. The difference did not matter in broad terms. Both sides were committed to the concept. The difference could have mattered in a legal challenge, partly because the impartiality requirements on independent radio and television in the Broadcasting Act are expressed more thoroughly than they were in the BBC Annex. But 1996 brought constitutional change. The BBC's new Charter and Agreement aims to put it on much the same footing as the commercial sector.

There is, though, still a difference of legal status. The Act, as statute law, imposes a legally enforceable duty of impartiality on independent broadcasting while the BBC Charter may not be legally enforceable in the same way. The point was not resolved in spite of a great controversial clamour in April 1995 when the Scottish courts stopped a BBC *Panorama* interview with John Major, as prime minister, from being shown in Scotland a few days before Scottish local elections. The BBC was accused by opposition political parties who brought the action of failing in its duty of impartiality. Their argument was that as elections were imminent an interview with the Conservative leader should be matched by similar interviews with other party leaders. In granting a temporary order to stop the programme in Scotland, the Scottish courts decided only that on the face of it the BBC had a case to answer. If the matter had gone to a full hearing the courts might have concluded that although the BBC had failed in its duty the courts could not do anything about it because the BBC, under a Royal Charter, is in a special position. The 1996 changes to the BBC's constitution will, however, encourage the courts in future to conclude that the BBC can indeed be held legally to account – on the basis of its own guidelines.

Legal status aside, the similarity of the basic commitment to impartiality used to hide detailed differences of substance between the BBC and the independent sector. The BBC made a very general statement, promising that its news and other programmes dealing with matters of public policy would treat controversial subjects with due impartiality. Meanwhile, the Independent Television Commission and, to a lesser extent, the Radio Authority are told by parliament in more detail what they must require of the people to whom they grant licences. For instance, the ITC, like the Radio Authority, must draw up a programme code to cover impartiality, among other things. Parliament says the ITC's code must explain, in relation to impartiality, what will be regarded as a 'series of programmes'.

This is to help make a judgement as to whether a series has been impartial overall. The code must also explain what 'due impartiality' calls for in particular circumstances. It must say how impartiality may be achieved in particular kinds of programmes. The 1996 changes put the BBC under an equal, politically driven obligation to describe its commitment to impartiality in some detail.

As a further refinement which, in its legal form, applied only to the commercial sector, the demand for 'due impartiality' is dropped, giving way to a ban on 'undue prominence' for some programmes of some local and other services. News at all levels always has to be duly impartial but the undue prominence variation applies to other local programmes dealing with political or industrial controversy or relating to public policy. Here, local independent radio and non-national independent television services have to make sure they do not give undue prominence 'to the views and opinions of particular persons or bodies'. The distinction did not feature in BBC statements, though programmes used it when relevant. For programme makers anywhere for most of the time there is no real difference between treating matters impartially and not allowing anyone's views to have too much prominence. But the two are not the same, and the difference eases the problems of a local station that genuinely can not locate a spokesperson for a particular point of view. A programme may fail to be impartial because someone is missing in spite of best efforts. In those circumstances, prominence for the view that does turn up is not automatically 'undue', a sensible concession all programmes deserve.

Previously, broadcasting regulation did not go as far as it does now. The most important point, though, may be that parliament does not try to say what impartiality is. It assumes it will be generally understood, if not always agreed in detail or how it applies in particular cases. In effect, it acknowledges that the law is not adequate to the task of defining it – and, most significantly, that it is not for politicians to have a detailed influence through rules they devise on how news is treated. It is left to the great and the good who become appointed to the ITC, the Radio Authority and the BBC board of governors to lay down rules and to pass judgements on programmes according to them, a loose rein that allows programme makers to proceed as they see fit – most of the time.

The nearest parliament comes to a description or a definition of impartiality is to say that it 'does not require absolute neutrality on every issue or detachment from fundamental democratic principles'. This is the language of guidelines. The sentiment is echoed or implied in the ITC Programme Code, the Radio Authority Programme Code and the BBC Producers' Guidelines.

In dealing with impartiality, these publications speak in terms of 'balance' while stressing that it is not to be understood in simple mathematical terms; they urge 'even-handedness' and 'fairness' and generally 'dispassionate' reporting; they call on programmes to recognise the relevant range of views on issues; and programmes should not 'editorialise' – unless they are personal view programmes, clearly labelled as such and operating within the permissible framework. The codes and guidelines acknowledge that impartiality, in the sense of presenting all significant points of view, may acceptably be achieved over a period of time rather than in one programme or one news broadcast. They state that with interviews editing must be impartial so that what remains after cuts fairly reflects the views of the person interviewed. Impartiality in political appearances means giving a fair amount of time to each of the parties or each noteworthy body of opinion. Reconstructions of real events in factual programmes must observe the precepts of impartiality. So must dramatised documentaries.

The Radio Authority is much the most severe about drama that dabbles in current controversies. While the ITC and the BBC haver in favour of creative talent, the Authority does not hesitate. It says 'Licence Holders must not broadcast fiction or drama designed to commend one side or the other in a matter of political or industrial controversy unless a further drama or fictional broadcast is planned to occur within three months which commends an opposing view.' The word 'designed' could be a loophole for the mischievous, offering acquittal on a technicality. The Authority's code forbids one-sided fiction on controversial issues being debated in parliament, a modern echo of the discredited and long-dead 'fourteen day rule', accepted under pressure by the BBC and eventually imposed by government in the 1950s, to stop broadcasters dealing with issues a fortnight before a parliamentary debate. The Radio Authority goes on to proscribe fiction that 'takes sides on any aspect of industrial relations during an important dispute'. Had the Radio Authority been the authority for all British radio, as it has at times urged it should be, this rule, plainly applied, would have stopped a number of illuminating dramas set in the coalfields and broadcast on BBC Radio 4 during the miners' strike of 1984–5. Distress moved the writers to side with the blighted mining communities, not with the government that encouraged pit closures nor with the police who tried to control the picket lines. Nor did the Coal Board, under its Scottish-American cost-cutting chairman, Ian Macgregor, evoke the sympathy of creative imaginations. The Radio Authority's zeal in this matter would allow impartiality to strangle creativity and may go further than parliament's intention, though it was the kind of thing a handful of right-wing backbenchers, particularly in the House of Lords, wanted and worked for as they sought to obstruct what they believed were left-leaning influences in broadcasting.

Of all the codes, rules and guidelines, the Radio Authority's do, though, use the expression that best captures the spirit of impartiality: it means not taking sides. It is the simplest way of putting it. Like the notion of balance, it is not a profound concept and is inclined to wither if taken too far. It is in the class of understanding which says the elephant is difficult to describe but easy to recognise. Total impartiality is accepted as not attainable because all journalism is affected by personal perceptions good and bad, by individual ignorance, individual insight, prejudice, personal preference, by lobbying and other slanting influences. The fallibility of human judgement denies complete impartiality. For believers, however, it is an ideal to be aimed for, best regarded as the spirit in which honest programmes are made, an approach that tries to be fair in very complex conditions. If journalists in public service broadcasting did not try to be impartial, if instead they could indulge their personal preferences without restraint, programmes would be polemics.

balance

Balance is not a concept to trouble newspapers much, although they all like to say a bit portentously that they take a suitably balanced approach to affairs. It is, though, a concept at the heart of the way British broadcasting is judged. It does not feature in the Broadcasting Act but years ago it acquired an official imprimatur through the now superceded Annex to the BBC Licence and Agreement, through the BBC Producers' Guidelines and in the programme codes parliament requires the Independent Television Commission and the Radio Authority to draw up. It features frequently in discussions about the quality of factual broadcasting and in complaints that programmes have not lived up to the standards expected of them.

Balance was never intended to mean 'thirty seconds for them and thirty seconds for each of the others', nor in newspapers to mean a sentence, a paragraph or an article to each of the contending views. Equality of sound-bite, the stop-watch version of balance in broadcasting, is favoured by the political parties when they believe their electoral chances would benefit from an equal quota of appearances. Other embattled interests suffering from adverse publicity in programmes also tend to interpret the concept in a mechanistic way. Programme makers regard these sceptically.

Balance is in fact a simple and straightforward notion, not profound, and not precise. It is closely allied to impartiality and fairness, and is used very often to mean much the same. These virtues of public service broadcasting are all quite ordinary and they impede, instead of helping, valid editorial effort if asked to deliver exact results. Sometimes the stop-watch is helpful, as during general elections when so much mundane party political comment is broadcast that the likeliest way to fair treatment all round is to stick close to quotas. Even then, the stop-watch is set aside when the news justifies more attention to one party than another. Stop-watch or not, experienced programme makers realise what interviewees find hard – that a cogent argument in thirty seconds is worth more than an ill-focused minute and a half. In such cases, equal time has low priority. To

44

decide whether a programme is reasonably balanced, the prominence of a contribution, how it is introduced, what follows it and whether it is directly rebutted by anyone else are all more significant than equal time.

For the normal run of programme making and newspaper reporting, balanced treatment means being even-handed, not giving one side of an argument unreasonable attention to its advantage or disadvantage. It means exploring issues in an uncommitted way so that viewers, listeners and readers appreciate all the important arguments, including the weight of support they enjoy. A balanced treatment of abortion, for instance, will recognise the passions that exist for and against without pretending that every argument is of equal weight and without every argument being given the same amount of air-time or equal column inches. It would recognise that some views on abortion are held by relatively few people but at times it may give minority views a great deal of attention because they are new, are developing, are particularly threatening or whatever. The dimensions of valid editorial interest are endless. Equally, balance does not mean allocating programme time or column inches according to the intensity of the belief.

It does not mean reflecting all sides to the argument every time the issue is examined. A newspaper feature or programme might fairly explore the growth of militant opposition to abortion that pickets vulnerable people outside clinics and might fairly try to understand the power of its belief without a word from the supporters of abortion. Even if the programme or station or paper had not explored any other aspect of abortion and did not intend to, it could still have dealt with the militants in a balanced way. The critical question would be whether the militants had gained unfair advantage or suffered unfair disadvantage as a result and, arising from that, whether the public was badly or well served.

objectivity

Objectivity is one of the partners of impartiality, often taken to mean much the same. It is a virtue expected of public service broadcasters, not required of newspapers. Programme journalists recognise that objectivity is not totally achievable but this does not allow them to abandon the idea that they must try to report events in ways that will survive scrutiny. Better to try to be objective as far as possible than to swamp people with partiality.

The idea is easily rubbished. Sceptics say it is dangerously misleading. It causes people to believe that certain news organisations are more to be trusted than others because they try to be objective and impartial when in fact their judgements are as selective and as biased as anyone else's. Overtly biased publications are, by this analysis, more honest because they do not pretend to be anything else and their prejudices are evident for all to see.

The actual performance of organisations that claim to be objective is also much questioned. Large numbers of viewers and listeners take objectivity to mean they will not hear or see anything done in a way that offends their idea of how it should be done. Claims to objectivity seem to encourage intolerance in its customers. When issues divide societies deeply, many people complain that coverage is partial, not objective, and that it will make divisions worse. The criticism was made persistently against the British media during the years of strife in Northern Ireland. What satisfied the nationalist community tended to disaffect the loyalists, and what met approval from loyalists in the neat terraced streets of east Belfast was scoffed at in the Bogside of Derry and the Catholic areas of west Belfast.

The same response greeted broadcast coverage of the miners' strike in 1984–5, the most bitter, the biggest and most protracted labour dispute in Britain for many years. Few people were neutral and many were suspicious of the news programmes. The miners' leader, Arthur Scargill, encouraged his members to the view that the news media were part of the enemy, active in a conspiracy to misrepresent the miners and to mislead the public. The belief was fostered when BBC television news inadvertently reversed pictures of a sequence of events during violent picketing at the Orgreave coking plant. Pickets were shown as charging the police and the police as retaliating when it was in fact the other way round. The mistake was later put right and the BBC apologised. But the human failure in the stressful process of quick editing was repeatedly, for years, paraded as evidence of bias, a damaging failure of objectivity that turned public opinion, it was said, against the miners. Those who claim to be objective, or are required to be so, are not allowed simple mistakes.

newspaper code of practice

Fears about the threat of legislation, particularly on privacy, pushed British newspapers and magazines into a code of practice in the early 1990s. They drew it up and the Press Complaints Commission ratified it. The Commission, a non statutory body supported by the industry, uses the code when considering complaints against newspapers. And as a development of compelling importance, a growing number of newspaper editors have the code written into their contracts: their conditions of employment require them to observe it. It is a simple document, a statement of principles and good behaviour, a preamble and eighteen clauses on two sides of paper, available to the public.

The code is professionally alert, as to be expected from the authorship, and it is, for the most part, realistic. Least convincing, in some ways simplistic, are the three opening clauses on 'Accuracy', 'Opportunity to reply', and 'Comment, conjecture and fact'. Like all such documents, the code has to make use of qualifications such as 'with due prominence', 'whenever appropriate', and 'when reasonably called for' if it is not to ramble on endlessly through a multitude of editorial possibilities. These decent, well-meant qualifications become escape routes for journalists reluctant to observe the spirit of the code. When the code says 'An apology should be published whenever appropriate' it leaves room for much argument, case by case, about whether it really would be appropriate in the circumstances.

The clause on 'Comment . . .' puts the hope of old fashioned standards before good sense when it says 'Newspapers, whilst free to be partisan, should distinguish clearly between comment, conjecture and fact.' Modern journalism in newspapers, as in broadcasting, only more so, blends comment, conjecture and fact in ways that take professional insight or special knowledge to detect and separate. Decently done, the mix enables journalism to cope sensibly with complex stories. It is also much abused. Human interest stories that seem to be most straightforward frequently do not bear scrutiny as statements of truth. Political news, the strongest area of newspaper partisanship, is notorious for bias wrapped up as fact, as the Labour party, one of the two big parties in British politics, would testify about tabloid coverage of its policies before the 1992 general election. Some voters were seriously misled by a scurrilous blend of comment, conjecture and fact in news reports of Labour's tax plans.

The code is firmly against journalistic intrusion on patients in hospitals, against journalistic intimidation and harassment, against pejorative references to race, colour, religion, sex and disability, in favour of sympathy and discretion towards people in grief, and strong on care in dealing with children. It is specific and uncompromising on references to children in sex cases. Clause 13 of the code says 'The press should not, even where the law does not prohibit it, identify children under the age of 16 who are involved in cases concerning sexual offences, whether as victims, or as witnesses or defendants.'

An important choice is made for reporting sexual offences against children. The code says the adult may be identified, that the term 'incest' should not be used and that something like 'serious offences against young children' should be used instead. That accords with long established practice, particularly in local newspapers where most reports of such offences are to be found. The disadvantage is that the British public does not readily learn from its newspapers of the extent of sexual abuse in the family because reports are disguised. And when public opinion is not well informed about a wrong it does not demand that it be righted.

Journalists who find themselves in conflict with the law of the land over confidential sources have the full backing of the code for newspapers. It says unflinchingly 'Journalists have a moral obligation to protect confidential sources of information.'

48

The code is emphatic on the public interest, a concept at the heart of disputes about journalistic ethics, most notably disputes about the privacy of public figures and about intrusive methods. The concept appears as a justification for otherwise questionable behaviour in five clauses of the code, on 'Privacy', 'Listening devices', 'Misrepresentation', 'Harassment' and 'Payment for articles'. It says of journalistic subterfuge, for instance, that it 'can be justified only in the public interest and only when material cannot be obtained by any other means'.

The cause of the public interest is regarded as so important that the code devotes its final clause to a definition of it. The clause suggests that the public interest may properly be invoked when crime or serious misdemeanour are being exposed, when public health and safety are at risk, and, in a provision of far-reaching significance, when 'preventing the public from being misled by some statement or action of an individual or organisation'. Government ministers who preach family values while keeping a mistress are among those who fall foul of that provision.

straight dealing

Journalists so often enquire into matters people do not want to talk about they soon develop methods of approach that are tentative, careful, oblique, roundabout, stealthy or sly. If it suits their purpose, they ask questions on the phone without declaring who they are, and if necessary pretend to business other than journalism. The description does not apply to all journalists all of the time but most, at some time, have behaved in ways most people would not regard as straight. It is one of the reasons for the poor reputation of journalists, competing as they do with politicians and estate agents for bottom places in the popularity list. It gives rise to the scathing image of the wheedling figure with the brown trilby, the grubby raincoat, the cigarette, the seedy complexion and the boozed features.

The phenomenon stretches back to the origins of journalism. First applied to newspapers, it extends to broadcasting though the conspicuous apparatus of television and radio might be expected to limit the opportunities for shifty approaches. Concern in the BBC that some programme makers were not as open as they should be about their intentions towards interviewees and other contributors led to rules about straight dealing being devised and being included as first chapter in two successive editions of the Producers' Guidelines. Complaints had generated the concern. On examination, a number left a suspicion that a small minority of producers, researchers or reporters had been less than honest or worse, a minority who compromised the reputation of all the rest. The concern was not confined to the BBC. It was echoed in complaints about other broadcasting organisations and it was a charge levelled more at television than at radio.

The need in broadcasting for comments to be literally 'on the record' encourages the problem. Where a newspaper journalist will make do with a comment from an unnamed source, in a reference dressed up to persuade as in 'a source in company headquarters', television strives to record it on video tape. And deviousness is used to persuade people to record when they might be reluctant if the real purpose is openly declared. After programmes had been broadcast, a repeated complaint from people interviewed was that the purpose of the interview and the programme were not made clear, that they were explained harmlessly in a generalised way. In one notorious case, a programme about a rape, the producer was accused of inveigling people into co-operation by telling them the programme was about trauma. Typically in cases complained about, the interview for the programme would be at length, half an hour or more, but with only a small extract used, an extract that at the time of recording seemed almost an aside but which assumed great importance in the different context of the completed programme. People felt the true intention had been deliberately kept from them. They had been enticed into talking about something they would have refused to talk about or would have talked about more circumspectly had the programme makers been honest with them. When the programme people admitted their guile, which was not often, they said it uncovered important truth which would otherwise have been hidden.

Another factor to make programme producers and programme reporters seem less than straight is that many people do not appreciate the need for a crisp 'sound-bite'. Practised politicians and other seasoned public figures do. They know the game. But people not used to interviews often feel cheated when only thirty seconds is used out of an interview that lasted thirty minutes. The harsh reality that it took thirty minutes of fishing to produce thirty succinct seconds passes them by.

People who complain are not always to be trusted. They too have hidden purposes especially when they are in significant positions. They are at times too slow to realise until after the event that the burden of telling an unwelcome truth is more painful when millions see you doing it on the television screen. The unguarded comment, the remark regretted cannot be denied when you have been seen to make it. The quote in the newspaper is easier to deny, or to charge as being used out of context, or to have been made 'off-the-record', a phrase of seriously uncertain meaning that can give credence to spurious complaint because it can mean 'not for use at all' or simply 'not for attribution'. The alleged victim of television has to make a more elaborate case against television journalists. The case is usually that the journalists misled them from the outset in one way or another.

Consumer programmes that routinely pursue commercial villains and exploiters might be expected to be accused of underhand dealing more often than others. In fact, they are among the least likely to be so accused. Apart from formally approved surreptitious methods, mainly secret recordings, they tend to confront their targets openly and to provide clear opportunities to answer difficult points, including allegations, though these opportunities may well involve 'foot-in-the-door' methods or scuffling encounters on the pavement. Consumer programmes are more likely to face complaint, obstruction and prevarication before transmission than after, the tactics of their victims, usually companies and corporations, occasionally informed by former consumer pro-gramme people who have become specialist advisers, poachers turned gamekeepers.

accuracy

Accuracy ought not to be an editorial issue. It is a fundamental value, deserving to be unquestioned and always applied as rigorously as reporters and editors can apply it. Instead, in significant areas of journalism, it is cynically manipulated, waved aside with the old jest that the facts should not be allowed to get in the way of a good story.

Even when intentions are good, accuracy is often much more difficult to achieve than non-journalists would believe. Reporters frequently depend, at best, on the eye-witness of others who have no training and who in newsworthy circumstances may become nervously unreliable or, worse, on honest but struggling third-hand hearsay, and worst of all, on the say so of people who want their partial version of events to be accepted as the whole truth.

News is also escorted by professionals through a variety of channels, shedding a bit of reliability every step of the way, mocking the experience of its handlers, the journalists. Picked up first by a seasoned freelance from a whisper, adapted knowingly after a call to police headquarters miles away, further embellished when rendered into journalese as the story is filed to an agency, snappily re-written before it gets on the agency wires, remodelled once more by a newsroom sub-editor, and then improved by a judicious word massage here and there from a more senior editor before it reaches the trusting public as a true record of what happened. By then the merchants of truth have delivered a reasonable approximation or, for all they know, a gross distortion.

Because of this propensity for news to travel badly, some American journals use 'fact checkers'. They check essential facts in copy by going back to primary sources or as near as they can get to them. Their remit runs from the momentous to the trivial. They are not confined to bald facts. They question judgements because they have to be justified by the facts. American media-study circles have referred to a 'fetishism of facts' and that fact checkers are 'obsessed with facticity', like accusing a doctor of being obsessed with cure.

By comparison, British and other European journalism seems careless of fact and scandalously lax in judgement. It is an exaggerated impression. There are lessons though. Getting it right is much harder than the public imagines and decidedly harder than some journalists realise. It is significant that on American news magazines the fact checkers check articles written by 'editors' or 'writers' in magazine offices far removed from the events they are writing about although using piles of copy from reporters and correspondents all over the world. For news magazines it works. The level of error in fact-checked publications is significantly better than in those that rely entirely on trust in the original reporter. But the way it works on weekly news magazines with time to consider each line would not fit readily into hurried daily news in newspapers or on radio and television. And when fact checkers were mooted for the BBC, staff derided the idea, saying they would accept only fat cheques.

It is a serious issue. Simple situations may be mildly misrepresented in the reporting; complex situations run the risk of being misrepresented very badly. To a greater or lesser extent all journalists re-write. They improve inelegant bits of reportage and without realising it introduce ambiguities. In further re-writing, ambiguities turn into falsehoods ready for public consumption. Moreover, when these inadvertent and other falsehoods occur in newspapers, they may be distributed yet more widely because they are at times recycled by broadcast journalists, some of whom uncritically accept what is printed in newspapers as automatically reliable. In a perfect world, no journalist would accept another's facts without independent checks. Another enemy is the background fact the journalist is sure of or takes for granted and does not even think to check. It may be a name, a person's age, an MP's constituency. It comes out wrong because a simple, cautionary check was not made. In the unattainable perfect world, journalists would check their own assumptions as diligently as they should check what other journalists have reported. Part of the problem is that the degree of checking and re-checking which is ideally desirable would slow down the process to such an extent that some of today's news would not be ready until the day after tomorrow.

good news, bad news

A steady stream of complaint from the public says the news is too gloomy, that there is too much bad news and that journalism is to blame because positive developments are ignored. Government sometimes develops the complaint, arguing that excessive bad news saps public morale by exaggerating failures and underestimating successes. Business joins in now and again with the argument that excessive bad news seriously damages the country's image and its commercial efforts abroad.

Broadcasting is a frequent target in this criticism, probably because the intimacy of the spoken word and the power of the moving picture excite people's anxieties more readily than do printed words and most still pictures. From time to time, broadcasting responds by making a special effort to report the positive, and even by introducing 'good news' programmes. The BBC television news presenter Martyn Lewis caused a flurry in the early 1990s when he sided with the critics. These evangelical efforts invariably run into the sand. Nothing much changes. A BBC Radio 3 'positive news' effort in the 1970s collapsed when the producer gave up the hopeless search for news stories that qualified. Other initiatives have gone the same way. But the criticism persists and because of it programme journalists continue to include positive reports in the news when they can.

In an important sense, the criticism is groundless. Even the worst news has positive elements. The famines and genocides of Africa arouse passionate concern and huge relief effort. The world has for ever suffered from heart-breaking disaster but only in recent times have humanitarian agencies moved consciences and supplies to the extent they do now. Reports of accidents show people behaving with courage and self-sacrifice. In other ways too and without riding on the back of disasters, the news media provide frequent insights into genuine human progress – in reports of medical advances, in reports of big commercial contracts for public works aimed at improving the daily lot of millions of people, in reports of human endurance and in reports of technological invention that relieve drudgery and danger. It is all there for people who care to look for it without bias.

A natural psychological factor creates the impression that the news is all bad. Most bad news has much more impact than most good news. Pictures of disaster and failure persist in the mind while pictures and information of positive developments have little impact at all or it fades rapidly. This would not be changed if journalists gave the positive more prominence, as the simplistic form of the criticism calls for. Specially placed good news would be unconvincing, a shift towards propaganda, and the bad news, still the most powerful, would continue to be the most remembered.

Accordingly, when people say there is too much bad news, they are, to an important degree, criticising their own perceptions. They also overlook the influence the news media, especially television, have as a force for the benefit of humankind against hostile or indifferent authority.

Birtism

No one really knows what 'Birtism' means. Even the man whose name has been hijacked, John Birt, would be hard pushed to define it and he, in any case, is said to dislike it as a term. The word took hold after he was appointed deputy director general of the BBC in 1987 and tended to be used as a criticism by people, particularly inside the BBC and especially inside BBC television current affairs, who did not like his ideas.

If it could be tied down to an editorial meaning, it would signify an unusually methodical approach to the making of serious programmes, probably also to the making of light-hearted programmes. It would put greater store on detailed calculation than on inspired insight. It would certainly expect great reliability, of perspective as well as of fact. It would put emphasis on explaining what things mean and why they are as they are, that is the attempt to get rid of the 'bias against understanding', the charge against television news, jointly prosecuted by Birt and the economics journalist, Peter Jay, in the 1970s.

Part of the calculating approach of Birtism is to try to make sure that 'built' programmes and features – those prepared over a number of days, weeks or months – work out clearly in advance what their intentions are and stick to them, instead of starting with a general idea and allowing the programme to go wherever the trail takes it. This involves strong research before anything is recorded. It is the aspect most virulently objected to by critics of editorial Birtism. They see it as a denial of robust journalism in that reporters and producers should be able to adapt their direction according to the facts they uncover, not to stick mechanically to a trail predetermined by earlier research. The conflict of view is, almost certainly, sterile, based on misunderstanding, some of it wilful. The issue is not whether broadcast journalism is to be allowed to follow the facts wherever they lead. The true disagreement is about the stage at which this should be done. The Birt way is for the conclusion to be as clear as possible before the programme commits itself to interviews and other recordings and to limit unpredicted directions to the minimum. Many journalists feel strongly that their job cannot be done properly without a large degree of continuing freedom to take whatever editorial turn they believe justified.

Birtism as a concept accrued managerial meanings before Birt became BBC director general in 1993. It now seems to mean any policy he encouraged, managerial or editorial, and which well-meaning, as well as ill-meaning, traditionalists do not like, for instance, the free market way of managing resources for programmes, known as producer choice.

identification

The disadvantages of being identified in the newspapers and in the news on radio and television are more widely felt than they used to be. One reason is that even a mild media interest these days means being approached, harried as the quarry sees it, by a squad of reporters, photographers and camera crews, bearing the intrusive weapons of the news trade.

56

When the interest is high, as when the media pursue well-known personalities or their lovers, alleged or actual, the squad becomes a small army and the weapons of the trade are augmented to include step ladders, listening devices and the surreptitious long lens.

Another, perhaps more powerful influence is that television has disclosed how disagreeable it all is. In the old days when newspapers ran around after the news, when the BBC did not bother much and when independent radio and television did not exist, only the victims of newsworthiness knew how much of an ordeal it was. The newspapers did not show the pursuit, or showed it only rarely. Now, millions of people who have never been newsworthy and who never will be can see for themselves, on the television screen, the intimidating insistence of the news hounds and the unseemly thrust of microphones and cameras. Many do not like it and the newsgathering scrum often distracts attention from the news being gathered.

It has all contributed to the belief that in the face of self-interested behaviour by the news media, often not justified by a genuine public interest, people need to be protected. Programmes and newspapers are honest enough to air the concern so that people who have been in the public eye for a few days or for a week or two are seen and heard to testify to the nature of the ordeal. The debate about privacy reflects the concern. In another aspect, the courts of law are increasingly sympathetic to the desire for anonymity on the part of witnesses and victims – and to defendants who face further trials – to such an extent that the principle of open justice is seriously qualified. There are suggestions that, as in a few other European countries, the names of people accused in legal cases should not be made public unless and until they are found guilty. Support groups talk about the ordeal of victims of crimes and accidents, with some opinion seeking to give victims control over they way their experiences are used editorially and, by implication, whether they should be used at all. Unless victims of crime consent, a number of police forces will not identify them to journalists when giving news of crime. In time of war, as in the 1991 Gulf War when American, British, French and Arab forces acted against Iraq for invading and over-running Kuwait, the Ministry of Defence in Britain and the armed services strongly protect the families of the dead, the injured and missing.

The issues of identification, harassment and intrusion merge into a composite problem. If names are not given in the first place, people cannot be approached let alone harassed. If they agree to speak only anonymously, their ordeal at the hands of the media is held to be lessened and in most such cases it is lessened because an anonymous witness is much less appealing than a witness of flesh and bone and tears. If these pressures advance in response to collective excesses the media will not act against they will damage the generally overlooked contribution news makes to knowledge. They would reduce the human element in the news and without the human element, reports of crime and disaster become cold, far enough removed from the suffering of identifiable people to fail to evoke compassion and understanding.

portrayal

Journalism is notorious for leaving individuals and groups with the belief that it has misrepresented them, not so much by getting facts wrong, though that occurs often enough, as by elevating a few facts and excluding others. Independent-minded journalism takes the view that it must portray people according to its purposes and as it sees them rather than as they see themselves or would like others to see them. Even without the distraction of political correctness, it is an area of genuine conflict between journalistic independence and social sensitivity.

Wilful as journalistic partiality sometimes is, it is mainly a product of the pursuit of 'the story'. Facts about people are relevant only to the extent they relate to the news story. People who appear in stories are partially portrayed because only part of them is relevant. A news reporter does not normally want their life story or even a rounded picture of them. If a person in a wheelchair is involved, say as a victim of a robbery at home, the fact of the wheelchair nearly always matters more to the story than the full-time job the person does. The wheelchair will be prominent because it adds interest, the full-time job at best referred to in passing because it is not relevant and, in the context, not interesting. This is likely to change only a little and slowly – not at all in some journalistic quarters. After a few years of hard-bitten experience, journalists come to dislike facts being wished into their stories for ulterior, non-journalistic purposes whether to appease a political or commercial pressure, or to concede a point to a well-intentioned lobby that argues for a better social image for single parents or for 'pensioners', the usual British label, for gays or for any of the other groups who feel misrepresented, misunderstood and – as a result, they say – badly provided for.

To that extent, clichés and stereotypes are inevitable, ensuring vigorous argument and protest. Journalistic resistance to pressure is well justified because there are so many 'image-improvers' keen to bend journalism to their purposes. Equally, decent social sensitivity, though liable to be scoffed at as politically correct, sees many instances of media discrimination on grounds of sex and sexual character, race, disability and age, failings that arise from general biases shared by journalists.

The issues may be more important for broadcasting than for newspapers, partly because the way people are heard and seen in programmes gives the impression of being authentic, partly because the structure of radio and television forces broadcasters to listen more carefully to criticism, and partly because of a belief that broadcasting, being a public service, should set an example. As a result, programme makers come under pressure over the position of women. The argument here is that discrimination against women is discrimination against half the population. It includes – or used to include – excessive portrayal of them as 'mums', shoppers and housewives, media images that helped to consolidate male domination, not just of top jobs but of middle and lower jobs. Pressure comes also from organisations and individuals on behalf of black people. They used to feature disproportionately as problems and still suffer from unfair generalisations promoted by white prejudice. Black people were hardly ever shown in responsible roles and few are now. Lobbies work on behalf of disabled people. They still tend to appear only in ways connected with their disabilities as though they were disqualified from 'normal' concerns and are all incapable of doing normal jobs. The case is that media images confirm the discrimination that disabled people are relevant only in terms of their disabilities. Older people – known considerately in politically correct America as 'seniors' – have campaigners too. They argue that older people are disregarded, sometimes demeaned, pensioners regarded as social passengers. AIDS and the rise of intolerance during the 1980s gave urgency to pressure groups for gays and lesbians. They are concerned that hostile and derisive words and simpering, one-sided images encourage homophobia.

The pressures call on journalists to make decisions on all of these issues. The arguments have to be recognised rather than accepted. Recognising them involves being alert, less to crude biases which tend to occur only if they are intended, than to unintended hidden messages in words and subtle, unconsidered slants in stories.

political correctness

Political correctness struggles to survive in Britain. It flourished for a while in what became known as 'loony left' local authorities where public policies passionately favoured minority needs, the dubious as well as the deserving. Elsewhere, it quickly became a wilting import from America where notions of equality and fairness are pursued more determinedly through rules, regulations, codes, quotas and policies than the British have stomach for. It was from the start a pejorative term in the British context, a counter-productive phrase that damages what its socially improving proponents try to achieve. It has, perversely, set back the causes of feminism and minority rights. Hostility to it has helped racism, sexism and other biased 'isms'. The case for journalistic care in the use of language – to avoid 'policemen' because there are 'policewomen', to avoid references to skin colour when it has nothing to do with the issue, to refuse to say 'dykes' and 'queers' in a hostile context – is now easily mocked by invoking the curse of political correctness.

The concern, shared by American commentators who do not enjoy riding bandwagons, is that determined political correctness prevents some problems being discussed at all or as frankly as they should be. However well-intended, it becomes censorship. Desirable sensitivities encourage a strong consensus in the media and in other places, a caring bandwagon of do-gooding that rolls on regardless of doubts. What is acceptable in language, attitude, social behaviour and collective policy and what is not become so firmly established that, like articles of faith, they are not questioned. Connected issues become taboo as matters for discussion. In this way the 'land of the free' sets limits on free expression in polite, liberal circles only to find that it has also set up a corrective backlash, voiced by impatient right-wingers, against 'preference policies' for disadvantaged minorities.

journalese

Journalese is poorly regarded, an abuse of language, cliché ridden, strongly contributing to declined standards of speech and writing, a baleful influence on the young, a source of exasperation to the middle aged and middle class, a banal form of writing that over-simplifies and which indicates an over-simplified view of the world. The word is dismissive. But journalese would not survive were it not successful. It justifies a different string of terms. Journalese is a vigorous form of expression, plain, straightforward, calculated to capture the attention of people who might otherwise ignore events in the world beyond their personal experience, a form that renders complex facts and circumstances simple because it sees no virtue in convolutions that deter interest.

In newspapers, easy writing makes easy reading and, in broadcasting, normal programme speech in news and other topical programmes is designed to convey meaning without distraction. The linearity of broadcasting means that listeners and viewers cannot go back over what they did not understand or what slipped by them because they were distracted by something else. The 'something else' can be the language used. If it is exceptional, exceptionally attractive or exceptionally ugly, the audience will pay so much attention to the form of speech that the message will be missed. A topical, non-creative programme fails if audiences notice the way they are spoken to rather than what they are told. The programme speech should be so easy as to make broadcasting seem easy.

The news columns of most newspapers are also written to be easily absorbed though people can always go back over what they have read. News journalists tend to see it as a personal failure if their work requires mental mastication. Gnarled news editors and chief subs who are not to be argued with insist that a difficult news story misses its target.

Journalese is purposeful. It has a function. It is not as it is because it does not know how to be better. It can, without doubt, go too far and become a parody. It happens. But journalese is also a joker who cultivates excess, especially in the biggest selling tabloid newspapers where exaggerated populism plays profitably on the connections between language and class in its 'Gotchas' and 'Worra lorra laffs'. 'Pop and prattle' radio exploits language in much the same way to appeal to younger people. At another extreme and in the long years of no direct competition, BBC Radio 3 cultivated a brand of lugubrious speech, supposedly of appeal to listeners who appreciate correct, grammatical talk along with other higher cultural values but which became so odd that a critic condemned it as the speech of a group of people talking to themselves while listeners eavesdropped. It was the excess of 'anti-journalese', a cure at least as bad as the ill.

Journalese gets implied support from experts in language who dismiss the idea of 'good usage' and 'bad usage'. When the test is the effectiveness of communication, journalese passes the test. It works because it communicates well.

journalistic rights and privileges

An old school of journalistic thought says journalists in Britain have no special rights and privileges and should have none. The argument is that journalistic rights are based on the rights of the citizen and amount to no more. A reporter watching a trial in court, for instance, is doing what ordinary members of the public in the public gallery are free to do and are, in fact, doing. That the reporter then writes about it in a newspaper or talks about it in a news programme is simply a difference of function, not a difference of right. The reporter's right to tell people what parliament is doing, though hard fought for many years ago, is equally ordinary. Nor is the reporter at the scene of an accident specially privileged.

The elementary argument is passionately held and has powerful implications. It becomes a case against the licensing of journalists and journalism, an aspect hotly argued at the time the Police and Criminal Evidence Act of 1984 was going through parliament as a bill. The argument was deployed in a dispute over plans in the bill to allow police to have access to journalistic material when they needed it as evidence in criminal cases. That aspect of the bill was strongly opposed by journalist bodies. As a concession, the government offered to introduce special terms for such access. That too was opposed by the 'old school' on the grounds that it would put journalists into a special position. Their material would be treated differently from evidence held by ordinary citizens. A slippery slope, said the old school, a historic and undesirable departure in the status of journalists.

The argument became fevered. If journalistic material was to be treated specially, it would have to be defined. It would imply a definition of journalist. Before long, it was feared, the law would have decided who was and who was not a journalist, regardless of what journalists and their professional organisations thought. Others argued for special treatment, exemption if possible, on the grounds that ready police access to journalists' material for use in criminal investigation and prosecution was more threatening than a theoretical chain of concerns about the status of journalists that was unlikely to occur in reality. Faced with this split, government went ahead anyway. The Police and Criminal Evidence Act provides special treatment for journalistic material. Police have to follow a special procedure to acquire notebooks, recordings, pictures and any other items through a court order if, as often happens, the journalist will not hand them over voluntarily.

To this extent and regardless of the ineffectiveness of the special treatment brought about by judges deciding in favour of the police at least 90 per cent of the time, journalists in Britain now have a legal right not given to ordinary citizens. In other ways too, the argument that the journalist is only a citizen with a special function is a sham. There are many privileges, perhaps not legally enforceable, but real enough. Reporters do not share court seats with the public. They have special arrangements, a press box. They have special arrangements in the House of Commons and the Lords and these include access to parts of the Palace of Westminster not allowed to the public. They are treated differently in a multitude of ways because of the job they do. Government offices, local councils, the police, hospitals, commercial companies and the entertainment industry all respond to journalists in ways denied to the public. The highest acknowledgement of the special position of journalism comes from the loftiest legal authorities, the Court of Appeal and the Lords, who, very occasionally, weave into a judgment a recognition of journalism as a vital function in democracy.

None the less, an enduring part of the old-style argument is the insistence that journalism is properly based on civil rights, not special rights. Like any good belief, it can be qualified here and there without being compromised. Most journalists could unite around the view that, as what they do is best done on behalf of the public, their position in society should be close to the position of citizen.

outside interests

Newspapers are much more liberal than broadcasting about the outside activities of their editorial staff, their liberality according with the freedom of newspapers to take sides. A newspaper may well tolerate one of its journalists siding with political or other controversial interests contrary to its own, provided those interests are not disreputable and do not slant the work of the journalist against the interests of the paper. It is not unusual for right-wing newspapers to have active left-wing journalists working for them and for some to be elected to the House of Commons on the Labour benches.

Broadcasting produces a fair number of MPs as well and, in spite of frequent condemnations that programme making is generally left-wing, most of the former broadcasters in the Commons during the 1980s and into the 1990s were on the Conservative benches. The important difference compared with newspapers is that while still in broadcasting, anyone with editorial powers must not actively engage in party political work or in favour of any other cause that seriously divides public opinion. It would put too strong a question mark over the broadcasters' duty to be impartial. Any broadcaster adopted as a prospective candidate for a political party in a constituency has to step down from editorial work that covers politics or other public issues. Professionalism and integrity would enable journalists to work impartially while working also for a political party but the broadcasting organisations are concerned that the suspicious public would see political bias. The policy may be summed up as 'If you would not want the public to know about it, do not do it; and if the public might get the wrong impression, do not do it.'

The stern approach covers many outside activities. A journalist in broadcasting, whether producer, editor or personality, who writes newspaper or magazine articles must not express committed views on divisive issues. The same applies to lectures and speeches. The rules also frown on public relations work or training by impartial programme makers for any organisation they might have to deal with for their programmes.

The protections for the sensitive virtue, impartiality, are not as well observed by programme people as the broadcasting organisations would like. Much work of a questionable kind goes on quietly, undeclared and undiscovered, sometimes doing no harm, but sometimes eroding reputation little by little. Some programme personalities, already well paid for their efforts, make a great deal of money 'on the side'.

payments

However hard the media watchdogs try, they cannot get rid of the cheque book in journalism. As in so many editorial matters, the prevailing journalistic attitude is pragmatic 'If you have to do it, you have to do it.' If you have to pay, you pay. But first, you try to get what you want without paying.

Local newspapers and local radio are probably the least frequent payers, not because they are more principled but because they are poorer. They expect to get as much news as they can without paying contributors for their time and effort, and when they do pay, the levels of remuneration are low. The biggest payers are the national tabloids. National television is modest by comparison. The tabloids regularly pay thousands to whisk away the newsworthy, an investment in pages of exclusive human interest coverage. Most payments are much less dramatic, a few hundred here, sometimes a thousand or two for a very desirable interview, more likely thirty or fifty pounds for a favour or a facility.

MPs not in government used to be paid a small fee as a matter of course for interviews in daily current affairs programmes on BBC radio and television but policy changed in the early 1980s. It was decided then that such appearances were part of political life for which a fee was not appropriate. The need for economies was an unacknowledged factor. The BBC wrote to all MPs to explain the change. A few, all frequent interviewees, complained for a time afterwards that they had not been paid. A few programme editors also worried that they would lose interviews they wanted unless they paid. What was and still is known as a 'disturbance fee' was allowed when an MP had been significantly inconvenienced and was increasingly used to circumvent the no-payment rule. Guidelines now caution against it.

personal views

Newspapers are generally tolerant of the public expression of personal views by journalists; television and radio are not. The difference stems from the demands of impartiality on the broadcasters, demands that are not made of newspapers. Though a radio or television journalist may strive to avoid any hint of a personal view in broadcast reports, people listening will suspect bias if the journalist is known for committed views expressed in magazine articles, interviews or talks. The problem tends to dog well-known newspaper journalists who join broadcasting, especially those who have written opinionated columns. They have a track record. They are known for certain views, a reputation that precedes them and trails behind them. It is not an insuperable problem but it gives rise to a rule that any newspaper article, speech or book by a broadcast journalist bound by the demands of impartiality should not stray beyond what would be allowed if they were to be dealing with the same subjects in an impartial broadcast.

personal view programmes

Programmes devoted to a personal view, whether of an individual or a group of like-minded individuals, are suspect creatures in public service broadcasting. The old-fashioned view is that any view can be quoted or expressed but that no programme should be made from the perspective of that point of view. It does not accord with the aspirations of some modern programme makers. They see strongly held personal views as a valuable resource to be exploited. As a result, personal views are often allowed a free run in programmes described as 'access' or 'community interest'. They may appear as short spurts like BBC2's *Fifth Column* which gave individuals ten minutes or so of screen time to press a point of view. They may appear as solid documentaries or features.

When well done they can illuminate a

subject in ways that often elude carefully balanced programmes. But they are on the face of it an offence against impartiality. They also give rise to suspicions that they are surrogates for left-wing programme makers to air views they hold themselves. The suspicion is fed by the strong tendency of personal view programmes to be against officialdom and authority. The views in most such programmes are not familiar. If they were, the programme makers would not be half so interested in them – for the very good reason that familiar views, orthodoxy that is, get abundant opportunity for expression in normal programmes.

Parliament was concerned to deal with personal view programmes during passage of the bill that became the Broadcasting Act of 1990. To some right-wing members in the House of Lords slanted programmes seemed to be an insidious threat. Rules were laid down for independent radio and independent television which are now reflected as they have to be in the programme codes of the Independent Television Commission and of the Radio Authority. They tell the programme companies that all personal view programmes should be clearly marked: listeners and viewers should be in no doubt what they are getting. Partial the programmes may be, but not based on false evidence. If they are part of a series, balance is to be achieved by giving other outstanding points of view a fair show in the same series, or by letting them be heard in early phone-ins or right of reply programmes. The programme companies have to be able to demonstrate to their regulators that over a reasonable period their programmes did not favour any side. In that way, parliament has edged towards a description of impartiality that was previously left to the broadcasters.

advertising

Promoters work energetically and inventively for product placement by mention, editorial publicity their prize. Reporters, editors and programme producers are expected to make sure their work recognises the real world of commerce while refusing blandishments to include references that are helpful to products and editorially gratuitous. Ever present temptations range from the frequently fallen-for sponsored survey, usually trivial and hardly ever worthwhile as a statistical statement, to a credit for an anodyne comment on the news from a commercial body, to the sponsored event.

Sponsored events are insidiously successful, with no editorial escape. In sport, the commercial interest has bought space for its name at the top of the scoreboard, on the outfield and in the name of the event. Organisers of events desperate for cash allowed commercial interests to attach their name to new or one-off events and soon it spread to established events. News learned to say 'The Cornhill Test' when 'The Test' had for decades communicated well enough. Now commercial plugs decorate editorial copy abundantly, justified by the belief that without them there would be fewer worthwhile events to report because turnstile takings cannot meet the costs.

News and current affairs programmes on television are less prone to product placement, as normally understood, than are drama and other creative work because they do not need to persuade the imagination by use of realistic props. When they show real goods, it is easier to make sure products shown are justified editorially. Factual programmes and newspaper pages that feature commercial goods as a matter of course, such as those about food, holidays and motoring, can only make sure that over a period of time they publicise a reasonable range without favouritism.

plugging products

Public relations officers are supposed to try hard to achieve it and journalists are supposed to try hard to resist it. The difference between a valid editorial mention of a commercial product and a plug can be so thin that the most experienced do not know the difference. To plug a book is acceptable, usually. To plug a film or play is tolerated, often. To plug a car is done surreptitiously in context. To plug a washing powder is a form of product placement.

Books, films and plays are given special treatment because they are entertainment or have cultural value. For programmes and newspapers they also provide lively content, interviews with famous or unusual authors, comments on and from notable actors. The different mediums of communication are hand in glove, doing each other a few favours to the benefit of the public. But in truth, new motor cars are reviewed and talked about in much the same way. That is probably because they are regarded as glamorous – more so than as dirty and damaging to the environment. New fridges and new washing machines do not get the same attention, and new washing powders would have to be truly revolutionary to be discussed.

There is no clear logic, perhaps no logic at all. If an editorial mention of a commercial product can be justified, then it is valid to mention it. Books, plays and films raise issues journalists and programme makers think worth examining. Motors cars are exciting but washing powders are boring.

industry and business

The news media, especially radio and television, used to be regarded by business people as antipathetic towards industry and business, and being antipathetic, were held to damage the wealth creating energy of the country. The case was that bright young men and women from the universities, wanting to live by supposedly higher values than those of industrial manufacture and money-making, chose to work in broadcasting and in newspapers, instead of in business. They preferred the arts, culture and intellectual values. Their values demoted business. The deleterious view they carried with them, so the argument said, influenced coverage to such an extent that it exuded hostility, or at least indifference, towards business.

The argument coincided with the period of industrial strife in the 1960s and 1970s and reflected concern that programmes and newspapers concentrated on strikes, go-slows, work-to-rule, overtime bans and other manifestations of industrial unrest and failed to recognise business successes. Bodies like the BBC's advisory committee on business, now abolished, heard heart-felt calls for special programmes to improve understanding of the world of work, even for a fictional serial that would do for business what the daily radio drama *The Archers* is reputed to have done for agriculture and rural life. No such serial was created, probably because no creative talent was moved by the idea and it certainly could not be summoned up, like a tray of fast food, at the will of committees dedicated to doing good. But programmes dealing with aspects of industry, business and commerce have burgeoned since those days. Serious financial journalism, a late arrival in radio and television, has thrived, moving on from dry reports of market prices and company results, and spinning off into incisive features and documentaries. Specialist reporters for economics, industry and business exude understanding, not ignorance or hostility. The argument is now little heard.

specialists

Specialist reporters, usually called correspondents, in well-paid seniority elevated to 'editor', are among the best of journalists when they really know their subject. Their specialist knowledge counteracts the tendency of journalism, predominantly a second-hand trade, to misunderstand and to misrepresent people and events. Their understanding of what lies behind the obvious helps them see significance in what appears ordinary. They have special access to the best sources of information and at their best they provide context, perspective and insight. As an acknowledgement of their value, many more specialists than before are employed by the news media generally and the BBC in particular.

The specialist's familiarity with the subject can work the other way. Where an enthusiastic, perhaps naive, general reporter sees a story, a well-informed specialist may think it old-hat, overlooking the ignorance of the general public about it. Worse, specialists can fall prey to the blandishments of their lobby, the system which gives them special accesses because they are trusted by confidential briefers. When the system is abused, which happens, specialists recycle uncritically the official line fed to them unattributably.

library material

Journalists use a variety of topical libraries. News information libraries are based heavily on newspaper and magazine cuttings. Programme archives contain programmes already broadcast, and they contain also original material, some of which may not yet have been used. Whether written or recorded for broadcast, material in these libraries goes back days, weeks, months and years. Cuttings and recordings are a rich source of background for journalists, an indispensable asset. They are used reputably and disreputably. Some stories and features are no more than cuttings regurgitated.

The library of newspaper cuttings and of broadcast news reports has one abiding drawback: mistakes persist. A date, someone's age, a statistical statement, a sequence of events, all these and more can be wrong, liable to be repeated, as reliable items on the record, many times. Even when a correction has been published, the correction may not be attached to the cutting in the library. More contentiously, a quote which may have made sense in the original article can carry a different meaning when repeated in another context. Worse, a quote that, on its first outing, was a dubious paraphrase or a merger of disparate comments can become a misrepresentation in later use. Innocent ambiguity in a news report can easily turn inadvertently into a falsehood when it is later repeated in words changed to what the user of the cuttings thought the original meant. Experience goes some way to lessening these problems but nothing abolishes them.

Reliable word for word quotes in print or in voice recordings also have limitations. They do not necessarily continue to represent the views of the person quoted weeks, months and years later. The individual may have had a radical change of mind, or may have adapted an opinion in the light of

72

developments. To recycle a comment in such circumstances as though it continued to be a fair statement of view is unfair. The only safeguards are to check whether it remains valid or to date it when it is used again. The dating does not have to be precise. To say 'Mr Bloggs said a couple of months ago that . . .' is often enough. Recordings in voice and vision from the past are normally labelled as such.

Television runs into a special problem with stock pictures used for background illustration. Shots of, say, a communal room in an old folks home, taken with permission, may be used more than once over a period of time as 'wallpaper' in reports of welfare cut-backs. The pictures distress relatives when old people shown in them have since died. It can happen with any stock shots – pictures of patients in hospital wards for news reports of health service changes, pictures of children in school classrooms for stories about educational reforms, scenes of shoppers in supermarkets as background for news of prices. Any such scene from days, weeks or months past may be a sad reminder for someone somewhere. The truth of the picture is miserably out of date. People are upset and angry when television intrudes in this way. The answer – expensively – is to shoot today's background today.

reconstructions

Television uses reconstructions frequently, radio less so, and the term is not really applicable to newspapers. It means re-enacting real events, usually to examine issues in dispute or, in crime programmes, to encourage witnesses to come forward with evidence by reminding them of scenes they may have seen but overlooked. The first consideration urged on broadcasters is that all reconstructions should be fair. Second, they are told they must not mislead people into thinking a reconstruction is real. Re-enactments are always to be labelled as such. Third, they have to take care over details. Even in very simple reconstructions some detail will not be known. It might be a facial expression that could prejudice perception of the event. If details have to be invented the programme should say so, as well as making sure they are fair.

Crime programmes have been criticised for reconstructing violent scenes more thoroughly and in more detail than necessary, thereby adding to the fear of crime. As a result, programme makers have curbed re-enactments of violent scenes in people's homes, say during a burglary, which could not trigger witness recollections because no one else was there to witness them. Violence in a public place that may have been witnessed is shown less disturbingly than some years ago.

news access

Once in the public domain, news is free for all. No one owns publicly known facts or has an exclusive right over them. No matter how long and hard and expensive it has been for a news organisation to secure information before anyone else, it ceases to be exclusive once published or broadcast. For that reason, national daily newspapers may withhold exclusives until later editions. It reduces the opportunity for competitors to rewrite the story to run it themselves the same morning.

Although publicly known facts are not owned by anyone, copyright law provides some protection for the form in which facts are first made known. The information can be used by others but generally not in the form in which it first appeared. The 'form' may mean all kinds of things: the page, the layout, the photograph, the film, the video, the sound recording, and the words used in the order they are used.

The copyright protection is qualified to a degree for purposes of news reporting. The normal need for permission to use the material is waived. There is no need either to acknowledge where the material first appeared. It is a cloudy area even for copyright lawyers because very little has been tested in court so there is a lack of case law and accordingly the extent of the waiver is not reliably known.

Lifting facts and re-writing them is no problem at all for the media. Facts are easily put into different words. But the waiver for news

74

reporting does not allow newspapers to lift photographs from competitors. Radio and television are, however, allowed to lift moving pictures and sound from others for purposes of news reporting. It must, though, be done within the terms of 'fair dealing'. It is the fair dealing provision that clouds the issue. The owner of what no one else has would argue that it cannot be fair for a competitor to lift hard won, frequently very costly, material.

Broadcasting organisations in Britain do not make use of the waiver, partly because it is an unclear legal right, mainly because they hate the prospect of their best material being lifted by competitors from easily recorded news programmes which is what would happen in a free-for-all in which everyone helped themselves to the best of what everyone else had. The gain would not outweigh the loss. ITN does not want the BBC to lift its best material though it would benefit from lifting the best of the BBC.

The case for lifting television news material at will was floated by Bruce Gyngell, head of TV-AM, the breakfast company that later lost its franchise in the ITV licence auction. He argued no one should own the news and as television is a medium of moving pictures that should mean pictures being freely available to everyone once they had been first shown. There was much more distaste than enthusiasm for the idea.

Some quiet lifting goes on in radio, small snatches of interview and other recordings, too short to be outstanding, usually not monitored or recognised by the station from which they were taken, and contritely admitted as a mistake when rumbled, though it might be within the law, but usually denied with indignant vigour. It is much less likely to happen on television because it would be more obvious. Instead, the television organisations reached an agreement in 1991 strictly limited to sport and strictly defined. It allows television to lift clips of sporting events from competitors, free of charge, but with a visual credit, available to be used only in general news programmes a specified maximum number of times and at a specified maximum length. The agreement headed off what might have been a messy free-for-all which would, almost certainly, have ended in the courts and which would have prompted calls for a procedure to be agreed to avoid disputes.

The television agreement on news access to sports material is appropriate in the sense that the television rights to show sporting events live and recorded are routinely bought and sold in a way that does not apply to general news events. No one buys the exclusive right to show a police news conference, a royal visit, a government White Paper, a ministerial speech or Question Time in the Commons. Exclusive interviews, paid for or not, and other news scoops are the result of journalistic initiative, not the same as deals for millions of pounds to cover well publicised events, such as premier league soccer or Wimbledon tennis, open to the fee paying public.

referral

All news organisations use referral in some form. At its most natural, it means turning to a senior colleague for advice, perhaps for a decision, when there is an editorial problem. The BBC has formalised the idea into a system where producers have to recognise issues with potential for trouble on which they should seek guidance or a ruling, and in a small number of specified cases – including exceptions to the rule that payments should not normally be made to criminals, secret recordings, interviews with terrorists, use of four-letter words, and co-funding of programmes – they are obliged to seek permission in advance, sometimes from very high level. The Independent Television Commission and the Radio Authority have, in effect, required a similar system in embryonic form in the stations they oversee. Their programme codes say permission must be obtained from senior staff on a number of issues, for instance, for recordings using hidden microphones.

Independent-minded programme makers, like all journalists, do not much care for obligatory referral. The reason for imposing it lies in the history of public rows about programmes.

> Some matters are so contentious that decisions on them have to be carefully and consistently calculated.

anticipation

Hectic journalists dashing to the unpredicted ignore the obvious – that problems are avoided or more easily dealt with by thinking ahead. For instance, some situations are more likely than others to produce demands for anonymous appearances: a television programme interviewing 'joy-riders' will almost certainly be asked to record interviews anonymously. This is easy to realise in advance and nearly as easy to agree a response in advance, in this case the question not just being whether to agree to anonymity but what device to use. If matters are left entirely to the wit of people on the spot, who may well be under other, more difficult, pressures, and as recorded material for broadcasting cannot always later be edited into acceptable form, the programme is very likely to find itself with material that is objectionable because it has been recorded in an unacceptable way but which it cannot drop without losing an important editorial point.

independent producers

Editorial problems are difficult enough when an organisation is coherent and makes all its editorial decisions within its own ranks. The difficulties are increased when editorial problems arise and are dealt with, or neglected, in teams that work independently outside the organisation but which provide programmes or newspaper stories. This has been the experience of British television since having to accept a government imposed quota of independent productions, and it has long been the case with newspapers when freelances are responsible for a story. It is almost impossible to be convinced of the detailed reliability of a story or a programme when it has not originated and been checked closely, stage by stage if necessary, within the organisation. Too often, especially with programmes which cannot be changed as readily as copy, and in spite of commissioning and tracking processes that keep

77

'in-house' executive producers in touch with the progress of independent productions, the broadcasting organisation is faced with a fait accompli which has to be accepted in its entirety or rejected entirely. The price could be a big bill for damages. The compensation is that independent producers and freelances have inspirations and ideas they would not have if they were not spurred on by the need to sell their talent.

cable programmes

Television and radio programmes on cable do not escape the regulators and the watchdogs. Though the Cable Authority no longer exists, its functions have been passed on by the Broadcasting Act of 1990 so that programmes carried into people's homes by cable are subject to the codes issued by the Independent Television Commission (ITC), the Radio Authority (RA) and the Broadcasting Standards Council (BSC), and to the decisions on privacy and fairness of the Broadcasting Complaints Commission (BCC). Programmes made specially for cable have to satisfy standards laid down on the entire range of issues by the ITC or the Radio Authority and the BSC. Aggrieved viewers and listeners can complain to one or more of the four bodies as appropriate. A cable service could be ordered to carry a statement as a result of a complaint and, if the matter was serious enough, could be fined or could even be deprived of its licence by the Radio Authority or the ITC. While the BSC and the BCC have powers to order statements to be carried in the cable service and published in newspapers, they have no powers to fine or to revoke licences.

satellite programmes

Many commentators refer to satellite television in Britain as being 'unregulated'. The comment is misleading. Satellite services are, to important degrees, as 'controlled' as the traditional, terrestrial channels of television. Any satellite service

78

originating in the United Kingdom has to be licensed by the Independent Television Commission and by mid-1995 more than seventy such licences had been granted though only about fifty of these had resulted in actual programme services. Much the most important and much the best known were the eight Sky services, including the twenty-four hours a day news channel, Sky News, provided by British Sky Broadcasting. The idea that these fifty or so services are not regulated is encouraged by the relative lightness of the regimes under which they operate compared to the regimes imposed on terrestrial television. They are not subject to the strong ownership rules laid down for the traditional channels; they are not required to provide certain kinds of programmes at certain times as the traditional channels are; they are allowed more advertising, though this may change. Satellite licences are granted virtually on request whereas the traditional licences are often competed for at vast expense with detailed business plans carefully laid out and detailed programme intentions described.

But Sky News and all the other fifty or so satellite channels have to observe the programme codes, as well as the advertising and sponsorship codes, laid down by the ITC. Importantly, the journalism of Sky News and of any of the other channels with journalistic output must observe the public service precepts of 'due impartiality' and accuracy in news and topical programmes.

In the same way, radio programmes by satellite have to operate under the Radio Authority and its journalistic code. Radio or television from Britain by satellite are subject also to the Broadcasting Complaints Commission and the Broadcasting Standards Council. The Council has to monitor programmes as best it can to pass general judgement on the taste and decency of them, on their portrayal of violence and sex, and whether they are paying enough attention to its code of acceptable programme behaviour. Satellite viewers and listeners can complain to the Council if they are offended. They can also complain to the Complaints Commission if they believe they have been unjustly or unfairly treated or if they think their privacy has been intruded upon without justification.

The regulatory regime, while lighter than for

traditional programme services, is significant. It exceeds the restraints on newspapers. At the same time, all the laws that apply to British newspapers – defamation, contempt, official secrets and others – apply also to satellite journalism as to all British broadcast journalism.

chapter four – trouble spots

privacy

The behaviour of the British media, especially of the tabloid newspapers, provoked bitter debate on privacy in the 1980s, a debate no nearer true resolution by the mid-1990s, despite the government decision not to bring in a privacy law. The essence of the issue is the extent – if any – to which newspapers, programmes, magazines and other parts of the media are entitled to make public facts about the private interests and activities of individuals who do not consent to the publicity. Issues arising from the main question include the methods used by journalists to discover private facts: harassment, long-lens photography, bugging, surreptitious recording, deception, use of stolen or leaked documents, trespass, persistent approaches to relatives, friends and colleagues. Concern over privacy includes concern for the feelings of people who are bereaved or who are involved in other distressing events. The right to grieve quietly is a matter of privacy. That people killed, accidently or deliberately, are not usually named publicly until their closest relatives, their next-of-kin, have been informed, is also a matter of privacy. So is respect for victims. Anonymity for people raped is a further dimension and the desire for privacy encourages anonymity in other contexts, from personal donations to political parties to big wins in the national lottery or on the football pools.

Television and radio, not absolved during

the British debate in the 1980s and 1990s, were not much blamed either, except that television was at times accused of intrusion by showing scenes of grief after fatal incidents or dwelling on them in close-up. Attention was to some extent focused elsewhere because the public already had an independent, statutory body, the Broadcasting Complaints Commission, to turn to on matters of privacy connected with programmes, and broadcasters certainly liked to think they were at the better behaved end of British journalism. The problem as perceived by most critics was mainly with the national tabloid newspapers.

Early concerns arose from a few notorious cases of distasteful intrusion. They included the case of Gorden Kaye, the actor. Reporters from the *Sunday Sport* entered a hospital room where he was recovering from brain surgery. They took pictures of him and recorded his rambling words. Not long afterwards, in 1988, journalists from newspapers were denounced also for what some did in the weeks up to the death of the television and radio personality, Russell Harty. As he lay ill, the newspaper people were gripped by the wrongful suspicion he was dying of AIDS. They insinuated themselves among his friends and neighbours and tried to wheedle information out of those who were caring for him. Popular newspapers then swooped on more august public figures. One was a homosexual judge in Scotland who used indiscreet haunts. Another was the leader of the Liberal Democrats, Paddy Ashdown, who in 1992 confirmed an affair with a secretary years earlier. A cabinet minister, David Mellor, was forced to resign later in 1992, after determined resistance, in the face of relentless, steamy tales of an affair with an actress. A few lesser politicians were victims to stories of sexual adventure. The newspapers seemed intent to topple people. They fell into an orgy of disclosure about younger adult members of the Royal Family – notably, about the Duchess of York, the Princess of Wales and the Prince of Wales. Other forms of sleaze in public life made many stories after allegations that some MPs would accept money to put questions in the House of Commons and that a few had done so. Stories of holidays abroad paid for by other people and of rewarding business connections led to issues of conflicts of interest, questionable financial connections and the extent to which MPs should declare outside interests being energetically examined in the columns of the papers. A number of the issues were adopted by an official inquiry chaired by a senior judge, Lord Nolan, into standards in public life. In the shadows of cases of tarnished public figures, the hurt of many ordinary people who felt traduced by the media was relegated, although members of a House of Commons select committee that examined privacy and media intrusion insisted they were mainly concerned with the harm done to non-public figures.

Far from agreeing on whether anything should be done and if so what, the contending camps could not even agree on the extent of the problem. Convinced backbench critics in parliament, moved by their own postbags as well as by what they saw in the papers, were in no doubt the press was out of control. They wanted a law to protect privacy and a statutory body, with powers to punish, to oversee newspapers. Reputable resisters in the newspaper industry argued that in proportion to the many thousands of stories in the papers unwarranted intrusions on privacy were very few with only a small number of journalists guilty of them. The Press Complaints Commission adopted this line in relation to complaints generally: they were a relatively small proportion, and of that small proportion less than 10 per cent related to privacy. The Commission emphasised what its work had done for 'people not in the public eye'. Critics reply that intrusions, seen in absolute rather than proportionate numbers, are considerable, that the degree of harm to individuals matters just as much as numbers and that like other forms of ill-treatment serious intrusions deserve redress. If only a few people were mugged, it would not be sensible to argue that the law should not punish muggers. Opponents of the privacy law demanded by the critics say it could not be precise enough to deal with such matters and that, being a blunt weapon, it would impede serious journalism in its public interest role more than it would help the victims of unethical journalism, that villains would use it as a shield and that important people would benefit most.

A general consensus probably exists on the view that private matters should be known about if they pertain to public duties. It does not take the argument far. It sticks on how, to what extent and when private matters do in fact pertain to public duties. The word 'pertain' is ambiguous. It could mean that private matters would have *adversely to affect* the performance of public duties before they should be made public. It could mean it would be enough that they *might* so affect them. If public figures with public responsibilities should be of the highest probity, it could mean that any private matter, favourable or unfavourable, *is relevant* to the public assessment of them. Public figures often allow favourable private matters to be known, at times exploited. Their consent should not be necessary, so the argument goes, for unfavourable facts to be taken into account as well. This approach says that when people vote for politicians they should be free to vote for the whole person, not simply for the authorised public image, that when they assess any public figure they should be able to take account, if they wish, of the entire persona, not only of the public face. Accordingly, any persistent sexual activity outside marriage by a politician should be exposed. Popular newspapers oblige in this when they can and when it is heterosexual activity. They do not, however, generally join in the 'outing' of gay politicians – that is of naming them as homosexual against their will – although people who cast their vote for the whole person would say they ought to be able to take account of heterosexuality, homosexuality, bisexuality, asexuality, marital fidelity, marital infidelity and anything else they judge significant. If certain facts are protected as private, they often cannot be taken into account because they often cannot be made known. When that is the case, people are told the protected facts are irrelevant. The effect of this is to tell people the grounds on which they must make democratic decisions.

The recognised core of the argument lies in the idea of 'the public interest'. When does the public have a legitimate interest in a private matter? Popular newspapers harm their case by some of their arguments. After long-lens photographs showed the youngest of the Queen's sons, Prince Edward, kissing his girl-friend at Balmoral, a newspaper editor argued that to show 'the affection they have for each other' was in the public interest. If they were to marry, people should know it was for the right reasons. One of the papers that named the biggest of the early national lottery winners in 1994 when he did not want to be said everyone could now share his joy! Another said people who put money into the lottery had a right to know who the winner was.

Journalists damage their case further when their stories go too far, as they often do. Tabloids have behaved as though the public interest argument stretches indefinitely, that once established it justifies anything. But a legitimate public interest in an aspect of the private behaviour of a public figure cannot automatically justify disclosure of any private information about the individual. Legitimate public interest certainly justified the story that the heir to the British throne, Prince Charles, the Prince of Wales, had had an affair with Mrs Camilla Parker-Bowles after his marriage. Public interest would probably also have justified the story, were it true, that Charles made love to Camilla at his home while his wife was upstairs. The case was compromised, though, by publication of pictures inside the Parker-Bowles home and bedroom against their will. They were not justified by a public interest.

The chairman of the Press Complaints Commission, Lord Wakeham, gave a strong warning to editors early in 1995 against abuse of the public interest defence. He said the Commission would not tolerate spurious use of the defence when considering complaints. Soon afterwards, the PCC severely criticised the biggest selling British newspaper, the Sunday tabloid, the *News of the World*, for coverage of the illness of Lady Spencer, wife of the brother of the Prince of Wales. The paper had shown sad pictures of Lady Spencer, taken evidently without her knowledge, while she was being treated for an eating disorder. No genuine public interest was involved and Lord Wakeham took the unusual step of writing to the owner of the paper, Rupert Murdoch of News Corporation, about it. As a result, Murdoch publicly rebuked the *News of the World* editor.

Specious and spurious arguments and dubious cases aside, the public interest defence is widely recognised as valid within limits. The committee appointed by government to examine media intrusion and headed by a lawyer, Sir David Calcutt, accepted it and suggested what public interest defences might be used. Journalistic intrusion could be justified if the information collected exposed crime, other wrong-doing or a danger to public health. The Press Complaints Commission adds a further consideration: intrusion can be justified if it would prevent 'the public from being misled by some statement or action of an individual or organisation'. This could be strengthened further by adapting the public interest defence that already exists in the Obscene Publications Act. An intrusion could be defended if the material gained exposed any matter of serious concern to the general public.

Critics regard generalised exceptions as weasel words designed to allow disreputable journalism to proceed unhindered. But plainly interpreted, a wide-ranging defence of the kind envisaged would offer some protection for public figures, would reduce the risk of commercial villains sheltering behind a privacy law and would not damage protection for ordinary people when they deserve it.

confidential sources

One of the few accepted absolutes in journalism is that confidential sources must be protected. A confidential source is simply someone who has given information or who has appeared anonymously in an interview on the promise that their identity will be kept secret. The information may have been given orally or in writing or contained in a document handed over to the journalist. The name of the source may be in the head of the journalist, known to no one else, or it may be written down somewhere. The journalistic rule that such sources be protected absolutely applies whatever the pressures on the journalist to renege. Although confrontations with the law in Britain on this point are rare, hefty fines are imposed when they do occur, as with the financial reporter, Jeremy Warner of the *Independent* and *The Times*, whose fine in 1988 reached £20,000 for refusing to identify a source of financial information – and prison for the journalist is always a possibility, as with Brendan Mulholland of the *Daily Mail*, who got six months, and Reginald Foster of the *Daily Sketch*, three months, in 1963, in both cases for refusing to disclose a source to an official tribunal that was investigating a spy scandal, and Bernard Falk of the BBC, who spent four days in the cells in 1971 for refusing to tell a court in Belfast whether an IRA man he had interviewed was the man in the dock.

When journalists run up against the law in this way, their problem, in nearly all cases, is the law of contempt, in other words, the actual offence is not refusing to name the source so much as defying a court order to do so. The punishment is, theoretically, unlimited as the contempt recurs with every refusal. A judge could impose a fine, of say £5,000 for first refusal, tell the journalist to come back a week later to see whether under punishment he has thought better of it, and then, when the journalist has not, impose a further fine, this time of perhaps £10,000 – and so on. The same could happen with imprisonment: Falk might have had recurrent spells of four days, or more, in gaol had the court not relented. One supposes, though without guarantee, that action so punitive would not be allowed to go on for long.

Legal action to compel disclosure may be triggered by any number of interests: by the police in pursuit of evidence, as in the Channel 4 hearings in 1992 arising out of a *Dispatches* programme shown in October 1991, *The Committee*, that alleged criminal connections in Northern Ireland between senior police officers and loyalist killers; by an aggrieved commercial company whose financial confidences were leaked, as with the trainee journalist, William Goodwin of the *Engineer*, whose ordeal at law started in 1989 and continued into 1990 when he was fined; by Department of Trade and Industry inspectors, pursuing financial wrong-dealing, as in the Jeremy Warner case; by a court facing a recalcitrant witness, the Falk case; or a tribunal with judicial powers also facing recalcitrant witnesses, the Mulholland and Foster cases.

An additional feature of the Goodwin case was that the company that pursued him relentlessly at law for months remained publicly unnamed throughout the hearings in the British courts. Goodwin had learned the company was negotiating a loan to help it over financial problems. As a good journalist, rather than report only what he had been told by his confidential source, he asked the company for comment. It was understandably alarmed. The editor of the magazine for which Goodwin worked was approached and agreed not to publish the story. That might and, in many cases, would have been the end of the matter. But the company was not satisfied. It insisted on knowing who gave Goodwin the information so that the leaker might be dealt with and further leaks prevented. When Goodwin would not break the promise of confidentiality he had given the source, the company pursued its insistence to court. Besides an order against Goodwin to disclose the source, an order was also made to stop the company's name being given during the reporting of Goodwin's protracted tribulations. The reasoning was that, as financial problems were at the heart of the issue, publicity from the company's legal attempts to find the leaker would have caused the very damage, with creditors and customers, it was desperate to avoid. To be named as the company pursuing Goodwin would have identified it as the company that badly needed financial support. The order meant that a young journalist whose story had been decently withheld by his editor was pursued by a commercial interest that did not have to answer publicly for its actions. The identity of the company was not made public until the Goodwin case went before the European Commission for Human Rights several years later.

A most difficult aspect of any case of a confidential source is that the individual journalist or programme maker may not be able or may not wish to pass the problem to the broader shoulders of the media organisation for which they work. The Goodwin, Warner, Falk, Mulholland and Foster cases are all of that kind. They are classic instances of the individual bearing the burden. The Falk case differed from the others only insofar as he was protecting the identity of a person who had appeared anonymously, back to camera, in a recorded television interview whereas the others had been given information 'on the quiet'. But the essence is the same: Falk was the reporter with the facts, he had promised not to identify the person and he had to carry the responsibility in defiance of a court, as had the others.

Channel 4 and the independent producer,

Box Productions, succeeded in lifting the weight from lower programme makers in the main hearings over the Northern Ireland *Dispatches* programme, a rare exception. They were able to do so because the police sought documents for which Channel 4 and Box were responsible, not a name held in the head of an individual programme maker which was the case in all the other instances. None the less, the zeal of the police, the Royal Ulster Constabulary, was such that a researcher was later arrested for perjury in the early hours of the morning, though eventually released without trial.

In nearly all cases, the reporter or producer has had to endure the force of the law from an early stage, albeit with considerable help from the radio or television station or newspaper for which they were working. This happens because it is usual with experienced journalists that only they know who the confidential source is. To make sure no one else can betray the identity, they keep it to themselves. They make the promise, they keep it. Better not to trust anyone else with it. And if no one else knows, no one else can be prosecuted. In any case, when more people know, it does not follow that someone else will be prosecuted instead of the reporter. It could mean the more who know, the more can be prosecuted, reporter and colleagues. When the information is in a reporter's head, not in a document, to pass it on does not wipe it out of the reporter's memory and therefore does not absolve the reporter. A court could pursue all those it had good reason to believe knew the name.

Historical perspective comes partly to the rescue of journalists made nervous by this issue. A sense of proportion makes it less alarming than it might seem. Very many confidences, significant and insignificant, are involved in journalism because reporting would be greatly weakened if promises were not made to protect the identity of people who are willing to give information but not willing to be named as the source – and hardly any of the cases come to serious confrontation. The risk that any such promise might develop into a punishing encounter with the law is small.
But risk it is.

While respect for journalistic sources, acting in the public interest, could be stronger in British law, the only early prospect that it will become so lies in the European appeal into the Goodwin case which ought to compel a change if Goodwin wins. But even if it were to be strengthened, it is not likely to become total. The issue involves an irreconcilable conflict between decent law that must pursue best evidence in the interests of justice and decent journalism that must honour promises.

An option always available to the journalist anxious to avoid judicial confrontation is to give no promise that cannot be kept. Better to be without the scoop. Once a promise is given, the foresighted journalist makes sure that as few people as possible know the identity of the source. The more who know, the more risk the promise will be broken. For close-knit programme teams, a particular danger is that the name or other identifying fact about the source filters down to junior members and a young researcher or secretary cannot be expected to stand unflinchingly in the face of the legal process to safeguard a promise they did not give.

Sometimes documents that would disclose the source are removed abroad, out of the jurisdiction, because documents may be seized. Sometimes they are hidden where no one would think of searching. These precautions are normally done at an early stage, before legally recognised moves have been made to disclose the documents. If not done early, removal, like destruction, adds to the offence in the eyes of the law.

Another danger is that a tell-tale document may be made available unawares: besides being in obvious notebooks, official papers and word processor disks, the name of a confidential source has been known to be on an expenses claim, filed innocently and routinely in the accountant's office, and easily discovered.

Journalists being pressed to disclose a name, are always able to go back to the source to check whether the promise can be lifted. A few sources have, in the end, agreed to be named. But not many.

off-the-record

What seems to be one of the simplest terms in journalism, 'off-the-record', has caused many problems and will cause many more. Its comrades – 'unattribu-table', 'not-for-quoting', 'for background only' – are almost as unreliable. Journalists do not agree among themselves what they mean and there is no consistency among the people who speak to journalists in those terms. When seeking information or when interviewing, some journalists make efforts to agree a meaning; some do not because they do not realise the terms are capable of different meanings; and others do not because ambiguity allows them to plead innocence when they quote an indiscreet remark that was not to be attributed to the source. The problems are probably worse for newspaper and magazine journalists who interview people discursively at length, whether about them-selves or about others, because public figures who relax can be remarkably indiscreet as though they were bursting to unburden themselves of fascinating tit-bits but without responsibility for them, and because such interviews are usually partly for quoting and partly not for quoting. To compound the problems, an interview which is 'on-the-record' in parts and 'off-the-record' in parts is likely to come with a further condition: that the interviewee be allowed to vet the finished piece before publication. That also may be left unclear, the journalist sidling out of an explicit commitment, the interviewee believing or hoping it to have been agreed – and recrimination the outcome when a candid aside makes headlines.

When a source says a remark expressing an opinion or giving a piece of information is 'off-the-record' it always means that the source must not be quoted as making it. But it is never automatically clear whether it can be quoted in disguise, as in 'A government minister said . . .', whether it must be a more distant disguise such as 'A government source said . . .', whether a bit of deceit is expected so that 'A source close to government said . . .', more dubiously 'Supporters of the minister say . . .' or whether the remark is not to be quoted in any terms and left to the journalist to assert. At times 'off-the-record' has been used to mean 'not for publication' which makes journalists wonder why they were given the information or the opinion in the first place.

A source who says that a remark is 'unattributable' has to be taken through the same questions. It is clear that the comment cannot be attributed to the source but not clear whether it can be attributed anonymously, again as in 'A government source said . . .' The positive and seemingly helpful 'for attribution' may not mean 'for direct attribution': 'You can quote the department but do not pin it on me.' The terms 'not for quoting' and 'for use without attribution' run up against the same questions. 'For background only' may mean 'not for publication' or 'not for use at all' and, in effect, 'I am telling you this so you understand the larger picture but you must not publish any of it.' That is always difficult to cope with. Important background, whether information or informed comment, has to become part of the coverage. If it influences the story, it is used by implication. What often happens is that journalists seek confirmation of the information from another source – or pretend they have had it so confirmed for use. It also happens that information for background only is held back for use after a while or perhaps used deftly in an opinion column. At other times 'for background only' means 'Use it on your own responsibility, not pinned on me or on the department.'

Disguised sourcing creates problems at times. A comment quoted in a disguised way may, in the context, be so transparent that it is clear where it came from. It is likely to offend a source as much as a clear breach of faith in a direct quote. In an ill-considered context, well-used labels such as 'A source close to the chairman . . .', which often means the chairman himself, have caused trouble from people close to the chairman who say it made it seem like them when they had nothing to do with it. The misery of the unwary journalist is complete when an 'off-the-record' source who is suspected as the source goes 'on-the-record' to deny responsibility.

crime

Crime reporting is less of a staple for broadcast news than it is for newspapers and it was frowned upon at the start of local radio in Britian after some stations tended daily to deliver a dismal catalogue of local misdemeanours. As a general fact, crime is less palatable when spoken about over radio and television than when read about in the local paper. But the occurrence of crime generally, its relentless growth in the later decades of the twentieth century, and isolated, untypical instances of serious crime, have to be attended to by any news organisation that wants to be taken seriously. It is a source of great social concern. It excites legitimate popular curiosity. It is, additionally, a rich seam for documentary programmes and feature articles to explore causes, motive, the extent of risk, the plight of victims, the wonders of detection and the efficacy of punishment.

The intimacy of the spoken word, delivered person to person into people's homes, encourages broadcast reports of crime against the person to be more restrained than reports in print. Another restraining influence on broadcasting is that people listening are not as free to select stories as they are with newspaper reports: they cannot fully decide what report to listen to next and what to miss out. They are more captive to the decisions of editors of programmes. Listening is passive, reading is active. The nature of radio and television combines with taste and decency to make broadcast descriptions of sexual and other assault very sparing. The aim is to say enough to let people know what has happened without feeding salacious curiosity or vicarious distress.

The differences between programmes and newspapers are matters of degree. For both, reporting court cases is difficult when much evidence is taken up with horrid detail. The reporter has no satisfactory alternative to leaving out a great deal of it. The governing principle is to include only as much as basic understanding calls for.

Fear of crime is a problem brought to the attention of the media only in recent years. Fear in some people is inflated beyond reason and the media have been urged to take the concern to heart. Programmes and newspapers are pressed to acknowledge a duty to keep a reliable perspective. The issue creates concern in journalists who feel they are being pressed to promote a convenient perspective. They recognise that the principle cause of the fear of crime is the occurrence of crime in large amounts. People fear crime because it exists.

Informed observers also know that perspective is personal. It is no comfort to the nervous middle-aged person who stays fearfully indoors to read that the most likely victims of assault outside are young men. It is no comfort to the old lady who has been robbed to be told by the radio that she is a tiny minority. And reliable, overall perspective is different again in neighbourhoods where over 50 per cent of families have experienced serious crime.

The issue defies generalisation. But as the personal approach of radio and television can excite more concern than print, especially in lonely individuals who look to broadcasting for companionship, and given television's ability to scare, programmes attract a greater expectation not to report news of crime in ways that distress people.

crime figures

The crime figures that get most publicity, those issued by the police, are not the most reliable. The police figures are of 'recorded crime' which is not the same as all crime. It is not even the same as 'reported crime', that is, crime reported by the public to the police. In conflict with reality, the news process projects the police figures without much qualification. The reality, put plainly, is that 'x' crimes occur, then 'x-minus' are reported to the police, and the police list only some of them: they record 'x-minus-minus'. By this time, the level of some types of crime in the police books is a long way from its level in the community.

Not all crimes are reported to the police because people at times think there is no point, the police cannot or will not do anything about it. This is particularly so with theft *from* vehicles, not the same as theft *of* vehicles, nearly all of which is reported. In high crime areas, not all burglaries are reported to the police, especially when it is the second or third or fourth time at the same address, a flat in one of the teeming and neglected parts of London or a house on one of the lawless hard estates in struggling cities up and down the land. Rape used to be seriously under-reported to the police, partly because victims were deterred by unsympathetic processes, but the level of reporting is now higher. There is no good reason to believe that the serious under-reporting of some crime is balanced by an equal amount of false reporting. People are much more likely not to report what has happened than to report what has not happened, so that, for some categories of crime, information reaching the police from the public, the victims, is very significantly below the rate at which the crime is occurring.

None the less, the police – for good and bad reasons – do not accept as reliable all reports of crime they are given. They discount some. When they discount them, they are not entered into their official, statistical records. And what is more, police forces differ in this judgement. Some discount fewer and record more than others, so there is no consistency from one police area to another, one part of the country to another.

So long as 'reporting' and 'recording' of crime are consistently done within individual police areas, the figures for those areas may show reasonably reliable trends from one year to another. They may reliably show that a particular category of crime has increased or decreased and the rate at which it has done so. But even this is uncertain when, for a variety of reasons, a shift occurs in the attitudes of the public towards the reporting of particular crime, as the greater reporting of rape has shown. The increased reporting of rape was encouraged by much more considerate treatment of victims when they went to the police, and by publicity, both about the crime and about the better treatment of victims. As a result, the increase in reported rape did not mean that more rapes had been committed. Similar variables affect other kinds of crime from time to time so that some evident increases are misleading: they are either not increases at all, or are smaller than the figures suggest. Even so, they mean that the level of reporting and recording comes closer to the level of the actual rate.

One of the effects of under-reporting is that when a trend is reliably recorded by the police, it is almost certainly and fairly consistently below the level at which it is really occurring in the community. The real trend, expressed as a developing line on a graph, will have much the same profile, but this real level will be higher along its entire length. So much seems to be well established by the 'British Crime Survey' (not really 'British' because it applies only to England and Wales), commissioned by the Home Office. It uses sample methods to arrive at what experts regard as nearer to actual levels. About ten thousand people are questioned for each survey. They are carefully representative of the population in terms of geographic spread, age, sex, socio-economic class and other factors. The experience of crime they declare to the Survey is then extrapolated into figures for all of England and Wales.

The Crime Survey suggests that during the decade of the 1980s, crime increased by about 50 per cent whereas the police figures for recorded crime put the increase at over 100 per cent. The difference is to be accounted for by a greater level of reporting by the public and a greater level of recording by the police at the end of the decade than at the beginning. Or put another way, recorded crime was even further below the true level at the beginning of the decade than it was at the end. Recorded crime is catching up with reality – with still a long way to go.

The Survey gives a total of about fifteen million crimes committed each year at the beginning of the 1990s whereas the figure for recorded crime was one-third of that, about five million. The public reported only half of crimes, about seven-and-a-half million, to the police, and the police discounted about one-third of those. One of the biggest areas of crime is the least recorded, that is, theft from vehicles. The police are told of little more than half of it; police record not much more than half of what they are told about so that less than a third of actual theft from vehicles is recorded. Badly reported categories include common assault, household vandalism and theft from the person. Well reported categories include theft of vehicles, burglary with loss and theft of bicycles.

All this gives news a problem. To be reliable about the truth of crime, reports of the level of recorded crime would have to be qualified and sceptical. They would make moderate, boring headlines. They would stir up apathy! They would make revealing comparisons with the figures in the British Crime Survey, and they would report the Survey fully when it is published which is now every other year. There have been five so far, for 1982, 1984, 1988, 1992 and 1994.

dealing with criminals

Journalists are like governments in the distasteful but necessary contacts they make. Both have to have dealings with rogues, thieves and murderers, and both say little about it. Journalists frequently venture into grubby corners of society and, in the interests of 'the story' which reflects an aspect of truth, make contacts decent people would normally shun. Journalism that investigates properly does not rely totally on reputable sources, the courts, the crime figures and the police, for its perceptions of criminals. It mixes with the criminals.

Dealing with criminals and doing deals with them are different, and journalists are under public pressure not to do deals, especially not to pay criminals. To pay them for information about their crimes is widely condemned outside journalism as rewarding crime. The code agreed by newspapers under the auspices of the Press Complaints Commission frowns on payments to criminals without forbidding it absolutely. Any payment has to be justified by a good public interest reason. BBC guidelines are similarly hedged. The codes of the Independent Television Commission and of the Radio Authority say nothing about payments. As with BBC guidelines, they do, however, caution against interviews with criminals regardless of whether payment is made.

Interviews are not and could not reasonably be ruled out. But journalists attract unfriendly attention when they give publicity to criminals. The charge soon translates into 'giving a platform to' a criminal or allowing the public enemy to 'glamorize' crime. Interviews, particularly on television, are held to 'legitimise' the individual being interviewed, even when the interview is realistic and when it is hostile.

There are not many opportunities for interviews with criminals 'on the run' or unconvicted, and even fewer occasions to go ahead with them. It is usually a matter of interviewing a criminal

97

who has been punished and who is now 'going straight'. This is usually when payment arises too. In these circumstances, payments are sometimes made. They are fairly small and are often written down as expenses for travel or time spent or as an ordinary fee for anyone who records an interview.

Interviews with criminals not yet convicted or who have escaped could fall foul of the law, particularly the Criminal Justice Act 1961 and the Criminal Law Act 1967. Contacts leading to an interview might be classed as 'assistance' to the criminal, itself an offence. Any payment could strengthen the possibility of offence as money might help a criminal to evade arrest.

Interviews with criminals sought by the police are likely to encourage the police to want information from the journalist. If journalist and criminal did a deal, say, not to disclose where the interview took place or when, the journalist might be heading towards a contempt and punishment for it. If the deal was that the criminal would be anonymous, the same danger arises for the journalist. Any confidentiality granted to a criminal is very hard to justify.

When the criminal is a terrorist, special and much more onerous legal considerations apply. They derive from the Prevention of Terrorism Act under which it is not only an offence to refuse to give information to the police, it is also an offence not to volunteer information that would help the fight against terrorism.

arrests

Besides the problem of knowing when someone is arrested, not just being questioned, injustice is occasionally done by the media naming people held by the police who are subsequently released without charge and without any justified suspicion attaching to them. The name may be leaked by a police source; it may be given, innocently or with forethought, by a relative. At times, the police formally announce details. They may also encourage media attention by letting reporters know that the individual's home and garden will be searched, a good photo opportunity. Sometimes public curiosity, driven by genuine concern over a notorious local crime, perhaps a series of assaults, is uncontainable. In such cases, a name may circulate freely among local people so that an individual is stained before the media can cause it, and as always, reliable fact from the media is better than untrustworthy gossip that may well implicate several names when only one person is under questioning.

The stain of being named in this way can dog innocent people for years and gossip is always ready with the cliché 'no smoke without fire'. For journalists, there is no clear way through the issues. What suits one case will not suit another. A decent option may be not to name suspects until they are charged – unless there is good, special reason to name them earlier. Competitive pressures – 'They are naming him, so I have to' – are not good reason. But a family protest in public, perhaps with the connivance of a solicitor, about unfair detention, as has happened, would usually be. As with nearly all editorial rules, this one is not hard and fast. It is, at best, an area for compassionate and considered restraint.

Animal Liberation Front

Journalists deal warily with the Animal Liberation Front (ALF), the most notable of the activist bodies in the animal rights movement. It has tried to mislead public and media over contamination scares and could have caused great commercial damage, including loss of jobs, for the price of a few phone calls to local newsdesks. Action of the kind tends to be local because ALF, like many such organisations, operates in virtually autonomous local cells, not monolithically with detailed plans of action handed down from a central command.

The problem for the news media is to know when a threat is a hoax and when it is genuine. As with the IRA which planted bomb hoaxes as well as bombs, ALF has mixed real action and hoax. It has carried out arson attacks and has also said it has contaminated products when it has not. At other times, products have been contaminated, whether by ALF members or other people. Failure by the media to alert the public to a threat that named products on a supermarket shelf have been contaminated could cause death and injury. Equally, publicity for what turns out to be a hoax causes commercial damage, public unease or panic, and, if it happens a number of times, damage to the credibility of the media and to their ability to serve the public properly.

Because of this, claims by ALF and by similar organisa-tions are dubious without corroboration from the police or other knowledgeable source. ALF will often produce convin-cing-looking evidence that it has, let us say, raided a laboratory where animals are kept for experiment. The evidence is frequently a video recording, made by ALF and supplied to television news programmes. The video could be a fake but it may be verified readily with the laboratory. Claims of contamination are more difficult but police and store owners usually help reporters and editors because their silence would jeopordise the public should the claim be genuine.

Interviews with ALF can also be a problem. The organisation now has spokespeople who will appear openly and identifiably but interviews with 'activists' who claim to have raided laboratories or to have planted incendiary devices are not given openly for fear of detection. Those interviewed insist on anonymity. Reporters tend to agree to it provided the insight to be gained is of real value. This risks conflict with the law if they know the identities. They have no privilege in law in the face of a court order to name an anonymous interviewee who has been promised confidentiality and the journalistic ethic does not allow promises to be broken.

How to allow anonymity is easy for radio: no names or identities are given in interviews. Newspaper pictures can readily be doctored to remove clues. Television finds it more difficult because a sequence of pictures involving visual clues has to be disguised. Back to camera or heavy shadow may be acceptable. Sometimes the 'activists' want to be shown in balaclavas and anoraks. This adds menace and is disliked by the broadcasting authorities. It may serve the terrorist purpose more than the public interest in knowing.

Programmes that allow ALF spokespeople to appear live take a risk. Unedited remarks may be inflammatory or may incite other people to action. Recorded interviews overcome the problem while recognising ALF as part of a serious body of concern about how animals are treated, a concern with a right to be heard.

bombs and bomb warnings

Bombs in public places are more than a story. The public has to be alerted to them, a job best done by the media, especially through the immediacy of radio and television, conscious all the while of the difference between alerting the public with straightforward facts and panicking them with excited descriptions.

As bomb warnings may be false, deliberately or unknowingly, news organisations usually seek guidance from the police. They can normally say whether the warning should be taken seriously. If a warning is believed to be a hoax, broadcasters and newspapers generally accept a duty not to serve the purposes of the hoaxer. If a warning has to be taken seriously, they have a greater duty to alert the public to the possible danger.

Terrorists frequently choose to leave their warnings with news organisations, with the result that many radio and television stations, national and local newspapers, and news agencies have developed procedures for dealing with such calls. The first rule is to waste no time in telling the police, bearing in mind that during the years of violence in Northern Ireland the interval between IRA warning and IRA bomb explosion, never generous, shortened. To inform the police well the terrorist message must be noted well. This means being able to report in full what the caller said. A code used is important; so is the time the call was made; it is in the public interest to be able to give as much detail as possible.

bomb hoaxes

Real bombs seem to encourage mischief makers and people with more evil intentions to pretend there are other bombs. Northern Irish terrorist groups, especially the IRA, included the hoax as part of their armoury of disruption. The media guard against this as best they can. The biggest danger is that if hoaxes are reported frequently, warnings of actual bombs may be ignored by the public. The hoax, in other words, can contribute greatly to the mood of uncertainty and apprehension terrorism aims to create.

The media depend inevitably on the police in this problem. They will usually advise whether a warning should be taken seriously. Hoaxes are often not reported. This is qualified though if a hoax produces significant, publicly evident disruption, say a shopping centre cleared and traffic seriously held up. In these circumstances, local radio and local newspapers, in particular, often feel they should let their listeners and readers know what is going on. This can be done without using the word 'hoax': traffic was diverted after a 'security alert', or the shopping centre cleared while a 'security check' was carried out. Blameless euphemisms are thought less likely to excite miscreants to imitate than the word 'hoax' which seems to act as a psychological trigger.

docu-drama

Unloved by broadcasting's governing bodies who find it difficult to answer for, detested by public authorities when it works against them, exclusive almost to television which is not always bold enough to use it, rarely heard on radio, hardly ever seen on the stage and inappropriate to newspapers who have their own line in invention, the powerful blend of fact and creativity, known as docu-drama or dramatised documentary, has scored remarkable successes. One of the most notable was the Granada Television programme, *Who Bombed*

Birmingham?, shown in March 1990. This was an investigation into the convictions of six people, known as 'the Birmingham Six', for the terrorist bombs that killed seventeen people in two pubs in Birmingham in 1974. The programme named other people it said were the real culprits and the doubts the programme cast on the convictions of the Six added greatly to the campaign for their release. Their convictions were quashed as being unsafe the year after the programme and the Six were freed after sixteen years in prison.

But the short history of docu-drama is also the history of controversy about such programmes. They are rarely shown without serious questions being raised about reliability. Questions are justified, in general and in particular cases. Some producers of drama who appropriate events in recent real life do not understand the disciplines of factual enquiry. Others are not willing to accept those disciplines when they do understand them. Some play fast and loose with facts and are casual with creative licence.

For all the failings of some of the practitioners, docu-drama can provide startling insight into recent and still puzzling events. The genre is not the same as 'reconstruction' though it is closely allied and often involves reconstructions. At its best, it is a form of investigative journalism dramatically, attractively and faithfully recreating scenes – and then, acknowledging that important facts remain undiscovered, perhaps undiscoverable, it uses the insights of creative drama to suggest what the hidden truth may be. It is perfectly valid for television and any other suitable medium to speculate in this way about what is not known but about which we would like to know.

The problem lies in the reluctance of television programme makers to mark in some obvious way those parts of their work that are factually reliable and those that are speculative. Unless special, perhaps obtrusive devices are used, it cannot be known when a docu-drama slides out of reliably known fact into likelihood through possibility and into invention. Viewers also cannot tell whether the invention is reasonable. These serious, unnecessary failings continue to damage the genre because creative programme makers are reluctant to take them seriously. When fact jostles with conjecture, people want to know which is which, however inconvenient it is to the conventions of programme making.

obituaries

Obituaries are a problem. It is difficult to be fully honest about someone who has just died. Even for hard-nosed journalists, the failings of the newly dead are usually to be spoken of softly, much more being made of the better side of the deceased. Considered generosity to the dead, unless they are foreign, is the rule. Only rarely is the rule seriously broken and then it stands a good chance of being regretted, provoking a rash of objections as letters to the editor or as a supplementary tribute. To praise when at all justified and to curb justified criticism is the norm. People who were sharply criticised in their lifetime are caressed in memory, the less desirable or more sensitive episodes and attributes sometimes ignored, sometimes glossed over obscurely, sometimes described gently in euphemisms. Causes of death are often ambivalently dealt with, the years of decline and the hardships of age unmentioned, unconventional lifestyle more alluded to than explained unless it was flaunted in life. Telling the truth candidly is left to the biographers.

National broadsheet newspapers take great trouble with their obituary columns and their approach has changed over the past decade. Though still rarely candid, they are more honest in their assessments, less deferential than they used to be. They are well written, at times indulgently so, more wordy than the news columns and allowed to meander. They are frequently the work of retired journalists, and when they are of very well-known figures they are on occasion, in the years leading up to death, carefully cultivated, updated, refreshed and polished, ready for publication as soon as the bad news is known. Decisions on who deserves an obituary can be very wilful. Obscure figures, well regarded by the obituarist, may well win a good many inches when more worthy characters have been neglected or given shorter shrift.

The quality of the obituaries in the broadsheet newspapers puts them well ahead of the 'biogs' of the big broadcasting organisations though they too take trouble to prepare for notable deaths. Much less air time than column inches is devoted to the purpose but, none the less, worthy lives are marked. Evocative clips of sound and picture footage adorn considered commentary to recall great deeds of the past. When the dead person was most famous, special programmes are made of the obituary material, with actuality from the archives and new tributes from colleagues.

Very occasionally, notable individuals ask to prepare their own obituaries. These are sometimes whimsical, useful only as an addition to the real job. As a further side issue, the Data Protection Act, which has been on the statute book since the mid-1980s, would allow anyone on whom an obituary has been prepared in anticipation of their demise to see it and to ask for changes to what they regarded as any mistakes, provided the material was stored electronically, not kept simply on paper in a filing cabinet. There are no publicised cases of the right being exercised.

opinion polls

Controversy dogs the opinion polls. When they have a bad run which they tended to have in the 1992 general election campaign in Britain they are mocked for misleading everyone – though journalistic hype of polls is at least equally to blame for people being misled. When they have performed well and have, in effect and in advance, described a 'no contest' to be no contest, they are condemned for influencing the result. They are said to have a bandwagon effect, that is to have encouraged people to vote for the likely winner. Poll-phobes call for publication of polls to be banned for some weeks before an election, as they are in France.

The case for suppression is usually dressed in the interests of democracy: people should be allowed to vote on issues and policies, not diverted by estimates paraded as predictions that

105

may, anyway, be misleading. Continued journalistic abuse of polls might conceivably encourage politically motivated restriction. But a ban would not stop political parties conducting polls for their own purposes, as they do now. It could not stop them alluding publicly to the results of their polls which they always say show their support to be firm or growing, never eroding. It would though stop newspapers, radio and television from publishing any objective check on party claims, and would deprive people of their right to vote on the basis of whatever considerations they wish, relevant or irrelevant, reliable or unreliable.

Journalists are certainly slow to behave towards opinion polls in a way their limited reliablility calls for. The embarrassment felt by broadcasters and newspapers when the general run of polls in the 1992 election campaign was confounded by the Conservative victory has not curbed the eagerness of journalists to use them liberally. They continue to be commissioned frequently and reported prominently. But in spite of excessive enthusiasm, exaggerated journalistic write-ups and the acknowledged failings of the polls – which are less than over-excited critics assert – they continue to provide the best available insights into the state of public opinion, a counter to confident claims on the basis of tiny and often partial evidence about what the public thinks. In political systems, such as Britain's, that deny the public a say in the conduct of national affairs except at elections every four or five years and then effectively restrict the choice to one of two or three, the opinion polls are virtually the only means by which people in authority learn anything like the true state of opinion in the country.

The limited reliability of opinion polls has long been well known to the pollsters. The recognised margin of error may make a result as much as six percentage points adrift, and the likelihood of a rogue poll once in a while may be adrift by much more than that. The poll experts often complain that newspapers and programmes present results too crudely. That is especially true of what are known as 'voting intention' polls at election times. These are the opinion polls that try to measure what percentage of people would vote for what party on the day they were questioned. The voting intention results are eagerly analysed by the parties, used as ammunition to attack opponents or as a spur to supporters, are proclaimed boldly by politically charged newspapers to whatever end they see fit, and exhaustively examined in television programmes as though they were the most captivating event of the day. The public is hooked on them as well. They give the appearance of precise and objective truth in a fog of political humbug. Objective they are. Precise they are not. And pollsters know that excited presentation in programmes and newspapers can make opinion poll figures, individually and cumulatively, seem more significant than they really are.

Precision and lack of it are much more important when trying to measure which party is ahead in the race for government than it is when measuring opinion on policy issues. If 70 per cent of people say the state of the economy is the most important issue, it matters little that the real figure may be 73 or 67 per cent – or anywhere in between. It matters a great deal, though, that the margin of error could make the true figure of support for one party not 40 but as much as 43 or as little as 37, while the true figure for its main opponent may be not 37 but 40 or 34 – or anywhere in between.

The polling organisations are forever examining, re-examining and refining their methods in the search for greater reliability. It is hard to believe that volatility in the electorate, cussedness and lies on the part of some voters who resent being asked what the ballot allows them to keep secret, a confusing overlap between the 'don't knows' who have not made up their minds and the 'won't says' who like to hide their hand, and the possibility of late swings of opinion will ever allow opinion polls to be much more reliable than they are now and have been for a long time. The problem is more one for journalists because without their agency the public would be much less misled.

phone-in polls

Technology has made the phone-in poll popular. Newspapers as well as television and radio set them up. Raise an issue, arrange a phone number for 'yes' and a number for 'no', allow enough time for plenty of people to call, and soon the paper or the programme has a good tale to tell.

The main problem is the tendency to make out that these polls are more significant than they really are. The temptation to declare, on the basis of a few hundred, maybe a few thousand calls, that the great British public has spoken, is strong. Whatever the numbers who called, there is never any reason to believe they represent the public at large. The people who phone, select themselves. They are not scientifically chosen. They are not likely to mix age and sex and social groups as they are mixed in the population. They may call mostly from certain parts of the country. As newspaper readers, they will represent a narrow band of people because the readers of any newspaper are not socially comprehensive. As listeners and viewers of the programme, their social spread may be better. But that they will have called in representative numbers is very unlikely. The people who call represent only themselves. There is even no good reason to believe they represent the general run of people who listened to the programme or who read the paper. It all does not invalidate phone-in polls. It says the results should be presented plainly.

paramilitaries

A belief in the power of words plays a big part in the reporting of the shadowy organisations that use violence to challenge authority. They are known as 'paramilitaries' quite often, more often as 'terrorists', especially by unfriendly, establishment media in democratic societies where the violence occurs, frequently as 'rebels' so long as they are another country's problem, occasionally as 'guerrillas', a detached term also generally reserved for armed rebels in other countries, and, from time to time when sympathy is strong, as 'freedom fighters', usually by their followers and foreign sponsors. The latter description reduces to 'fighters', a euphemism frequently applied to groups in the Middle East during the decades of conflict between the Israelis and the Arabs. The abbreviation is favoured in the highly regarded BBC World Service from Bush House in London, reflecting an aversion to 'terrorist' on the grounds that the word takes a stand and that today's unspeakable terrorist may be tomorrow's lauded dignitary.

The number of groups operating in any situation tends to flourish as much as the variety of descriptions given to them. They multiply through splits and breakaways as disaffected followers who want better results set up new groups. They give themselves dramatic, sometimes mysterious names as the catalogue of the past few decades testifies: the 'Red Army Faction' (RAF) in the former West Germany, the 'Red Brigades' in Italy, the 'Tamil Tigers' still current in Sri Lanka and 'Shining Path' active in Peru. They may simply take a name from heroes or members like the 'Bader Meinhof Gang', or be known mainly as followers of a fanatical leader, like Bhindranwale in whose name Sikh extremists fortified the Golden Temple of Amritsar in 1984 to make a base for terrorist acts.

In Northern Ireland, where authority, believing strongly in the significance of words, often countered with publicity rather than policy, they were never publicly referred to as anything other than 'terrorists' or 'paramilitaries'. All the Northern Ireland paramilitary organisations had strong links with the past, as befits the historic resentments of the politics. The group that was to become the most proficient terrorist organisation in the world, the IRA, rarely known by its full name of 'Irish Republican Army', split into the Official IRA and the Provisional IRA at the beginning of the 1970s. The 'Officials', as they became known, virtually disappeared and their founders sidled into legitimate politics. The 'Provisionals', known often to the security forces as 'PIRA', became the terrorist force that mattered. The split spawned also 'Republican Sinn Fein' which struggled to exist whereas plain 'Sinn Fein' flourished as the political wing of the Provisionals.

Other groups came and went. INLA (Irish National Liberation Army) achieved infamy as the killers of the prominent Conservative politician, Airey Neave, a close associate of Margaret Thatcher, then leader of the opposition in the British parliament. Neave died when a bomb exploded under his car as he was leaving the underground car park at the House of Commons in London in March 1979. INLA had originated as a split from the IRA and eventually its members turned violently against themselves. IPLO (Irish People's Liberation Organisation) was a breakaway from INLA. Little known bodies like Saor Eire (Free Ireland) and Fianna Eireann (the Youth Movement) led shadowy existences, very often so shadowy as to seem non-existent.

All these republican groups who favoured Irishness instead of Britishness were opposed by their equivalents on the other main side, known collectively and variously as unionists, for the union with Great Britain, or loyalist, denoting loyalty to the Crown, or Protestant, a sign of deep dislike of the papacy and the traditional though declining Catholic hold on much of Ireland. The UDA (Ulster Defence Association) was the biggest of the loyalist organisations and there was doubt about how close or distant it was to terrorism. It was eventually made illegal, proscribed, a declaration that the authorities regarded it as violent, whatever else it was. The UVF (Ulster Volunteer Force) admitted to acts of violence on behalf of the loyalist cause, as did the UFF (Ulster Freedom Fighters).

Rebel movements the world over have complex connections and some are as complex as the Irish. The tangle of Middle Eastern politics has created tangled connections. The PLO (Palestine Liberation Organisation) has many dimensions, some of them violent. Few journalists understand the mysteries of these organisations. Whether a terrorist group belongs to and is controlled by its parent organisation is often a matter of doubt. Terrorist groups often operate autonomously in cells with untraceable connections to an overall command. That way the capture of one or two people leads only to the cell, not the start of a long trail to the very heart of the organisation. The central organisation may still answer for its autonomous parts, as the IRA usually did, and the organisation clothes itself in the descriptions of the established military, referring to its 'brigades', its 'commanders', its 'units' and even its 'quarter-masters'. The terms are all part of the paramilitary belief in the power of publicity, attempts to create an aura of significance and legitimacy. The organisations are not monolithic

110

in the ways their organisational claims would suggest. They are very loosely organised, at times disorganised. When the peace process in Northern Ireland was underway, the very long interval before the IRA was able to call a ceasefire testified to the looseness of its organisation and to the problem of making sure the activists would go along with what the leadership wanted.

Police Federation

The Police Federation – the police officers' trades union – looks after the interests of its members vigorously. As part of its job it helps police officers accused of bad behaviour. The help extends to action against the media when called for. The Federation has sought injunctions to stop programmes it believed would prejudice the case of officers accused of offences – even when the programme was concerned with a different albeit similar case. An oblique connection may be enough to prompt legal action by the Federation. Actions for defamation against newspapers have been started and some have been successful though the offending stories have not named officers against whom complaints of misconduct were made. Typically, an arrest is made, no charge is brought, the person is released and complains about wrongful arrest, perhaps about harassment or discrimination. This is reported in the local paper. The arresting police officer is not named by the paper, so the public at large does not learn who it is. The complaint is investigated and rejected. After it is rejected, the newspaper faces action for defamation, action backed by the Federation which agrees to meet the legal costs of the officer.

The Federation argues that police officers are particularly vulnerable to charges of defamation, a fair point in view of the front-line nature of their work. It argues further that although an officer may not be named in a defamatory news report, the officer's colleagues none the less know who it refers to. Damage may be done professionally. Colleagues may condemn the officer. A stained reputation could harm the individual's prospects in the force. It is a moot point that damage, if done, would not depend on a news report because in the closed world of the police station, as in any closed environment, gossip does not depend on published news.

Few of these actions get to court. Most local papers believe the risk of losing an expensive court case is worse than paying a smaller amount long before that stage. Some editors also say that some stories of alleged police misconduct are not reported in the papers because of the threat of financially supported legal action against them. The Federation replied vigorously in the *Guardian* newspaper that newspapers could avoid the problem by exercising 'elementary professionalism in ensuring that what they print does not offend against the laws of libel'. Experienced journalists will regard this as simplistic. If a complaint against a police officer is not proved, the newspaper that reported it in good faith is just as vulnerable to action for defamation as the police officer is to defamatory comments in the first place. In such conditions, the only safe journalistic course is not to report complaints until they have been officially investigated – and then perhaps only to report those few that are upheld, a course to keep the public in the dark most of the time.

requests for material

Journalists have a problem when police want their material. The problem occurs also though less often with other official investigating authorities – financial inspectors from the Department of Trade or customs officers. All can get legal orders for material to be handed over whether the journalist likes it or not. Wherever the request comes from, it can apply to the full range of journalistic material – reporters' notebooks, papers they have acquired, names they have only in their heads, still pictures, video recordings and sound recordings. Requests from people who have no special rights of access under the law are more easily dealt with, whether refused or granted, though a court order is always possible if justice calls for it.

Journalists usually resist requests from the police for material that has not been made public.

They sometimes also resist requests for material already published or shown in programmes. They have an extra problem if material handed over would break a promise of confidentiality. Whether already published or not and whether for confidential material or not, the requests arise usually in connection with the investigation and prosecution of crime or other actionable wrong-doing and many journalists, not all, dislike being treated as an arm of the law. They say it conflicts with their duty to observe and report events independently. When their material is used to convict in a court of law, they say it makes them seem like a 'copper's nark'. Reporters and picture takers who need to be tolerated as observers in violent situations such as street riots and militant protests believe they are more likely to be turned on by demonstrators the more their work is exploited for purposes of the criminal law. They cite ugly street scenes after a football match when a camerman was grabbed by the throat and his video cassette seized. In the end, the gathering of information for the benefit of the public becomes more and more difficult, at times impossible. The public interest in a flow of reliable information is ill served. The law replies that like all citizens news people have citizens' duties. They have to contribute to the high public interest in justice being done. The main danger to journalists, so the legal reasoning goes and as voiced by the former law lord, Lord Denning, is from the pictures shown not the pictures ordered to be handed over.

The power of the police to acquire journalistic material is formalised in the Police and Criminal Evidence Act 1984. This is the act normally used though occasionally in the special circumstances of Northern Ireland journalists have faced demands under powers given in the Prevention of Terrorism Act. Under the 1984 PACE Act, police need a court order. To this end, they have to persuade a circuit judge that what they want falls under the terms of the Act. It is a stiffer process than they have to go through for a search warrant which needs the signature of a magistrate. But they have little difficulty persuading the judges. The police have to satisfy the judge they are investigating a serious arrestable offence, that the material they want would be of 'substantial' value as evidence, that they cannot get the material in any other way and that it is in the public interest for them to have it. In the dozens of cases since 1984, the police have lost only a handful – three or four at the most.

Counsel for national and local newspapers, for independent television, for Sky News by satellite television, for news and picture agencies and for the BBC have pleaded the media case repeatedly in the courts, as they did when Scotland Yard applied for news pictures of poll tax riots in Central London in 1990. The judge ordered vast amounts of material to be handed over. In a case arising from a violent demonstration connected with a racist attack in south-east London not many months later, the judge decided the journalistic material was 'crucial'. Of the argument on behalf of the journalists, he said 'I do not see how the integrity and impartiality of those involved should be affected when it is an order of the court.' Photographers and reporters who have to go close to street violence to do their job of informing the public attest otherwise: they face added hostility because their work helps the police. The same judge, Gerald Butler, in a case arising from a violent anti-nazi street protest, agreed there was a 'very great' public interest in full and free reporting – but the public interest in the arrest and conviction of rioters who had injured 200 police far outweighed the increased risk, real as it was, to photographers.

The balance of judicial decision is almost invariably on the police side. In the few cases where the media have successfully resisted – one a BBC case at Southwark in London, another a Central TV case in Oxford – the judges did not favour the public interest case of the journalists over the interests of justice; they decided the police had failed to prove the material relevant. The journalistic argument wins rarely and wins only on a technicality.

News organisations continue to object though there are signs of fading willingness to argue in court: local newspapers and regional television stations shrink at times from the expense and a number of national newspapers sit back, taking no part in the legal contest, content to hand over material if an order is made. They say they have no desire to impede the process of justice. They also recognise a lost cause.

sexual offences

The British media are reasonably well behaved towards the victims of sexual offences. What journalists call 'good stories' are curbed out of a desire not to cause further harm to people, especially children, who have been sexually assaulted. The law goes a long way to protect, providing anonymity for victims of rape, people who are victims of a number of other sexual crimes and for children generally. Media rules add to the protection. The newspapers' code of practice says 'The press should not, even where the law does not prohibit it, identify children under the age of sixteen who are involved in cases concerning sexual offences, whether as victims, or as witnesses or defendants.' BBC guidelines go further. They say it was BBC policy not normally to reveal the identity of victims of sexual crime long before the law was changed in 1992 to extend anonymity for rape victims to the victims of a range of other sex crimes.

The scene is not entirely satisfactory. In the late summer of 1994, a woman who had been raped accepted out-of-court damages of £10,000 from a freesheet newspaper group for a report that gave too many clues about her identity without naming her. The report had named the street in which she lived, a short street; it said the woman was in her fifties and implied she lived alone. Neighbours and friends realised from the facts given that she was the victim. Cases of that kind are caused by unthinking journalism, not by mischievous reporting. In another case, a report of a trial in a serious broadsheet said of a rape victim that she was single, 25 years old, had two children, one a 3-year-old boy, had recently split from her common law husband, lived in a flat and named the town near to where she lived, a list of facts too revealing for her anonymity. The same effect is inadvertently achieved when different news reports in different media give different facts which, put together, point firmly to the identity of the victim, a phenomenon known as 'jigsaw identification' and against which the media have tried to guard.

Another problem was in dispute for a number of years. It concerns the victims of incest and other sexual crimes in the family. For many years the reporting tradition was to name the accused and, so as to avoid identifying the related victims, not to name the offence, to say instead that it was 'a serious sexual offence'. The disguise ensured two effects: that the victims were protected – and that the general public did not know just how frequent were cases of incest in Britain. Allegations of sexual abuse in the family and a number of notorious cases, some large scale, accordingly caused much consternation in a society that did not know these things had been going on for many, many generations, that thought it was part of a new decline and that was ill-prepared to know how to respond.

The alternative to a policy that in effect suppresses news of incest is, exceptionally in the system of open justice, not to name accused or victims and to specify the crime. Local newspapers, the main reporters of sex cases and always keen to include names because 'names sell newspapers', opposed this. The best part of their argument was that in a decent society no one should disappear from the streets into prison without the public knowing. People sent to prison should be named. The national newspapers, not so dependent on naming names and knowing that at times it may be more important or just better copy to specify the offence, were not keen on a hard and fast policy. Now, however, the newspaper code says the adult should be identified, the term incest should not be used and that the offence should be described as 'serious offences against children' or similar. Chances are that when the story calls for it, the national newspapers will go in a different direction from the locals, broadcasting will be at sixes and sevens – and the young victims of abuse will be identified by default.

statistics

Good statistics lie only when they are badly presented. The television or newspaper graph of price rises can easily make inflation seem worse than it is because the gradient is steeper the shorter the time-scale base line of the graph and the longer the vertical price line. Devise the graph differently – lengthen the time line and shorten the price line – and inflation will seem gentle. In written or spoken statements, selection of one figure over another can render statistics equally misleading: 'A record number of jobs was created last month' takes on a different significance if it is also true at the same time, as it could be, that 'Thousands of jobs in traditional industries were lost last month.' Convenient statements to suit political ends can be plucked from any of the sets of official figures which are taken as indicators of the state of the nation, be they for crime, prices, wages, imports, exports, manufacturing output, agricultural production and unemployment.

The faults are easier to describe than to correct. The best journalism goes for a sense of context, the larger picture that often belies the excited headline. Sensible context may mean newly issued figures for the month are best compared with the same month of the previous year rather than with the previous month or better still, at times, with the trend over the past year. That is often true of unemployment figures which are prone to seasonal variations. The variations may obscure a trend. As a result, the bald figures are accompanied by an analysis in which they are 'adjusted for seasonal factors' and which puts some emphasis on 'the underlying trend'. Longer term comparisons of unemployment figures – say the level now against the level fifteen years ago – are more difficult because the methods of counting have changed so much. Even so, the official treatment of unemployment figures and the briefings on them for journalists are more sophisticated than for other officially issued figures. Crime figures are probably the worst, being notoriously unreliable because they state the levels of crime recorded by the police which are much lower in some categories than the actual occurrence of crime in the country, some of which is not reported to the police. Recorded rises and falls in some crimes, particularly violent crime, can be false. Recorded rape rose some years ago because more victims came forward, confident of better treatment, not because more rapes were committed. Yet, journalists and politicians still seize on changes in the crime figures as though they were of funda- mental importance. Statistics are made to lie because they are partially presented.

117

trade names

The journalists' trade journal in Britain, the *UK Press Gazette*, often devotes several pages towards the back to a list of names registered as trade names exclusive to the product they describe but which are often used, in journalism as in ordinary speech, as a generic term for all products of that kind. The *Gazette*'s effort is cautionary. Many journalists have fallen foul of trade names. It is not surprising as journalists are best when they live in the real world, the world where ordinary people say 'hoover' meaning vacuum cleaner (which should be suction cleaner), where ball pens are still sometimes referred to a 'biros' and where temporary offices and toilets are 'port-a-cabins', very close to the trade name 'Portakabin'.

Manufacturers generally enjoy the benefit of their product being the generic parent. It amounts over the years to considerable publicity without payment. But they do not like it when the reference occurs in an adverse context. All very well when your product gives its name to all portable buildings but when two people die in a fire in another manufacturer's temporary structure use of your product's name is a calumny. It could be costly for the journalist, a trade defamation.

chapter five – violent events

effects of violence

The debate about whether media portrayal of violence encourages violence in society has centred on fictional violence, not on the images of real-life violence shown on television and in newspapers. A few voices complain about ill-effects of violence in the news but they are a small minority. Pictures of factual violence provoke many more complaints on grounds of taste so that when newspapers and television curb what they show, which they often do, they do so on those grounds, not on grounds that excessive scenes might encourage or incite others to violence. Many newspapers, especially local papers, are reluctant to show bodies, and when they do show them it is rarely in close-up. Traditional television is the same. The motive is to avoid upsetting and offending people. Occasionally, when a picture not shown is of a mutilated victim who might be recognised by a reader or viewer, an editor will say people deserve dignity in death. Exceptions occur when the bodies are foreign and when editors decide people should know the full force of terrible atrocities. Even then, the worst is rarely shown, always a matter of taste and decency.

People are genuinely upset and offended when pictures are more explicit than they believe they ought to be. Many who complain believe it enough to be told scores of people died dreadful deaths without having to see the bodies. Warnings on television – 'Viewers may find some of the pictures disturbing' – remove less than all of the offence. Long and wide shots reduce distress without eliminating it. The public service aim is to move people, at times to shock but not gratuitously. Television was very restrained in its pictures of people crushed to death during the Liverpool soccer match at the Hillsborough ground in Sheffield in 1989 when ninety-four people were killed, so restrained that some television journalists felt the awful truth had been too much diluted, and yet no other pictures in recent times have caused so much justified distress. Restraint was evident too in the pictures of the fire that consumed a stand for spectators at the soccer ground in Bradford in 1985, killing forty people, but no one could fail to be moved by the horror of it. Although deeply distressing pictures were shown of the fatal scenes after the violence at the Heysel stadium in Belgium also in 1985 when forty-one people were killed at the game between Liverpool and Juventus, much worse was held back. Pictures shown on television in Britain of the destruction of the Pan Am airliner blown out of the sky over Lockerbie in the south of Scotland by a bomb in 1988 were dignified by the care taken to convey the horror without exploiting the carnage of 270 dead. It happens day after day because television newsrooms now receive many more pictures of violence and its aftermath than they used to in the expensive days of film that had to be developed. The video camera, cheap to buy and cheap to equip with tape, is everywhere, never far away when newsworthy violence occurs.

If television news editors in Britain, still largely observing public service ideas, did not show restraint, the country's screens would be full of bloody pictures every day. People who call for more restraint would be aghast at the close-up horrors shown frequently on television in Italy, France and other little restrained parts of Europe. By comparison, British viewers are protected from harsh realities. At the same time, they see more of the human toll of civil wars and civil disasters than ever before. The bad events of the world seem worse than they were when, in fact, they are simply being shown to be as bad as they ever were. Famine in a foreign land did not mean as much when it was described as when it is shown. People comfortably at home, warm, well-fed and satisfied did not graphically understand the truth about the swollen bellies, the bone-thin legs and the flies pestering the dying eyes of small children when they could only read about it. Nor were they driven in such large numbers to contribute their charity to alleviate it. Whatever charge may be levied at real-life violence on television it has acted as a force for humanity. It may be beyond the capacity of the best motivated governments to put right and evocative pictures do not will a solution to problems. But the sight of starved children expiring in the dust and of refugees fleeing from the shells fired on their homes from the hills have added to the urgency of relief efforts and to the work of peace negotiators. Without modern communications the efforts would be less.

Attitudes among editors in television are not as fixed as they used to be. In conditions of competition and easy technology, more explicit pictures are shown more often, partly because more exist, mainly because traditional restraints are less observed when editors say of their rivals, 'They will show it so we will have to.' Regional news programmes tend to dwell on stories of personal violence, muggings, rapes, and murders. National news programmes, unused to witnessing so many civil wars with so many killings as in former Yugoslavia and discontented parts of the Russian empire after the collapse of European communism, are also more likely to show the ugly aftermath of violence, charred and mutilated bodies and people still alive in hospital with legs and arms blown off. The public concern it causes is not based on taste and decency, nor on a fear that such pictures encourage violence. It is a concern about the cheapening effect of frequent exposure to the nasty images of violence. The point quickly becomes emotional, expressed with more passion than clarity. News pictures of violence 'degrade' viewers. Worse, they 'brutalise' them.

The point is difficult to grasp rationally, partly because good evidence is absent, partly because it expresses a sweeping generalisation about an alleged common effect on millions of individuals. It imagines or speculates. It does not state what is demonstrably known or reliably suspected. But it raises a powerful concern. It also echoes reasoning long used by

121

public service broadcasters – that the more violence is shown the more people get used to it. Gruesome pictures have a diminishing effect. At first, people are very shocked, then less so, then hardly at all. Once the chain of effect is established, the pictures need to be more and more shocking to move the people who see them. Before long, great suffering induces great indifference.

The best to be said for the validity of the argument is that 'it stands to reason'. What indications there are do not support it. Very large numbers of people continued to be concerned over the fighting in former Yugoslavia in the mid-1990s as the months and the ceasefires went by. Any lessening of concern was more likely the result of exasperation than of a diminishing failure to be shocked by pictures of the umpteenth outrage. And after that, people were greatly moved by the sight of the brutal Russian shelling of the Chechen capital, Grozny, as 1994 gave way to 1995. The outstanding impression is that after several decades of increasingly explicit television news and after many examples of brilliant television journalism (as well as many examples of brilliant newspaper and radio journalism) from the world's trouble spots people are increasingly disturbed by events in the world, an effect opposite to that feared. Editors may have to answer the charge that they make people over concerned, an echo of the meretricious claim that people fear crime more than they should. There is more than a touch of paternalism in these arguments. They are rarely advanced by people who say they themselves have been 'cheapened', 'brutalised', made unduly fearful or had their consciences blunted by over-exposure. The concern is for others, the mass of people who, by implication, must be overwhelmed in one way or another by the images of violence fired at them by irresponsible editors.

terrorism

Journalism in a terrorised society faces a persistent and fundamental criticism, as it did in Northern Ireland during the twenty-five years of violence up to the anxious peace of the late summer of 1994: that it encourages the terrorism. The criticism has echoed across the years. To an extent, it reflects exasperation and despair, the old swipe at the messenger with bad news. It has more considered adherents. They say publicity is one of the principal aims of terrorists. They kill, not so much to persuade authority to give them what they want there and then, but to win headlines which eventually will erode resistance to their demands. Every killing reported publicises their cause. In publicising it, the cause is elevated, inflated beyond its worth. Publicity makes it stronger than it really is and, then, keeps it alive.

Authoritarian regimes seem to accept the analysis, as they did in the party dictatorships of eastern Europe before the collapse of communism. News of terrorist acts such as kidnaps, killings and hijacks, was suppressed, as was much other bad news. It appeared to work. Terrorism in those countries did not grow, which may have had more to do with the oppressive presence of police and intelligence services but which owed something to the suppression of publicity. There is also no reason to believe the spirit of violence went away. It festered quietly. The issues were suppressed to such an extent that people in the west were surprised at the chaos of conflicting causes that tore apart the countries of the former Soviet Union, causing in twenty-five months many more deaths and many more injuries than were caused in twenty-five years of violence in Northern Ireland.

A branch of the argument against publicity for violence concerned broadcast interviews with terrorists. They were held, in a speech in 1985 by the British prime minister, Mrs Thatcher, to provide terrorists with the 'oxygen of publicity'. The argument persuaded few programme makers in Britain. Interviews with terrorists were rare and the main vehicle of publicity for terrorism was unquestionably news reports of terrorist acts. Terrorists gained publicity because people were told the facts. And telling the facts hardly ever included interviews with terrorists.

The case against coverage of terrorism was often extravagantly stated. The extreme version was that television and the newspapers 'glamorized' terrorists. Use of the word 'glamorize' was emotional, not reasoned and not satisfactorily explained. It seemed to mean that terrorists and their violence were elevated to a prominence normally achieved only by people of legitimate power. Though front page splashes and dramatic television pictures were always accompanied by condemnations, usually in the words used – 'outrage', 'murderous', 'evil', 'monsters' – the publicity was still held to glamorize. It seems to mean nothing more than the more moderately stated form of the argument about publicity feeding the cause.

A sophisticated form of the argument was used by the British home secretary, Douglas Hurd, when he sought to justify the legal ban the government imposed in 1988 on British broadcasters which prevented them using the voices of Northern Ireland terrorists and their supporters in programmes. Although he said interviews allowed sympathisers to 'justify and glory' the violence, his emphasis was elsewhere. Radio and television provided an 'easy platform' for terrorists and importantly, in doing so, allowed them to draw 'support and sustenance'. Direct access to programmes gave terrorists and their supporters an 'air and appearance of authority'. This spread the 'ripple of fear' of terrorist acts in the community. 'The terrorist act creates the fear and the direct broadcast spreads it.' Although related to events in Northern Ireland, Mr Hurd's analysis is readily applied to terrorism wherever it occurs. It could be adopted and adapted by authority everywhere as the classic case against any form of publicity for terrorism.

The other side of the argument troubled journalists with responsibility for covering events in Northern Ireland, in the Middle East, in former West Germany, in Italy, Sri Lanka and wherever terrorists were active. If, in response to criticism that they encouraged terrorism, they downgraded or ignored violence, they would also be downgrading or ignoring events that gravely troubled ordinary people. Worse, if publicity faded, it was likely that the bomb which killed two people would, next time, kill five, then ten. Violence would escalate until it could no longer be downgraded or ignored.

A new dimension of criticism against the media arose in the aftermath of the bomb that killed almost 170 people in a United States federal government building in Oaklahoma City in 1995, an outrage of immense proportions, much greater

than anything that had afflicted Northern Ireland, comparable
to the worst of terrorism anywhere, and particularly shocking to
Americans who had little previous experience of terrorism on
their own ground. Followers of an extreme right-wing militia
were blamed. Some critics pointed accusing fingers at 'shock
jocks', the uninhibited, often angry, libertarian presenters of
right-wing radio station phone-in programmes. The critics said
these over-excited proponents of individual freedoms, including
the right to bear arms and the right to be left alone by
increasingly overbearing, tyrannical government, had encouraged wild fears about the collapse of fundamental American
values and in so doing had fed extremist attitudes.

An aspect to trouble journalists and troublesome in a
different way to authority is that some terrorism is carried out
by official forces or agents. It is referred to as 'state terrorism'. It
exists. There are strong suspicions that the security forces in
Northern Ireland committed terrorist acts, part of a black
campaign to discredit avowed terrorist organisations. In
Rhodesia in southern Africa after the unilateral breakaway
from Britain and during the guerrilla war in the 1970s that led to
the creation of Zimbabwe, there were many claims that security
forces, usually units of the highly trained 'Selous Scouts', had
committed atrocities in remote areas. The Scouts, it was said,
had pretended to be from guerrilla groups in order to discredit
them in the eyes of black people. The claims were made by the
African nationalist parties whose terrorist/guerrilla fighters
readily killed black rivals. The claims were reported without
evidence at the time. Information months later, in cases years
later, supported some of the claims when originally all were
disbelievingly received. State terrorism is like that. Journalists
can hardly ever identify the perpetrators of it at the time.
Circumstantial evidence often takes weeks to gather, especially
from frightened people in the bush, and remains inconclusive
whereas avowed terrorists proclaim their murders.

The tension between the media and authority over
terrorism continues unresolved. It is not resolvable
in the present state of knowledge. But just as the
Northern Ireland troubles influenced society at
large – security precautions all over the United
Kingdom, special laws and special courts – so they

influenced journalism. In the twenty-five years of the violence, British journalism made concessions to authority in the interests of the fight against terrorism. The homes of people known or likely to be targets of the IRA or of loyalist terror groups were not identified; the number plates of their motor cars were obscured in pictures; the movements of VIPs on business and sometimes on holiday were not disclosed, especially not in advance. There were also many rows between government and broadcasters about programmes. Programmes were dropped or changed and critics who believed the broadcasting authorities had behaved cravenly would not accept the explanation that most of these programmes were judged to have genuine editorial faults. The destructive power of terrorism diminished everything it touched.

hijacks

The 1970s were a decade of hijacks. They virtually petered out during the late 1980s as police, with other law and order agencies, developed counter-techniques and precautions, as the political will to resist grew stronger, and as hijackers realised their violent and frequently murderous missions achieved little. A few incidents in the mid-1990s reminded everyone that security weaknesses would be exploited by fanatics willing to sacrifice their own lives for no evident return. All the while, there was official and public concern over the role of the media, a concern aroused equally by other, continuing terrorist acts. The concern predated but was encapsulated in the well-remembered charge that media coverage provided terrorists with 'the oxygen of publicity'. The remark was prompted by a Middle Eastern hijack in June 1985. During it, television showed close-up pictures of one of the hijackers holding a pistol to the head of the pilot of the American aircraft grounded at Beirut, while pilot and hijacker answered questions for the camera. It was a deeply disturbing scene, the closest television news pictures have come to proving that, in making an incident on a remote runway in the sun into a

126

public spectacle all over the world, media and terrorists encourage each other.

The point is not proved or disproved. The criticism will pursue journalists whenever politically motivated violence occurs and, quite often, over the reporting of ordinary, non-political criminality. It is an issue journalists have to answer.

Insofar as the 'oxygen of publicity' outburst by Mrs Thatcher, the British prime minister of the 1980s, was aimed against interviews with terrorists it was misdirected because the incident at Beirut that provoked it was so unusual. The scene was without question distasteful in the extreme. Many people found it very disturbing. Television editors could have justified a decision not to show it or to present it in such a way as to reduce its impact. That, however, is not the same as saying the interviews encouraged those actual hijackers or other potential hijackers. If media coverage encourages – different from causes – terrorism, as is likely, perhaps even certain, the influence lies elsewhere. It lies in ordinary news coverage. Reports of bombs, shootings, kidnaps and hijacks are much more significant than the occasional interview. Headlines whether large or small, news reports whether excited or restrained, and dramatic pictures in close-up or long-shot of the aftermath of outrages are the main encouragement for the terrorist psyche. To refuse to conduct interviews with terrorists would not change that and if reports of actual events were suppressed or unnaturally subdued in an attempt to stop terrorism, terrorists would make their terror more horrifying to compel better attention. The existence of television, radio and newspapers in free societies is the encouragement.

During hijacks and other incidents involving hostages, such as sieges, broadcasters contend also with the possibility that what they broadcast will directly affect what happens in the incident. Although aircraft hijackers do not have newspapers delivered, they are able easily to tune in to radio broadcasts and miniature television sets make television coverage readily available. The danger that hijackers might retaliate against hostages was openly acknowledged when a hijacked aircraft was on the ground in Cyprus. Radio stations were asked not to speculate on the state of mind of the hijackers for fear it agitated them. Broadcasters usually co-operate with requests of that kind because, if they do not, the price of a few frank words the public can do without might be a dead hostage.

riots

The course of public protests that turn to riot may be influenced by the media, especially by television. Some protesters are encouraged to be at scenes by the knowledge the media will be there. Then once the protest is underway, the sight of the cameras, microphones and the rest of the paraphernalia of the news gatherers is believed at times to encourage greater excitement leading to violence than if the protest had been unobserved. Demonstrators against the poll tax in the centre of the normally peaceful English city of Norwich in the late 1980s started to smash windows of shops when television lights were switched on.

Television and radio which are more evident at many newsworthy scenes than newspapers because of the prominence of their news vehicles and recording equipment are alert to the risk and do what they can to reduce it. Technology helps. Cameras that need no additional light and small video cameras are more discreet than the traditional bulky shoulder-borne instruments. Reporters and camera crews are told to be as low profile as possible. But they cannot become invisible and their new technology remains obvious. Whatever is done, the presence of the news media at tense events is liable to have an influence. The options are stark: tolerate the risk or keep the images of protest and the policing of protest away from the public.

copycat behaviour

Many people assume that bad behaviour shown on television is copied in real life, an assumption often aggressively asserted as though it were a proven fact or, at least, so obvious as to be unchallengeable. Good evidence is, however, lacking. But the makers of programmes are not allowed to shelter behind that. They are urged repeatedly to take the matter very seriously. The broadcasting regulators and watchdogs certainly do. So does public opinion. More importantly, the unproven possibility of a causal connection disturbs any decent conscience. At the heart of the concern is the belief that only one death or serious injury caused by imitation is one too many and cannot be accepted.

The issue is not one sided. Concern about copycat could propel programmes into unreal stances. For fear of bad effects, they could distance themselves – and their audiences – from the real world, so guarded as to be anodyne, careful to the point of deception.

The weight of concern falls mainly on television because of the belief that to see something happen is usually much more influential than to hear about it or to read about it. In effect, television viewing simulates direct experience and causes the vast majority of people to see so much more than they would from real direct experience. But if there is a copycat effect, radio is likely to cause some of it, and newspapers cannot be absolved. Copycat is a problem for all of the media, with television in the forefront.

In some ways, factual programmes and fictional programmes have different problems. The news cameras and microphones are normally not able to replay the moment of violence or other act by an individual that might be imitated – muggings or snatch-and-run raids on shop tills – because they were not there at the time to record it, whereas drama inventively recreates such incidents. The news is, however, frequently present for predicted or prolonged violence by crowds and groups, as with street demonstrations and roof-top prison protests. This suggests the possibility that fiction may be more likely to influence an individual to dangerous imitation while the news may be more likely to influence groups.

In both cases alleged copycat is not credible without the significant influence of other factors. A brooding, probably lonely psyche, disturbed enough to be triggered to violence by a television drama, would, in the absence of a television stimulus, have been triggered by something else – a video, a newspaper report, a personal experience. Equally, when crowd violence in one inner city area is followed the next day by similar violence elsewhere, as in the urban riots that afflicted more than thirty British towns and cities in the summer of 1981, there had to be common social elements in addition to any propensity to copy what had appeared on television and been reported dramatically on radio and in newspapers. In the same way, shared discontent over conditions in gaols, with other factors like good weather and the ready availability of food, were highly influential in causing and prolonging prison violence in many parts of the country in 1990, whatever additional influence there was from the attentions of the media so manifestly enjoyed by the prisoners, especially at Strangeways gaol in Manchester in northwest England.

When the authorities are concerned that media attention is making matters worse, it is for them to do something about it, if they can. It is a better first option than for media organisations to be expected to censor themselves. Remembering that the rebellious Strangeways prisoners enjoyed also the attentions of people in the street who saw them clearly from the road below next to the prison walls in Manchester, the authorities might have been able to erect tarpaulin screens to prevent the prisoners seeing out and public and media from seeing in. They did that for the siege at the Libyan People's Bureau, the embassy, in London in 1984 after police officer Yvonne Fletcher was shot dead in the street outside. The Libyan building was shrouded from view. The media were allowed guided viewings. In Manchester, however, an official screen might have provoked the protesting prisoners to more violence.

In the complexity of considerations relating to copycat violence, the responsibilities of factual programmes and newspapers cannot be clear. However necessary it is to say they must do nothing to encourage or to increase crime and violence, as the codes of good practice insist, it is inadequate when no one can know confidently, nor even suspect reliably, that significant outbreaks of violence would have been avoided if earlier instances had not been reported. Nor is it believable that scenes of imitable and manifestly undesirable behaviour will have only a one-way influence. They are as likely to serve as an awful warning to some people. They may deter. They may encourage others, parents perhaps, to help prevent more by exerting pressure on young delinquents. Positive effects of this kind are rarely asserted and would be extremely difficult to establish. But negative effects, though much asserted, have not been reliably established in spite of much effort, and there is really no good reason to believe in one more than the other – with some reason to believe in both.

It was certainly very easy to believe in the copycat effect during the British urban violence in 1981 and the prison riots in 1990. A connection between the reporting of one event and the later occurrence of another like event seemed obvious and, years later, it cannot be refuted. The response of programme makers and newspaper editors has to be that copycat cannot apply without other factors to encourage it, that a great deal of care is taken not to provide overt encouragement to violence, other criminality and other bad behaviour, that the voices of condemnation are always given prominence, that good but hidden effects are also likely, and that people must be told what goes on in their society. At the end of this trail of counter-argument to the critics and social improvers who want media restraint in the interests of social policy is the bald likelihood that some copycat effect may, unavoidably, be a price an open, informed society has to pay.

suicides

The evidence is not extensive and what there is is nowhere near conclusive but reported suicides may encourage other suicides. That is not the same as saying reported suicides 'cause' other people to take their own lives. There has to be a predisposition as with other forms of suspected copycat, and it may be that a suicide following a report of a suicide would just as easily have been triggered by something else, that in the circumstances of unhappiness it would have occurred anyway.

A suspicion persists. Coroners have occasionally asked reporters not to publish explicit details of unusual suicide methods disclosed at inquests in case they are copied and have included remarks at the end of inquests intended to counteract the influence an inquest report might have on a potential suicide. Such remarks are usually reported, mainly because they add to the newsworthiness of the inquest, and requests to curb explicit details of suicide methods are often agreed to. Whether either deters any suicides is not known.

accidents and disasters

Accidents and disasters are big stories, taking up very large amounts of broadcasting time and of newspaper space, not entirely to good effect. The good is that they inform instantly; public opinion is immediately engaged, and so are special interests; coverage makes people aware of dangers; it encourages charitable responses, and it puts pressure on authority to act.

It is also often overdone, frenetic in manner and providing information of such an extent that it excites editors and reporters more than it interests readers, viewers and listeners. Broadcast reports, in particular, cause anxiety in some people, and offer opportunities to instant unreliable punditry. Suggestions about causes are at times seriously awry. Initial estimates of dead and injured may be seriously wrong, especially figures from earthquakes and huge floods.

Charges of intrusion on private matters are nearly always made against the news media after accidents and disasters. They are provoked by pictures and sound of grief stricken people or badly injured victims. It does not seem to matter that the bereaved and injured have co-operated. British people are ambivalent onlookers to grief. Their curiosity struggles with a cultural preference for the emotions of bereavement to be private, whether out of regard for the bereaved or because they themselves become too upset. When distressed people co-operate with reporters, critics say their condition clouded their judgement; they should not have been approached. In other words, 'Do not show grief.' The argument has a little merit.

132

But it is not likely to prevail. Reporters, photographers and camera crews see distress as part of the reality and if it is not portrayed the truth is not fully represented.

Whatever journalists do they will be criticised and there are always a few, driven by competition, who go too far but some news organisations decently hold back. Their reporters and picture-takers are told to accept clear refusals by distressed victims to be interviewed, not to pursue victims who try to avoid them, and not to use the long lens to sneak up on people's emotions. Long and wide shots are often acceptable and less intrusive. The same organisations edit sympathetically, refusing to use intrusive pictures. On television, editors often forgo lingering shots of people in distress.

After accidents involving large numbers of people, air crashes especially, television viewers and newspaper readers complain about pictures of victims in hospital. To head off the concerns, reports may say the cameras were allowed in by the victims and the hospital authorities. Reporters find that glad-to-be-alive victims are at times pleased to appear in pictures, especially when it is a way of reassuring far-away relatives and friends they have not suffered too badly.

A next-of-kin problem of another kind often arises. It is a problem mainly for radio and television with their ability to make information instantly public, though news late in the day makes it a problem for newspapers as well. The problem is that near relatives sometimes learn bad personal news, either directly or by clear implication, from a programme: when an identified airliner with a given flight number crashes with the loss of all on board, many people know that their daughter or son, husband or wife, mother or father, was on that flight and that they have been killed before any names have been made known. There is no totally satisfactory way of dealing with this problem. The traditional responses to distressed relatives that important news must be given and that names are withheld until next-of-kin have been informed do nothing to assuage the sense of emotional injury. The dilemma is that excessive restraint by the news media in the face of increasingly vigorous promotion of the interests of distressed relatives would curb news reporting to an extent that society becomes less well informed. Withholding news altogether until it is harmless is a sure way to manipulation and ignorance.

Other failings afflict the news media after major accidents and disasters. Too often they are overcome by the big story, careless of what can reliably be known in complex situations. For their part, radio and television become unmindful of the fact that, besides being more immediate than print, they are more personal as well: to be told distressing news by a newscaster or reporter is more shocking than reading it. Reports of scenes of distress on radio and close-up scenes on television are more likely to be more upsetting than reports and pictures in newspapers. Even the most careful broadcasting will cause distress, and, when it is not careful, the public purpose is more difficult to justify.

The news media can do little about complaints that their clamorous interest puts extra pressure on the authorities at a time when officials need all their energies to cope with the accident. No one can reasonably expect broadcasters and newspapers not to enquire. And if effort is not made to keep the public informed quickly and fully, which can only be through the media, rumours of all sorts of failings flourish, making bad situations seem worse.

military action

Honesty of reporting military action depends frequently on whether the news organisation's own country is involved, whether it is action inside the country or outside, whether it is action involving an ally, whether it is someone else's civil war or whether it is between faraway nations. News organisations are often not able to report military action by their own country as they would like even when it is well short of war. Apart from pressures from varieties of the national interest, including national security, and pressures to take account of the interests of 'Our boys', the soldiers, and of their families, they are greatly limited by the problem of getting good information reliably. Reporters may not be able to witness military action as it happens, reporting instead in the aftermath. They rely heavily on the military and on government or on others with interests to promote. The state's desire to put the best face on its actions is at its keenest when it is using its ultimate power, through its armed forces, against external enemies or against home grown rebels and terrorists, branded emotively as the enemies within. And these enemies of the state, in turn, are keen to turn publicity to their advantage. Both sides manage the flow of news. Facts are partially selected for release to journalists and access to areas of fighting is strictly controlled, usually on the stated grounds that it is too dangerous to allow ready access or would jeopordise the military operation. Restrictions also hide failures and excesses.

chapter six – special treatment

anonymity

Respectable and disreputable people alike with something they would rather not disclose are more likely now than in the past to want to appear anonymously in programmes and in print. They are also more likely to be allowed to do so. It is partly because the television camera, the radio microphone and the newspaper reporter find their way into intimate corners of human life which, for a long time, they were denied or denied themselves and which in less frank times were not even approached as possible. As with many things in the media, anonymity is infectious so that justified cases have encouraged unjustified cases.

A touch of credibility may be lost when someone appears in shadow or back to camera, and the broadcaster especially has to face politically motivated wrath, perhaps regulator's censure, for allowing criminals or other undesirables to speak unidentifiably. It can also lead to severe problems of protecting sources if the interview interests the police. It is sometimes possible to allow anonymity on publication while agreeing to disclose identity later to police or a court for a legally valid reason. When this is not possible, a confrontation with the law is as likely to result from anonymity given lightly as from requests carefully considered, agreed to only rarely and only when there is good reason.

'Good reason' covers many situations. A victim

of sexual or other assault, feeling embarrassed or ashamed or shocked or all three, is usually protected from public gaze on request and without argument, and may still make a significant contribution to a programme or article. A relative of a convicted person might be able to illuminate an issue without being willing to be exposed to the greater gossip that follows an identifiable appearance in a programme or in print. Donors of body organs for transplant are not now named publicly, and no public good would be served in most cases by disclosing their identity.

An argument that surfaces, usually in America, that anonymity encourages unwarranted shame in victims, particularly the victims of sexual crime, is received in Britain as unconvincing, a self-serving rationalisation by American media people who use it. A name given against the wishes of the victim adds injury to injury.

The case for the privacy of victims is easy. It is a great deal more difficult when the guilty want to hide in the shadow. It is also much more likely to cause a law and order problem for newspapers and programmes. A firm rule is tempting but is bound to be arguable. The media might firmly refuse anonymity to anyone confessing to a crime or convicted of one – and be applauded for it. There would, though, be times when this would lose an important contribution, a missed opportunity to enlighten. The worth of a scruple not to allow the guilty to hide their identity cannot adequately be measured against a failure to advance knowledge. But as factual programmes, newspapers and magazines are in the business of advancing knowledge and understanding, then if the contribution is remarkable, not routine or predictable, anonymity for an unrepentant criminal can be justified.

Anonymity is more easily accorded in radio and in newspapers than in television because it usually means no more than not putting a name to a voice or a quote. Sometimes, however, a person interviewed for radio will ask for voice to be disguised or even for someone else to speak the words so there is no risk of the voice being recognised. A newspaper may also decide to disguise faces in a picture.

Television has more complex problems as it uses many more pictures and sound as well. It has, accordingly, more complex devices for the problems. The individual not to be identified may be elaborately 'made up', in effect disguised with extra hair and face colouring, which can be done very successfully given enough time. This happened with a former police agent in Northern Ireland who infiltrated the IRA and who was shown in extensive interview in a programme in 1992 called *The Informer* in the BBC series *Inside Story*. Interviewees may be shot back-to-camera, or in deep shadow. The job can also be done artfully by using shots very close up – the right ear, cheek and not much more, or the mouth and chin from over the shoulder. The individual may need convincing that it works.

Another method, pixillation, now also used for newspaper pictures, hides identity by breaking up the face in the picture into a mosaic of squares. A thumb-print, a smudge or what looks like a heavy mist over the face are other techniques. These devices tend to be used when anonymity is an after-thought.

Balaclavas or scarves wrapped round the head are sometimes used, especially by bad lads and worse. These dramatise and add bravado which some viewers resent.

Television programme makers have to make sure they deliver the anonymity they promise. There have been cases of people filmed in shadow being identifiable on screen because the shadow was not heavy enough. Pixillation, too, is not always successful. A few people say that by screwing up their eyes when looking at the screen they can reconstitute the pixillated face. This is a significant risk when the pixillated face is known to the squinter. Coarse pixillation using larger squares seems to overcome the problem.

Television, like radio, will also sometimes have to use voice disguise. The effect can be risible, creating a 'Donald Duck' distortion. Even when not absurd, it is a distraction. Only a light change to the pitch of the voice sounds natural and this is not usually enough of a disguise. Although programme makers tend not to like it, it is more successful to have the words read or acted by someone else.

A combination of techniques is sometimes used for fail safe effect. A man and wife protesting against psychological methods they said had given rise to false allegations of sexual abuse of their daughter were seen back to camera, in low light and with their heads in a fog.

jigsaw identification

The jigsaw effect occurs when two or more news reports added together inadvertently point to the identity of someone whose name has not been given in any of the reports. This effect that no one wants, though rare, is most liable to occur with regard to victims of sexual crime, especially abuse within the family and rape. This is what happens. Radio, television and newspapers generally respect the need for anonymity of the victim. They accept that publicity is likely to add to the ordeal of the assault. The law reinforces this attitude by banning publication of a victim's name and any other identifying personal facts in nearly all cases from the time the offence is committed. Each news organisation decides separately what other facts about the victim and the case it will publish, each careful not to give away too much. One report, in a local newspaper for instance, may say of a rape that the victim was blonde and 23 years old. Another report on the same case, perhaps on local radio, says the victim lives with her parents in a named district of the town, and yet another report, possibly on television, in another newspaper or on another radio station, says she was attacked while getting into her green sports car. Facts of this kind may be given all on the same day or they may emerge over a number of days. Separately, they do not betray the identity of the victim. But together they say enough for people of the locality to work out who she is.

The problem is most frequent for the local news media, that is, local papers, local news agencies, local radio and regional television, because there are many cases of sexual crime that do not interest the national media. Easier as it ought to be for relatively small numbers of news organisations in a locality to come to an agreement on how to avoid the jigsaw effect, they find it hard to agree. When the story interests the national newspapers and all the national media, the chances of an agreed approach are negligible.

The problems of co-ordinating news coverage among extremely competitive organisations were highlighted after a widely reported rape in London in 1986, a case in which the victim agreed, months later, to talk openly about the assault on her. It happened at a vicarage. The victim was the daughter of the vicar. Immediately after the crime, no news report named the young woman. But many reports were published and broadcast, locally and nationally, over an unusually protracted period. Different reports contained different facts. Some identified the vicarage, referring to the victim as a woman in the house at the time. Some referred to the victim as a vicar's daughter 'in London' without giving the locality of the vicarage. It was not long before many people realised who the victim was.

The case was so troublesome that newspapers, television and radio met under the auspices of the Press Council, predecessor of the Press Complaints Commission, the body that at the time considered complaints against newspapers and concerned itself with journalistic standards in newspapers. The meeting drew up guidance to try to prevent the same thing happening again, an aim practised journalists saw as unattainable.

The guidance was re-emphasised some years later. It made the obvious point that an address, though without a name, was a strong pointer and should not be given, as now forbidden in law. It urged news organisations not to describe any link with another person in the story. It also cautioned against information about any link between the victim and the scene of the attack. The advice may have avoided some cases of jigsaw identification but knowledge of it fades with time as the journalistic population changes. It is the kind of thing that has to be pointed out repeatedly, and even then, there will be unforeseen coincidences of factors in which inadvertent identification occurs though everyone diligently observes the advice.

The surest way to prevent the jigsaw effect would be a very restrictive law, one that specified the few facts that could be reported, with everything else forbidden, as with reports of preliminary hearings in courts when reporting restrictions are not lifted. Such a law would prevent the victims of sexual crimes from being widely identified. It would not, though, prevent local, street knowledge which is part of the suffering for victims and which travels, not through the news media, but along the whispering grapevines of gossip and rumour. At times, such a restrictive law would also prevent important information from entering the public domain, not by design but because restrictive laws invariably stop more than they intend, doing specific good and indeterminate harm.

emergencies

People in authority know more about the media interest in emergencies than they used to. But many officials or officers, in the police, local councils and other bodies involved in dealing with emergencies, have difficulty accepting that the media must be dealt with as well, that one of the worst things is to ignore the approaches of reporters and photographers. Newspeople, persevering against the problem, often have to rely on hearsay or, at best, unofficial reports in the first hours of an emergency while local people are buzzing with rumour. Officials, stressed by the demands of the emergency and concerned for immediate victims, may fail to see that a wider public in the area is anxiously concerned, that it needs good information and that the quickest way to give it is through radio, television and the newspapers. As experience in Northern Ireland has found, exaggerated rumour and destructive gossip take over when reliable information is slow.

Newspeople covering emergencies are usually expected to agree to restraints, to accept, for instance, conducted early visits to the sites of big air crashes to avoid damage to evidence, or, as another example, to withhold personal details, normally names, of dead and seriously injured victims until next-of-kin have been informed. When large numbers of newspeople are clamouring for information, officials may seek 'pooling' arrangements. This allows a few reporters, camera crews and photographers to a restricted scene in return for an agreement to share their material with all the journalists who cannot be admitted. Interviews with victims willing to talk and pictures of them may be arranged as a precaution against intrusion. During widespread and continuing emergencies, for instance, those caused by very severe weather, local newspapers and local

141

radio are often asked to carry special, extended announcements, perhaps lists of schools closed or traffic routes blocked.

There are many reasonable deals between media and authority which are in the public interest, easier for helpful officials than for obstructive officials to achieve, but always requiring journalists to be alert to any attempt to hide scandalous facts.

blackouts

The British media, newspapers and broadcasting, operate news blackouts from time to time. They are usually, but not exclusively, agreed as a result of an approach by the police and in connection with matters being pursued by the police. Threats to contaminate goods in usually well-known stores are often 'blacked out' unless there is reason to believe actual contamination has occurred. Occasionally, blackouts are agreed over sensitive military events or preparations. They are likely to be asked for during small sieges, that is, when an individual, usually in a highly agitated condition, holds a hostage, frequently a former girl friend, under threat in a house or flat surrounded by police. Prison authorities may seek a blackout when a prisoner, barricaded in a cell, is threatening another, a form of siege.

The risk in sieges is that news reports, if heard or read, might jeopardise the captive victim by agitating the already highly charged captor. The police are able to stop newspapers reaching the captor in a siege but they may be able to do nothing about broadcasts. In some other incidents when the captors and their whereabouts are not known, newspaper coverage could be as dangerous to the victim as a revealing broadcast. A blackout may be total in that no news at all is given of a particular event for an agreed period or may be partial in that some facts are left out of reports for a while, in some case permanently.

The best argument, some say the only valid argument, for any blackout is that without it life would be lost or seriously jeopordised. This is the spirit behind many blackouts. But short term blackouts lasting a few hours have been observed for other reasons. In one case, news of the arrest of a criminal was withheld by programmes and newspapers until police had picked up others in the gang who might have been alerted had the news been made public right away. In another, the news media kept quiet about an arms find in Wales until the arrest weeks later of terrorists who came to collect the weapons. Had the find been reported earlier, the terrorists would probably have learned of the reports and would not have returned to the spot where the cache was buried.

Journalists are reluctant to agree to blackouts. They dislike the idea of being hand-in-glove with authority and their credibility, rated lowly anyway, could be reduced further when they are discovered to be. But deals have been done as long as journalism has existed. They will go on being asked for and being agreed to. Most editors believe them justified as a rare occurrence so long as they are not imposed by outside authority, so long as the news organisations are genuinely persuaded by reasons given and so long as the blackout is publicly acknowledged whenever possible after the event, a gesture to keep faith with the public.

No self-respecting editor would admit, at the time, agreeing to a blackout as a favour, nor to spare the embarrassment of a public figure. Candid confessions by editors who have granted a favour are rare even long after. But it happens.

contamination scares

Media organisations in Britain censor themselves over most deliberate contamination scares when they believe them to be false. Some threats are never reported; some are reported only after an arrest has been made. But known actual contamination is reported, and has to be, because of the duty of newspapers, radio and television to alert the public to true danger. The main problem is to know when a threat is false and when it is real. A number of false threats are designed to cause commercial damage by scaring people away from certain goods or stores. Other false threats are malicious hoaxes, carried out for perverse personal satisfaction, or 'try-ons' that might lead to ransom demands. Even real threats are not straightforward because they can mean that products will be contaminated if a demand is not met, or that goods, usually on supermarket shelves, have already been contaminated and that more will be.

There is no totally satisfactory approach for the media on this issue. One way lies encouragement to extortionists, including terrorists, and to mischief makers, with a strong additional risk that the reporting of empty scares would make people indifferent to occasional warnings of real danger they should take seriously. The other way lies a negligent failure to give adequate warning that would help people avoid disfigurement or disablement and perhaps death.

Public response to contamination reports in newspapers, and on radio and television shows what a peculiar problem it can be. In 1989 a remarkable series of cases in Britain developed the features of an epidemic. Contamination of a relatively small number of jars of baby food was widely reported. First reports said glass had been found in some jars. Over the following weeks, several hundred cases in many parts of Britain of broken and ground glass, pins, bits of razor blades and other sharp objects in jars were reported to and in the media, or to the police, or to shops and stores. It was concluded in the end that only a handful were genuine. A few people had found dangerous objects in jars without knowing how they came to be there. But the vast majority, into hundreds, were of contamination by the people who purported to have discovered it. Some of these people were trying to cash in through compensation. Others appeared to want attention or sympathy, or publicity and notoriety.

A year or two later, the Animal Liberation Front phoned a number of television, radio and newspaper newsrooms in the English Midlands one morning to say it had put corrosive fluid into shampoos on the shelves of a number of branches of a named and well-known chain of stores in different towns. It was, it said, in retaliation against products being tested on animals. No contaminated products were found. It was a hoax which ALF hoped, on being reported, would scare people away from those and like products in any of the stores. The plan failed because the hoax was not reported.

On another occasion, large quantities of a soft drink were removed from display because it was believed some might have been tampered with. The precautions were widely reported in the media with the reasons for them. These recurrent threats of contamination encouraged manufacturers to add a security seal to the packaging of goods that, without it, could easily be contaminated. Manufacturers may not have done as much as quickly without the pressure of unwelcome publicity.

The reporting by the news media of all contamination threats would be good only for the perpetrators. Usually no reporting goes ahead unless a check suggests that a particular threat should be taken seriously. The police will usually say when they believe it should. The actions, more so than the comments, of the commercial victims, manufacturer or retailer, may give a further steer. The public interest comes first and the final decision on this – to publish or not to publish in the interests of the public – is for the media, regardless of the occasions on which their decisions are bad.

sieges

The course of sieges, small scale or large scale, are liable to be influenced by news reports. The anodyne phrases 'the course of' and 'influenced by' can have terrible implications. When terrorists hold hostages, as in the six-day siege at the Iranian Embassy in London in 1980, innocent people may be killed or injured or exposed to greater terror by news reports on radio or television that agitate or displease their captors. When a lone gunman, distraught and unhinged, holds an estranged girl friend hostage in her flat, he may be driven to murder or suicide by what is said about him on the radio. The police can stop newspapers being delivered to buildings under siege but the jamming of radio and television could provoke as much anger as the news being jammed. Because of the problems, broadcasters often leave out information and speculation the

145

police believe could be provocative, such as information about the crates of equipment taken into the building next to the Iranian Embassy during the London siege. News of high profile incidents that may last for days cannot be left out altogether but news of low level, domestic sieges that are likely to be over in a few hours often is. Journalists, never keen to suppress interesting facts, accept that no great public harm is done by withholding particular information for a short time or for as long as necessary, that no great public good would be served by insisting it be included and that the story is not worth the possibility of harm to individuals at risk.

kidnaps

An understanding on kidnaps has existed between the media and Scotland Yard since the early 1970s, and this understanding became an explicit agreement with all police forces in England and Wales in the mid-1980s. The agreement does not formally apply to the police and media in Scotland because of the different legal standing of criminal investigation there. Nor does it apply formally to the Northern Ireland police, the Royal Ulster Constabulary, because of the complications of terrorist crime which dominated Northern Ireland at the time. But the terms of the agreement have been used in both countries.

Representatives of local and regional newspapers in Britain had doubts, in principle and in practice, about making a formal pact with the police. They stood aside from the mid-1980s agreement but local and regional papers have co-operated in all cases where the agreement has been invoked. The agreed terms are not publicly divulged, though they have to be known in the news organisations.

It is a unique agreement between police and media. No other on any other topic exists. There are no formalised restraints, voluntary or otherwise, on crime reporting generally. Even at the height of the violence in Northern Ireland and its spill-over into the British mainland, there were no signed agreements on terrorism though understandings on a few sensitive details were observed. Restrictions on a range of stories are agreed with all of the news media from time to time as special one-off arrangements and, as they always have been, quiet deals are done between particular news organisations and particular police forces.

conditions

Some public figures are notorious for trying to impose conditions on their appearances and, because of the nature of radio and television, the problem is much greater for programmes than for newspapers. The principal offenders are politicians, though by no means all politicians, some of whom are so eager for publicity they would pay to appear.

All manner of conditions are sought. Sometimes it is that a recorded interview be used in full or not at all, sometimes that the editing be approved before broadcast, at times that the interview be live. A few try to dictate where in a programme their interview should be used. Some, usually government ministers, demand the last word or that no other interviewee be allowed to speak during or after the interview. Ministers quite often refuse to join a discussion, saying they will accept only a one-to-one interview. Occasionally, they try to decide who should interview them. At times, they call for detailed questions in advance – and insist on no departure from them. The politician or other figure to be interviewed may demand that certain questions are not asked or that certain topics be avoided altogether. Front bench speakers, very conscious of status, especially when they are in government, often refuse to appear on an equal footing with a lesser opponent: the frontbencher will do an interview but will not appear in a discussion with a backbencher.

Ministerial minders in the departmental press office or in the minister's private office are usually the conduit for such conditions. They are at times the inventors of them and, quite often, they are more obdurate than the minister.

Conditions are not always introduced in

advance of recording or in advance of the visit to the studio. Interviews have been recorded, then followed quickly by a demand they be used in full or not at all. Trouble-free arrangements for a live discussion have fallen through at the last moment after one of the participants insisted on an interview – or, a favourite device, claimed an understanding that it was going to be an interview and declared that, unless it was, would not take part. Chicanery flourishes when politicians try to win the best conditions for themselves.

Programmes sometimes surrender to these pressures. They do so because they are desperate for the contribution, and because the pressures for balance, which imbues all of British broadcasting and under which all sides are owed fair representation, are thought seriously to limit the ability of programme makers to be tough with people who seek unreasonable conditions. Programme makers and the broadcasting authorities have made the problem worse than it need be and worse than it would have been had they refused consistently from the start to compromise. Balance does not require contributions to be geared to public relations needs and editors can insist on journalistic imperatives.

Not all conditions must be refused. Detailed questions have reasonably been supplied in writing in advance when the topic is complex and has a long history, so that the interviewee can check details and references. There are no good reasons, though, to stick absolutely to advance questions: some answers inevitably call for elaboration. Conditions of the 'questions in advance' kind are more likely to be appropriate for more considered programmes, say a documentary, than for daily, highly topical shows where experienced people to be interviewed have ready answers to any question. Special conditions have been agreed for long considered programmes given unusual accesses, whether to individuals who are not normally interviewed or to places normally closed to journalists. For instance, in a series of interviews with normally anonymous and therefore unpractised government officials, civil servants, who had been given permission to speak publicly in a programme, it was agreed they could be allowed, while recording the interview, to take a question again and be given a promise that no use or reference would be made to the redundant, perhaps gauche, answer.

Conditions accepted have caused rows after programmes because they were not carefully worked out and written down. Written or not, they are another short cut to dispute if they are open ended. The unpractised government officials, for example, were allowed to change any answer so long as the recording continued and so long as the interviewer was on the premises but the exceptional right ceased once the recording team had left. Only the most powerful reasons allow an answer to be changed some hours later or the next day.

Special conditions are invariably sought when cameras and microphones are allowed into confidential places to record sensitive processes, like interviews in police cells, briefings for soldiers or case conferences of social workers. The police, for instance, often argue that they will have to be allowed to see a programme before transmission to make sure nothing in it would prejudice a fair trial. This is an area of dispute and is by no means as clear cut as when police or the army wish to protect the identity of undercover officers. Programmes frequently argue that they and their lawyers must be responsible for *sub judice* matters, as with any other legal aspects. The police have, however, had serious trouble from courts for not protecting the integrity of their part of the legal process. This emphasises the need for well considered agreements. In the end, the programmes decide whether the price asked, a compromise of editorial independence, is worth the prize offered.

For the normal run of topical programmes, when an unacceptable condition is refused and, as a result, an interview lost, programmes reserve the right to say on air why an advocate of a particular point of view is missing. Producers call it 'empty chairing'. It has been used aggressively in retaliation against recalcitrant, missing interviewees. Properly used, it is as a service, by way of explanation, to listeners and viewers. Fair explanation matters when saying why a place in the programme is empty as busy public figures cannot always meet a programme time, and there is a significant difference between on-air explanations that 'The minister refused to be interviewed' and 'The minister was not able to appear.' The problem for the well-intentioned producer is that it is often difficult to know when a reason given is valid, not an excuse.

As it is rarely true to say that only one person is suitable for interview, programmes frequently work hard to find reasonable substitutes for refusers. If they do not, the broadcasting authorities may foot-fault a programme, on complaint, and perhaps without much sympathy for the realities of programme making.

deals

Many people try to do deals with journalists. Politicians, especially those in government using cohorts of press officers, are assiduous seekers of journalistic concession. They are not alone: trades union leaders, business executives, other public figures and even ordinary citizens all try to fix things in their favour. The favour may be editorial or in kind. They ask for stories to be dropped, for unfriendly facts to be put aside, for their names or mention of their company to be left out; they ask for payment or for copies of pictures. The more important the deal-seekers, the more likely they are to insist their contribution is treated specially, not processed solely according to journalistic imperatives. They ask for interviews to be used in full or not at all. They ask to see copy before publication or to hear edited interviews before broadcast.

Any deal is difficult. No deal is the best deal. But some deals are inevitable. Experienced journalism takes the hard nosed attitude that the deal to be done must provide something of value for the journalism. It could mean an editorial concession if it is the best way of making sure that coverage is not lost. It might mean refusing any concession at all, going ahead regardless, as best able, and ignoring the noisy wrath of people who feel they own something of the story of which they are part.

The journalistic attitude is pragmatic, not principled. If appropriate, what has been conceded to one is refused to another because one editorial prize to be gained is well worth the concession while the other is not.

previews

Requests that develop into demands to see material before publication or broadcast offend journalistic propriety and are hardly ever welcome. But they are frequent. They are also quite often agreed to. They are never made disinterestedly, just out of curiosity. They always have an intention to influence content, at times to control it. An editor under pressure may oblige a journalist to agree to a preview or the journalist facing a decision alone on the spot may agree out of eagerness to secure the story, and the promise made, whether it should or should not have been, is a promise to be kept in all but the most exceptional circumstances.

A preview demand can be made at any time, in a small or in a weighty matter, and can refer to part only of a programme or article or to all of it. It may amount to no more than a need for a convincing assurance that a comment is used properly in context. To this end, the person who gave the quote wants the completed passage in the script or story read over the phone to satisfy them, easy to meet, difficult for the journalist to concede. Many demands are more onerous. People interviewed may ask to read the finished report of the interview before it gets into the paper or to hear the edited recording, sometimes complete with introduction, before broadcast. The process in radio and television becomes more complicated when clips of interview are spread across a programme. Interviewees have insisted on seeing a programme before broadcast because they wanted to make sure their comments were given a fair show when juxtaposed against the recorded comments of other people, a concern especially strong over programmes dealing with controversial issues.

Certain situations encourage requests for a preview. With newspaper and magazine interviews a request is most likely when some of the comments made are not to be quoted. In such cases, interviewees want to make sure their indiscretions are not attributed to them or traceable to them. Special facilities granted, including access to events not normally witnessed by the public, often come with a demand for preview.

This is very likely to happen when, for instance, a journalist or programme team is allowed to follow and to record official child carers investigating reported cases of neglect. The police, the army and other security services will usually want previews if they are to allow programme makers to record undercover operations or any activity not normally observed.

Experienced authorities like the police and army will make preview a condition before access is agreed: no preview, no access. Less experienced organisations or individuals may ask for a preview as an afterthought, the information, interview or facilities sought by the journalist having already been given. Journalists have no legal or ethical obligations to agree to late requests for material to be vetted before publication. It is a matter of discretion. Some such requests are agreed for no better reason than keeping on the right side of a frequent source. When a preview is demanded in advance as a condition, it is a matter of calculation: is the material to be gained worth the concession? When the prize is extraordinary access to highly interesting confidential operations, the answer is usually eager: 'Well worth it!' Many outstanding television and radio programmes are made on that basis.

Regardless of whether it is a condition in advance or an afterthought, seasoned journalists do not agree to previews in an open-ended way. The purpose of the preview has to be made clear and mutually accepted. Least acceptable is that the previewer wants to decide whether the journalist has done the job properly – that facts are correct, that the report is fair, edited reasonably and includes an acceptable sense of context. These are always matters for journalists to decide, no one else. Purposes given are rarely so bald and they vary from authority to authority. The police normally want to make sure no undercover officer is identified, no other security secret disclosed and no *sub judice* risk incurred. The army are also concerned about security. A social services team will want to protect vulnerable individuals. A manufacturing company may want to protect a valuable commercial secret. These are all reasonable precautions. It is also reasonable for officials not to want to leave them to the good sense of the journalists.

Reasonable precautions readily develop into

an unreasonable desire to make sure the programme or report is entirely to the liking of the people who allowed it. A few rare figures, like the Queen, may have been granted a comprehensive veto. A few others try to achieve it. The government of India, bureaucratically elaborate as ever, was outstandingly persistent when considering permits for television documentaries and features. Its conditions for permission to film in India included, on occasion, a 'guide' to accompany the team throughout its work in India and an allocated adviser to be paid for by the television team. It insisted also on a preview of the completed programme, usually a fortnight in advance of broadcast. The final condition was for a promise that anything the government objected to in the previewed programme would be removed or changed. At least one programme team stayed at home in Britain because it could not inveigle an acceptable compromise to the promise. A high legal group in England asked for the same unqualified editorial power and was also refused with the result an important access was lost. The judicial authorities in Scotland were not so demanding. Negotiations to allow BBC television cameras into their courts resulted in an engrossing series on BBC2 towards the end of 1994 with a criminal trial shown in Scotland before that. Judges could have previews to make sure the interests of justice were not harmed.

Politically motivated requests for preview are made from time to time. Politicians who ask usually want to interfere and to make a fuss if editors will not make changes. The demand is almost certain to come in disguise: 'The programme will make news and we want to be able to answer calls from reporters properly.' Policy is that such demands are resisted at the outset – if they are not, no one acknowledges it.

Stiffly principled journalists totally dismiss the idea of previews, politically motivated or not, however well founded they are and however well considered the conditions for them. Americans talk about it in an absolutist way. The strong instinct of their newspaper people and television networks is to refuse on the grounds that it must damage editorial independence. Though not a hard and fast attitude, it is less flexible than in British journalism. Accordingly, British television has been allowed accesses in the United States not achieved by US cameras.

And the best American journalism has an enviable reputation for integrity, better than the general reputation of British journalism.

embargoes

Journalists observe embargoes as lightly as possible. Embargoes are broken, the facts leaked or the release time wheedled out of if the story is worth it, if the journalists can think of what sounds like a good reason for doing so – and, of prime importance, if they think they can get away with it without later retaliation. Journalists' self-concerned approach matches the nature of many embargoes. The motive of the people releasing the information is often to maximise publicity or to make it easier to handle, at times to control, the media interest. Instead of having to field dozens, maybe hundreds, of unco-ordinated and repetitive queries, a pre-arranged news conference deals with most of them, and, immediately afterwards, the radio and television reporters queue up for their interviews. Clearly, this benefits the media, to some extent, as well. But it is a system that encourages news manipulation. As the simplest device, an unfavourable report can be held back and embargoed because another event known to be coming up will overshadow everything else in the news that day. A favourable report can be pushed forward for greater attention when news is quiet.

Ploys are natural and they will naturally give rise to attempts by journalists to circumvent them. Embargoes on the most official reports, like government White Papers which may be delivered to news desks days ahead of publication, are observed and effectively evaded at the same time. Reporters given them under strict embargo prepare reports of varying degrees of diligence for publication some time ahead while others are busy with their contacts, extracting what they can for publication ahead of embargo. Very few embargoed reports of any real news value remain fully confidential until publication time.

Authors of reports often co-operate in judicious leaks. Their co-operation, leading to publicity for their report, sometimes takes the form of interviews on the breakfast shows, hours before publication, on the understanding they will talk opaquely about the report without disclosing what is in it. Sometimes the authors or the commissioners of the report are behind those well-informed, embargo-busting leaks, mainly in newspapers, that titillate interest. In such simple ways and in other more complex ways, the system of embargoes encourages journalism and authority to conspire in their own interests.

chapter seven – disputed practices

journalistic licence

It is impossible to say how often journalists wilfully make things seem different from what they really are. A bit of licence here and there is a professional self-indulgence practised by many. It starts acceptably and slides bit by bit into deceit. A television programme showing a presenter, reporter or interviewee against a relevant skyline when all that is really behind them is a plain board, part of the studio set, is using a technical convention of programme making to add a mild sense of presence to the picture the viewer sees. In radio, the sounds of a school playground in the background to a report on an educational issue may have come from the sound library. They may have been recorded by the reporter and added later as background to create an impression of 'on the spot'. Licence is used more questionably by those radio reporters who record 'links', that is, commentary between clips of interview and other recordings, in a street outside the studio to use in the programme in such a way they seem like the natural noises of a location in another part of the country or in another country. The little deceits are to add credence. So also is the licence that pretends the newspaper war despatch came from the battlefront when the reporter was miles away. The slippery slope leads to a few chronicled examples of television reporters giving the impression their piece to camera was done at the trouble spot when in fact they were in a studio or other safe location against a background of 'wild track', pictures and sound shot earlier at the scene. The slippery slope includes comments in a newspaper interview recycled by another paper in such a way that makes it look fresh, at times exclusive. The slope ends with blatant examples of facts knowlingly being bent to improve the story. And a journalist who responds 'Don't let the facts get in the way of a good story' uses the old adage only half in jest.

journalistic trickery

Journalism frequently operates on the edge of moral acceptability. Journalists keep bad company when the search for facts calls for it; they trespass on privacy; they ignore the law occasionally; they use pretence and guile when it suits them. Journalistic codes and guidelines reflect this dimly by having remarkably few hard and fast rules. The ethical framework of journalism is kept exceptionally flexible to allow journalists to justify their behaviour if at all possible, which may seem a contradiction in people who are at the forefront of demands for strict moral justifications for the behaviour of professionals such as doctors, lawyers, social workers and politicians.

Few journalists, if any, are morally grubby all the time. Few, if any, are morally upright all the time and the moral ambivalence of their position is necessary to the service they provide to society. In the British system, they are already strongly confined by the law and by the hold authority has on the flow of information. To confine them further by strict and elaborate moral codes would allow officialdom to be more secretive, politicians to be less accountable and business to do as it sees fit with less risk of being exposed when the customer is exploited.

The heart of the matter is whether deceitful journalistic means, when not against the law, are justified by more important ends and the extent to which this is so. The connected question, which is just as important, is to whom or to what journalists should be answerable for their behaviour when it is within the law but may be undesirable. A few deceits are widely condemned by journalists themselves: one was the taking of sneak pictures of a popular television actor, Gorden Kaye, while he was in hospital in the late 1980s critically ill after an accident. The consensus was that no good was served. Mostly, underhand methods are professionally accepted and socially tolerated when the results are significant enough.

The incidence of journalistic trickery for good ends is common. Reporters and photographers have posed as cleaners to test airport and airline security in time of terrorist threat. When they find controls are lax, they have served the public interest by exposing a dangerous weakness which far outweighs, in importance, the deceit they used and which would not be admitted by authority without the firmest of evidence. The *Sunday Times* disclosure in 1994 that two British members of parliament were prepared to put parliamentary questions in return for payment rested heavily on a pretence that a journalist who approached them was a businessman. The pretence angered a number of other MPs who accused the *Sunday Times* of 'entrapment', that is of creating a false situation to induce wrong-doing. But many examples of journalistic trickery for good ends amount to entrapment and without it many acts of wrong-doing that harm innocent people or the public good would not be exposed. The Press Complaints Commission sided initially with journalistic thinking in deciding the *Sunday Times*'s method was justified in the public interest.

The position of politicians in parliament is particularly important in this thinking. Only they could impose enforceable curbs on journalistic behaviour, laws to make journalists worthier than required by their adopted ethic, a topic that has exercised the politicians for many years, especially when privacy is invaded. At the same time, one of the most important functions, possibly the most important function of journalism in a free society, is to report on and to assess the doings of people who exercise political power. It follows that whenever politicians fundamentally limit the power of journalism they may limit the extent to which they, themselves, can be examined. Political power would be used to protect politicians. They

158

would, in fact, be one of the main beneficiaries of legislation to protect privacy unless such a law declared that politicians, because of their public positions, are not entitled to privacy, a negligible prospect.

Scams to trap undesirables extend beyond politics and security to many commercial corners of society. Consumer programmes on television and radio along with watchdog columns in newspapers expose dodgy kitchen salesmen, double glazing pirates, devious insurance sellers, dubious timeshare promotions, loan sharks and many other exploiters by posing as ordinary customers or their friends to make recordings that are very hard to challenge. The method is entrapment and all entrapments involve a lie. The lie is used to uncover a truth. Journalists say the lie is small and the truth is important.

Good evidence is what matters to well motivated journalists involved in pretences that have a good public purpose. They have been told often enough by lawyers that the kinds of allegations they are investigating are serious defamations that have to be proved. Reporters and their editors learn from experience that other people's testimony may be unreliable, or reluctant. Some witnesses melt away, on fearful second thoughts, when faced with the prospect of giving evidence in court. Allegations of commercial deceit relying solely on the testimony of aggrieved customers often have no documentary or other objective support. Media lawyers occasionally advise journalists to record relevant phone calls without telling the person at the other end because they make denial difficult.

Worthy journalistic organisations expect evidence acquired by underhand methods to satisfy two other conditions. The first is that there should be substantial grounds for suspicion, not as strong as legal proof, before underhand method is used. The reporter should not be engaged on a speculative 'fishing trip'. The second is that the evidence could not be acquired by clean methods. That is often a matter for experienced judgement because it is very easy to wreck an investigation by premature, open approaches to the suspect, family or colleagues.

Unpalatable as it is to some people, the prevailing journalistic ethic says devious dealing to expose devious dealing is justified provided the

159

actions being exposed are significantly more serious than the method used to expose them. Journalists see the choice as being to secure good evidence or to allow many practices that work against the public to continue to flourish.

secret recordings

Recordings in sound or vision made without the knowledge of the people being recorded are important for journalists seeking to expose wrong-doing. A large part of the power of secret recordings is that the truth of them is difficult to deny, crucial when a programme or a newspaper is alleging misdeeds. And the vindication for covert methods is that truthful incriminating recordings are not likely to be made with the co-operation of the guilty. Secret recordings do good work on behalf of victims of deceitful commercial methods or of criminal activities when open methods would fail. They are also an editorial temptation, themselves a deceitful method, liable to be seen as counter-productive if the target is insignificant. Because secret recordings (known also as concealed, hidden or covert recordings) are underhand, many people want to be satisfied that the method is justified, otherwise, the journalist becomes the villain.

Many news organisations regard a recording to be made secretly as a last resort. It usually means that research has already established wrong-doing and that the journalist needs legally acceptable proof. It means that the likely purport of what is to be recorded is known. The main justification is that important facts, whether in words spoken or in acts, which deserve to be made public, could not be recorded openly and known for certain.

A variety of factors works against open recording. It is obvious that commercial cheats will behave abnormally, that is, honestly, when they know the cameras or microphones to be on them. It is important, for instance, when capturing unacceptable sales methods. Similarly, journalists and programme teams allowed to follow undercover police or

160

customs officials, say on the trail of drugs dealers or smugglers, cannot allow the presence of their cameras to be known. Journalists would be in danger at times if they recorded openly, particularly when investigating criminals.

The guiding rules – that a secret recording is justified if the subject matter is important, not trivial, that what is being recorded is necessary to the editorial purpose, and that it could not have been recorded openly – have prevailed for well over a decade. They are, though, not absolute and there is always room for judgement. The complaints commissions may regard a secret recording of an individual as grounds for taking seriously a complaint that privacy had been infringed. The final judgement would depend on whether the infringement was regarded as justified, probably hinging on whether the public interest had genuinely been served.

Although a secret recording may contain conclusive proof of wrong-doing for which there is no evident justification, the people recorded are usually given a chance to speak for themselves, confronted with the evidence. In the face of a complaint, the Broadcasting Complaints Commission or the Press Complaints Commission could conclude that the recording was justified but that the programme or newspaper was at fault for not seeking a response.

As concealed recordings usually relate to wrong-doing, the police and other investigating authorities are frequently interested in them and any connected material. Extra police interest is aroused because there is, nearly always, more material available than was actually used and with newspapers police value the original material, not the form in which it was printed. Police approaches for information and material tend to be an acute matter of conscience among journalists who are not used to it. But, when no confidences are involved and when all the material was capable of being used, reporters who are used to it take the view that material be made available to the police because there is not much point in exposing villainy while refusing to help convict it.

doorstepping

Doorstepping adds drama especially in front of the camera, sometimes adding drama to an undramatic situation. It means confronting newsworthy individuals – usually people who have been up to no good – without advance warning as they leave their office or their home, or their lovenest, putting them in a position in which 'No comment' seems as exciting and as significant as a confession.

It is a favourite device of investigative reporters who, having gathered the evidence surreptitiously, as they usually have to, may choose to present it to investigated villains (their victims) when they are not expecting it and, to reduce the risk of legal obstruction, at the last minute. Often though, the investigative reporter with a dossier of substantiated allegations against a target will have first asked for an interview or statement. The more villainous the target the more likely they are to have refused to talk, to have refused even to acknowledge the request. Many requests for considered comment are evaded or ignored when the context is unfavourable to the person being asked to talk. It may be a politician hiding disreputable financial connections, a commercial con-merchant who has gulled ordinary people, or a drugs baron who exudes respectability. In such cases, the rough methods of the doorstep are justified as the only hope of getting any comment at all, though very often the comment is insubstantial – but the pictures or the sound are dramatic.

The ill-considered doorstep may draw a complaint to the Press Complaints Commission or to the Broadcasting Complaints Commision and they may decide that the action was an unwarranted intrusion on privacy. The governing bodies of radio and television, being composed usually of non-journalistic outsiders, sensitive to charges of bullying by the media, tend also to take a dim view. In the BBC, doorstepping outside the news context requires special approval.

The forest of microphones and cameras that greets people after a newsworthy meeting is a form of doorstep. It is widely accepted as part of the lot of experienced public figures who court

162

public attention. There is, though, much public sympathy for blameless people thrust into the limelight who cannot be expected to find it anything other than an ordeal. Nothing much can be done about this. The journalists will not go away when there is a legitimate public interest – and quite often when there is not. The individual journalists usually behave reasonably well and occasionally, to reduce the stress for the victim of the media's attention, it has been agreed that only one reporter will put questions. This does not happen naturally and would not be accepted by journalists as desirable if it were to happen routinely. When it does happen, it is because the individual has an authoritative guardian who can negotiate terms in return for an appearance. The event is then no longer a 'doorstep'.

eavesdropping

Without eavesdropping, some of the world's best stories, important truths as well as trivia, would be lost. Eavesdropping does not have to involve the breaking of a confidence by the journalist who receives the overheard information, as some critics argue. The eavesdropper does not always seek to eavesdrop and cannot be held to have a responsibility to protect what others would prefer to keep confidential. It is for indiscreet chatterers to take precautions, not for the journalist to shield them.

If the journalist has no source other than the eavesdropped, reports are easily denied, so the eavesdrop usually has to be the means by which the information is gained in the first place, then confirmed by quotable evidence. Sometimes, the eavesdrop is based on recorded material that cannot be denied. This has happened when television or radio has kept microphones alive while technical checks are done after recording an interview or speech. Normal conventions place a responsibility on the broadcaster not to use anything said in these unguarded, after-the-event moments when politicians are apt to be indiscreet and will often make remarks they would not make at the time on the record. Hundreds of newsworthy remarks have been made in such circumstances and very few have leaked. One leak occurred in the early 1990s when John Major as prime minister referred to right-wing 'bastards' in his cabinet. The television interviewer honoured the convention but word of the prime minister's indiscretion emerged by other routes. Whoever broke a confidence, it was not the journalists who received and used the information. They were not part of the understanding between broadcaster and interviewee. News was made and the public was given a startling contemporary insight into what lies behind smooth, public relations manipulated and civil service protected cabinet relations. Normally, we have to wait for memoirs, years after the event, to learn the truth in such matters. As journalists will eavesdrop when they can, it is for imprudent talkers to curb themselves.

lobby journalism

Journalists with access to lobbies tend to value them as providing privileged insights for 'trusties'. Journalists excluded from them or who exclude themselves tend to decry them as a perversion. The lobbies involved have nothing to do with 'lobbyists', people who try to influence MPs, government ministers, government departments and other official bodies in favour of whatever cause they are paid to represent. Lobby journalists are correspondents for newspapers, periodicals and broadcasting who are allowed special access to official sources of information and comment. The most important – and notorious – use of the lobby system in Britain is the twice-daily briefing by the prime minister's press office, usually in the person of the press secretary, when the views of Ten Downing Street are made known to the correspondents allowed to attend and who accept the conditions of access. Some information given and comments made can be attributed to Number Ten as agreed at the time. Often information and comment, though freely for use in stories, must not be attributed directly to the press secretary, to the prime minister, to Number Ten or to anyone. At times, what the lobby is fed is not supposed to be used at all, being for background only, 'Just to make sure you understand the context, you understand!' Similar lobbies, though less important and less frequent, operate in other areas of government business – in transport, health, agriculture, defence, foreign affairs and so on. Accredited, specialist correspondents allowed to attend them are given briefings, facts which they can use without attributing them to any particular minister or official, and often not to the department.

The system excites hostility. Journalists opposed to it say it allows government – and any other authority operating it – to spread their views without taking responsibility for them. Information and comment too sensitive or too embarrassing for open disclosure are slipped, in effect with a nod and a wink, to a few journalists who can be trusted to deliver it to the public to the benefit of the source but without the source having to answer for it. Lobby sources cannot readily be challenged or interrogated in a proper way by journalists outside the lobby. Worse, it enables the source to deny responsibility. Worse still, the lobby correspondents – so it is alleged – often do the government's dirty work for it by reporting uncritically as hard fact what they have been told by partial sources not checked against others.

The criticisms are in some ways well founded. Correspondents sometimes recycle what they have been told unattributably as though it was impartial, unchallengeable truth. That is, though, a failing on the part of correspondents who do it rather than on the part of the system. The criticisms are also suspect in that if the system was not formalised it would operate in an informal way. A few journalists will always develop special relationships with sources allowing them to receive special privileges. Further, given the abiding confidentiality of approach in the British system of governance, some important facts and some important judgements would not be given to the public if the lobby system did not exist or, more likely, would be given through the agency of a smaller number of journalists for a smaller number of news organisations to a smaller public.

conflicts of interest

All journalists are liable to experience conflicts of interest, even when the range of their activities outside their work is small. A simple desire not to do an old friend harm can get in the way of a story. A conflict may arise when a frequent source expects, as a favour, a story to be overlooked or unnaturally pruned. Journalistic professionalism copes with these pressures as best it can.

British broadcasting faces more serious forms of conflict of interest. Personalities it has created, being commercially valuable as household names and, to a lesser extent, producers it has trained, are offered large sums of money by commercial interests while they are still in programmes. Most are careful not to compromise themselves, especially when they work for news and topical programmes where trust would be damaged by commercial connections. A few are not careful enough. The true extent of the problem is impossible to know because many of the activities that earn big money are not declared and are not publicly obvious.

The blandishments are great. Companies pay handsomely to have their corporate videos presented by a programme personality known to millions and produced by experts. They also pay very well to have the radiance of a personality in the chair at their company conference. They pay a great deal, additionally, to buy professional coaching so that their executives can cope well with radio and television interviews. All this is promotional work, serving the interests of a commercial paymaster, just as much as doing the 'voice-over' for an advert, or for declaring the super-store well and truly open. If the programme people who do this work also on news and current affairs, or any topical programme, their reputation for an uncommitted approach and the reputation of their programme is compromised to some degree because their talent has been used to promote an organisation or a product they might have to deal with impartially in their programme. The point is not that video work corrupts them and, being professional, they are not cravenly in the pocket of a commercial interest. They can and do put tough questions in a programme to the very same people. They can and do examine issues robustly, without favour. But public perception may be intensely sceptical. When the public learns of these things, they lose trust, a little or a lot. The reputation for impartiality is reduced, not surprisingly. Interviewers are meant to be uncommitted and a cheque from a newsworthy corporation implies a commitment and casts a shadow.

Media training, including lessons in how to do well when being interviewed, for business executives and others liable to be in the public eye is an unresolved area of problem. Professional coaching is in demand. BBC guidelines are firm. They say no presenter or editorial person in news and current affairs and other topical programmes should coach people in how to be interviewed. Editorial people keen to earn fees outside their programme work would prefer a more permissive view. A minimalist rule would say only that no programme journalist should coach anyone for an interview already arranged by the organisation for which the journalist works.

Other forms of commitment by people in significant editorial roles have long and firmly been ruled out. These include working for a political party, campaigning for a controversial cause, and taking a stand on a disputed matter of public policy (other than a broadcasting issue). To take a stand – or to seem to take a stand – for a commercial interest is just as undesirable because it impinges on editorial detachment.

Programme people have been known to take the view that quiet commitment, out of sight of the public, is acceptable, their argument being that what the public does not know about does not trouble it. Against this, viewers of a corporate video are television viewers as well and knowing that a presenter has taken their company shilling could stain their view of the presenter on the programme. No secret is safe anyway. Popular newspapers, doing their jobs properly, can find out about them and if, in the popular view, these quietly undertaken activities were not questionable they would not be news either.

People determined to remain editorially clean follow the rule that if you would not want the public to know, do not do it – nor allow others to do it.

freebies

Some journalism depends heavily on 'freebies', that is on trips and facilities such as the use of motors cars and hotel rooms, free of charge or at low cost. Rare the journalist who has not occasionally had the pleasure. The energetic press relations, public relations and image-making businesses court media attention with a fat cheque and the relationship is, at times, editorially suspect because commercial and other interests enjoy publicity they would not get if they did not pay for it. It is a natural state of affairs in which the antidote against undue editorial influence is the integrity of the journalist. The issue is not whether freebies win publicity, which they clearly do, but whether the freebie causes a favourable gloss when there should be no gloss or when it should be unfavourable.

Given that free facilities need not mean slanted coverage and that some events could not readily be covered without facilities provided, few journalistic organisations forbid freebies absolutely. Many, however, assert that editorial coverage cannot be bought. That is too bald because, in effect, it *is* bought. An image on the television screen which might be a brief shot of an airline symbol on the tail-plane, a mention in a radio programme and a line or two in the newspaper columns may be the extent of the reward, and it is not always favourable. But it is there. The public have had their attention drawn to it because journalists were entertained or helped. The influence occurs often at the soft-end of journalism, for instance, in cheerful features about holidays. It can, though, appear anywhere. Much of the time it is harmless. Some of the time, it fails the public because editorial scrutiny is relaxed. The proper journalistic stance is that, whatever facilities are provided they will be declared, no conditions will be accepted, no editorial favours granted and the nature of the coverage decided independently.

Occasionally, especially when hard news is involved, a news organisation insists on paying its way or will join a facility only if it is generally available to journalists. The usual attitude is not so puritanical. If it was, the number of available freebies would be much reduced and the public would not be better informed.

chapter eight – politics

interviewing

Interviewing is one of the successes and one of the failures of modern British broadcasting. With other forms of 'invitation' broadcasting such as phone-ins, it has succeeded over the years in bringing multitudes of people in front of the camera and the microphone to talk about their experiences and to give their views which are then heard widely when previously they reached hardly anyone. The variety of public opinion is heard as never before, compelling public authorities, including government, to pay more attention to it. The process contributes to public scepticism of authority which is less able now to disguise incompetence. It contributes hugely to freedom of expression, providing added value when opinions are heard through the media by large numbers of people rather than by a few.

The failures are equally important. Legions of public figures have been quizzed on radio and television and the accumulated experience has taught them techniques of self-justification, rebuttal and evasion to such an extent that the more they are held to account the more they cloud the issues. Seasoned public figures, most notably politicians of government, are so programmed by experience, by their advisers, public relations officers and image-makers that in broadcast interviews weak cases are made to sound strong and arguable cases presented as unchallengeable. The practised use of statistics, pulled as though out of a hat, confound interviewers. Assertive, over-elaborate, verbose questions with many assumptions allow the interviewee an easy ride because they are easily rubbished. Factual errors in questions from presenters of pacey news programmes who have too much else to think about open escape routes for government ministers when they are cornered. Clichéd questions, often beginning 'But surely, Minister . . .', have the sound of a challenge and the substance of squeak. The same question is put three or four times, in slightly different ways, and frequently fails to extract an answer anyone wants to hear. It is a particular fault of reporters who do not recognise the difference between a news interview to extract information and an interview to explore issues. Besides being unproductive, repetitive questioning tends to exasperate the audience, evoking sympathy for the person being interviewed. Important interviewees will use indignation or a superior manner in retaliation when it suits them. They will answer questions at excessive length or in round-about ways that waste time – and against which the broadcasters have developed no effective antidote.

Another factor works against the interviewers. In a culture which values politeness, it is very easy for a prevaricating public figure to make the interviewer seem rude and ill-mannered. The BBC chairman, Marmaduke Hussey, reflected the concern of polite society when he called for fewer interruptions during interviews and, in so doing, played into the hands of the evaders and obfuscators. They were helped too by the later intervention of the BBC director-general, John Birt, when he expressed regret about 'disdainful' interviewers, about the 'ritualistic encounter' turning into a 'brief opportunity to bicker' and about the emphasis on personality at the expense of issues. He had a wider concern: that the demands of the media for quick reactions and instant headlines cheapened public debate and the entire political process because it worked against 'cool and measured judgement'.

The solution lies mainly in the hands of the public figures rather than in the approach of the interviewers. Public figures could restore integrity to public debate by giving direct answers to direct questions. Even the best interviewers combining courtesy and persistence with time and back-up

171

for good research, and with enough programme time to explore issues thoroughly, do not overcome the ability of determined public figures to avoid the point of questions they do not like. Mrs Thatcher, as prime minister, was never interviewed successfully on serious political issues. She was unable or unwilling to give short answers and hardly ever addressed a question directly. In some ways, she was protecting herself. When she was appointed Conservative party leader, Mrs Thatcher was poor at interviews. She was inexperienced. Early in her leadership before she came to power in 1979, when the news media were eager to explore the range of her views, an extended interview being recorded for radio down a line to London from a studio in another part of the country was abandoned. She could not put her argument coherently. She stumbled, hesitated and dried up in spite of repeated re-takes. The case illustrates what is liable to be overlooked: that being interviewed at length on complex issues with millions of supporters and opponents intent on every word is an ordeal. It is not easy. Being interviewed is as difficult as interviewing. The job of the interviewee is as hard as the job of the interviewer. It is made more difficult when the questioner is a disembodied voice through a pair of headphones. Politicians are expected to undergo the ordeal many times. They have to learn how to cope. Instead of learning how to satisfy the purpose of the interview, which is to provide the people they serve with information and reasons for policies, they learn how to survive the interview. The more probing the interviewers become and the better equipped they are with good questions backed by good research, the more public figures become skilled at hiding what they do not wish to disclose and careful to deposit only those tit-bits they regard as safe.

There are a few exceptions. Douglas Hurd, as foreign secretary, confident elder statesman, answered questions straightforwardly. He addressed the issue as put to him, not another, though he would at times go on to point out that the real issue, as he saw it, was different. He dealt informatively, as well as equably, with interviews even when they were gauche.

News programmes on radio and television are likely to continue to favour the quick interview of anything between two and six minutes rather than extended interviews that evolve slowly over a longer spell, and it is easy to underestimate the contribution of the shorter dash. They add spirit, especially when live, and they often contain a nugget, an important insight, which is later quoted in other programmes and in the papers. As individual interviews, they are frequently unsuccessful as a way of exploring complex issues. The more such interviews in a programme, the greater the demands on the presenter-interviewers and the less likely they are to be well briefed. However hard they try, the politicians are better briefed and, usually, more nimble. None the less, an accumulation of relatively short interviews in a programme or collection of programmes and perhaps over a number of days often succeeds in excavating what really matters. Like digging for gold, finding one or two nuggets creates great piles of rubbish.

Extended interviews of the kind Brian Walden conducted on *Weekend World* on ITV on a Sunday or those on *On The Record* on BBC Television also on a Sunday worked hard to come closer to the heart of issues. Given the programme time and research time devoted to them, they did not, however, produce many truly candid responses. Had they done so, they would have made news more often, as *Breakfast with Frost* on BBC Television, another Sunday programme, usually does and as Jimmy Young has done for years during the week on Radio 2 with a relaxed style of interview unfairly mocked by brash current affairs journalists. For all the successes of Young and Frost, extended interviews at a considered pace would never appeal to enough people to equal the accumulated contribution to public debate made by 'shorter dash' interviews on the daily news programmes.

Newspaper and magazine interviews are rarely an issue. Much more news copy is provided by broadcast interviews than by interviews for print. Occasionally, a print interview provides startling copy, as when one of Mrs Thatcher's cabinet stalwarts, Nicholas Ridley, made incautious remarks about Germans in an interview with Dominic Lawson of the *Spectator.* The indiscretion had a typical aftermath, not so much in Nicholas Ridley's resignation, but in a dispute between interviewer and interviewee as to whether the xenophobic remarks had been on the record or not.

government bias

As a general rule, inevitably though not invariably, governments get more coverage than opposition parties and other expressions of opposition. This applies in free societies, as in countries where newspapers and broadcasting are politically controlled. Although in controlled countries it occurs to a much greater degree than in free countries, in neither does it stop governments complaining about media bias against them.

A bias in amount of editorial attention is fitting because governments affect the lives of people to an extent that oppositions cannot. They take money from people; they improve their standard of living by good economic management; they lose them their jobs by mismanagement of the economy; they bring in laws that help and hinder people; and in many other ways they are a burden and a blessing. Notions of balance and impartiality cannot override the reality, though they should qualify the bias in amount to prevent it becoming or to reduce its capacity to become a bias of presentation. The distinction is not always appreciated, the objective not always achieved.

In the British system which imposes a duty of impartiality on broadcasters, opposition parties often complain about the amount of coverage given to government. They seem indifferent to any difference between amount and presentation. They argue for equality. Radio and television go some way to meet this to the extent that broadcast news often contains insubstantial, ritualistic reactions from the official opposition and from the Liberal Democrats that contribute little to their standing and hardly anything to audience understanding. Longer news programmes like the early evening *Channel 4 News* and *Newsnight* on BBC2 do better because they have longer interviews, discussions and features, demoting the soundbite. Oppositions that feel neglected do not regard this as adequate

174

compensation because *Channel 4 News* and *Newsnight* have much smaller audiences than the news programmes on ITV and BBC1. There is not much to be done about it. Quotas to counter the effects of normal news judgements damage news programmes and their reputation without benefiting the political parties, the political system or the public.

dealing with government

Not only does government get the lion's share of attention, it profits from armies of advisers, civil servants with detailed expert knowledge as well as press officers who devise ways of making weak cases sound strong. The government machine is massive. By comparison, opposition backup is rickety. Its research is never of the quality of government's.

The Thatcher governments of the 1980s exploited these advantages to an extent never seen before in British politics – and strengthened them ruthlessly. Departmental press offices became aggressive engines of partial publicity. Some civil servants in the information ranks abandoned the stance of disinterested adviser to become political advocates. They pressed the government case with passion. Public money was used in favour of political causes. The government's hold on official information, which allows no right of access to anyone else, was an added advantage for ministers who were often able to proclaim best knowledge based on their Whitehall briefing papers. The selective use of statistical figures became another weapon. Few inquisitors, on television, on radio, for a newspaper – or in parliament – had the ready knowledge to challenge the stream of pointedly placed assertions by government ministers of the kind that said business investment in Britain was increasing at a greater rate than in any country of the European Union, or that Britain had created more new jobs, or that hospital waiting lists for serious operations had been reduced by a significant percentage.

During radio phone-ins and sometimes for other radio appearances, government ministers had advisers alongside to help them with facts and figures and arguments. When an issue being journalistically investigated was very adverse for government, a carefully prepared statement rather than an interview would be offered, bad enough for a newspaper but worse for a programme of 'talking heads' wanting voiced answers to criticisms direct from a minister.

Newspapers and programmes have many examples of the rigmarole they can be involved in when challenging government on complicated and contentious issues. While any organisation can cloud issues, few can match the ability of the government machine to obfuscate. Frequently, little can be done in the short term to overcome it. The best that topical, news-related programmes and features are able to do is to expose evasion. In the longer term, persistent digging has some success. Too often the digging produces a relic of a dead story.

ministers

The media put enormous pressure on the government machine and its principal minders, government ministers. Democratic accountability in countries like Britain and America, with aggressive newspapers and advanced broadcasting systems, now works more through the media than through parliament. The importance of the media channel of accountability is reflected in the time and effort devoted to it, in the considerable armies of press officers in government departments and in the trouble taken to help ministers perform well. Experienced ministers become very skilful, so much so that their skill has outstripped the skill of journalists to question them effectively. In one-to-one interviews in programmes, it is unusual for government spokespeople to come off second best. When they are exposed, it is more by their own glibness than by effective questioning. They mostly survive challenging interviews respectably. When they face assemblies of reporters and correspondents at news conferences, they are rarely in real difficulties. They are exceptionally well briefed on the subject and extremely well coached on how to conduct themselves.

They and their advisers work hard to achieve the ascendancy, so effectively that, as a perverse consequence, the public interest is ill served. Skill in dealing with journalistic enquiry is not the same as honesty of explanation. Facts are selectively presented in interviews and judgements angled to suit the moment. Even the best informed journalists cannot be expected to have enough detailed information at their fingertips to challenge well there and then. There is no instant or fully successful counter. The best available is good reporting that digs into difficult facts for as long as it takes and which questions suspect gloss. Newspapers are generally better at it than broadcasting because they are bolder, not inhibited by regulators' niceties such as impartiality, and are better vehicles for it because the complicated expositions of investigative journalism are best absorbed when studied in print than when fleetingly received in a broadcast. In radio and television, longer, well researched programmes are better at the task than the short leash daily news programmes which have much bigger audiences.

elections

General elections in Britain demonstrate and, to a degree, exaggerate the differences of approach between newspapers and broadcasting. The partiality of British newspapers is boasted and the impartiality of British broadcasting is stretched beyond sense.

Newspapers are under no enforceable editorial obligations of objectivity or fairness. Any they impose on themselves, unilaterally or through the Press Complaints Commission, are lightly interpreted. They are free to take sides and virtually all do so, and are free to select news to suit their politics as most do. Their political characteristics are widely accepted as part of a vigorously free press. Though the news copy and the comment columns usually press overwhelmingly in favour of the right, it is not an issue that disturbs the public anything like as much as it disturbs the disadvantaged political parties. Public indifference stems partly from the well recognised preference of many

177

people to buy the newspaper which expresses their beliefs and prejudices and which, in turn, means that nearly all of those whose vote is influenced by what they read in their newspaper are simply being nudged in the direction they want to go. If the effect of the strong pro-Conservative bias had been more than marginal, Britain would never have had a Labour government.

Television and radio are subjected to close election scrutiny. It includes internal monitoring and much self-examination. It includes minute assessments by the political parties. The newspapers, ever watchful, are ready to intervene loudly, part of their service to Conservatism. The public make many phone calls and write many letters, very few of them favourable, and they come from all political directions. Programmes dealing with the election are required by laws, codes, guidelines, self-imposed ordinances and publicly expressed pressure to adopt whatever contortions it takes not to favour any candidate or any party, nor to work against anyone, not even the 'loonies'. In the weeks a general election is known to be imminent and in the few weeks of the campaign proper, programme makers and broadcasting executives spend huge amounts of time applying the templates of fairness.

Whatever criticisms are made of a system that includes unconfined newspapers and confined broadcasting, the mix of partiality and impartiality is beneficial. One seems to encourage the other. As an effect or as a coincidence, British voters have a bigger kaleidoscope of election coverage than people in most countries. British broadcasting is less governed by the election soundbite than are American radio and television with the result that arguments get better airings. British coverage is more vigorous than in more regulated systems. Driven by political commitment, British newspapers express the passions of an election campaign more vividly than broadcasting does. The political fervour of the national newspapers exposes disagreements more sharply than do the choreographed exchanges of the politicians. There is no reason to believe the public would be better informed or better apprised of the issues if the politicians had more control of the campaign, if the newspapers were less partial and if broadcasting was less constrained by rules.

Election programmes on British radio and

television are still growing up. They were non-existent or very inadequate until the 1950s. They advanced during the 1960s and greatly during the 1970s. They developed more strongly during the 1980s in spite of recurrent rows, though in the run-up to the 1992 election, the unnecessary postponement by the BBC of the programme on the economy by its economics editor, Peter Jay, was a set-back rooted in earlier rows. In the late 1990s and beyond, broadcasters are set to continue the developments started thirty years earlier, largely a process of realising that the limitations on programme makers, including the Representation of the People Act (RPA), are by no means as inhibiting as they were earlier thought to be. Politicians may also begin to realise that the RPA is not as strong a weapon in their hands as some of them believe it to be.

The biggest problem for programmes is how to satisfy impartiality. The political parties tend to see it in terms of an allocation of air-time. Since the days of the alliance of the Social Democrats and the Liberals in the early 1980s, the parties have failed to agree on the details of a three-way allocation in the one area where they are allowed to make a decision on election air-time, namely the allocation of party election broadcasts (pebs). The decision in this regard used to be made by the committee on party political broadcasts. It is a committee of the parties which acted on recommendations from the main broadcasting organisations, that is, the BBC and the regulators of independent television and radio. The committee decided what should be the ratio of party election broadcasts. These broadcasts, made by the parties, usually five to ten minutes long on television and five on radio, are the campaign version of the party political broadcasts (ppbs) that appear at non-election times. A ratio has to be decided for each general election.

Before the rise of the alliance parties, the ratio used to be five:five:three – five broadcasts on national television and five on national radio for the Conservative party, five also for the Labour party with three for the 'no-hope of power' Liberal party. Special arrangements for pebs were and are made for the SNP in Scotland, for Plaid Cymru in Wales, and even more special arrangements, a substitute for pebs, for the parties in Northern Ireland. Also, any other party that fights more than fifty seats in the election qualifies for one television broadcast and one on radio. Under that rule, the National Front had broadcasts in 1983 and the Green party subsequently.

Agreement on the ratio failed after the rise of the alliance of the SDP and Liberals. They wanted equality, a ratio of five:five:five. Labour and Conservatives disagreed. The committee reached no decision for any of the three general elections of 1983, 1987 and 1992. So, the broadcasting organisations applied what they had recommended. In 1983 it was five:five: four, in 1987, five:five:five, reverting in 1992 to five:five:four.

These are modest arrangements by comparison with decisions in the former communist-run countries of eastern Europe which are emerging into democracy. The broadcasting organisations are not allowed to decide election matters for themselves and are frequently denied any influence. Constitutional rules and electoral commissions decide what spaces the political parties will be given, usually generous to the parties and punishing for viewers and listeners. In the first general election in Czechoslovakia after the 'velvet revolution' and before the split of Slovakia from the Czech Republic, the allocation of television time to the parties was so onerous that for a month two hours a day, from 5 o'clock in the late afternoon to 7 o'clock in the early evening, were given over to party election broadcasts. Here and in some other newly democratic countries, all parties were treated equally, no-hopers being allocated as much time as major contenders. The allocation in former Czechoslovakia included one party election broadcast of half-an-hour for each party. Naked self-service by the parties prevails. In Bulgaria, for the election towards the end of 1994, time was allocated only to parties in three coalitions in parliament – and apart from brief news reports, public radio and television were not allowed to cover the election. Journalists from newspapers were to provide the journalistic input for the allocated discussion programmes. Professional broadcasters were forbidden, the reason given that in the tensions of an election campaign their impartiality might be impugned!

In spite of the modest nature of the arrangements in Britain, the major parties have an inordinate influence on who gets what in broadcasting. For years, the BBC, and ITV to a lesser extent, used the ratio of party election broadcasts as a guide for election programmes. If the ratio of allocated time was five:five:four, then amounts of time given to appearances by each party in news and current affairs programmes was, more or less, of that order. It was never a strict rule but it had a significant influence. Live or recorded extracts of speeches, interviews, walkabouts, news conferences, contributions to discussions, insubstantial photo-calls and other actual bits of electioneering were noted. Any candidate or spokesperson seen or heard was counted, though mentions by a reporter or correspondent were not. It had to be a contribution in voice or vision by the people and parties in the election. If a party fell below the ratio or raced ahead, an editor had something to be concerned about – but not if there were good reasons for the discrepancy. Labour party disagreements over Europe imbalanced the quotas in one of the general elections in 1974 (a year when there were two general elections), and when in 1987 Labour refused to put up a spokesperson for a discussion in the Radio 4 breakfast news and current affairs programme, *Today*, on defence – another abidingly divisive issue for the party – there was no question of compensating it to keep the coverage nearer to the ratio.

Editors tend to regard any ratio for programmes as an editorial strait-jacket. The feeling found expression in the 1992 election campaign when Independent Television News (ITN) said it was determined to make its decisions on the basis of news values and the BBC stressed that the ratio was only a guide. The connection between programmes and the peb ratio will, almost certainly, grow weaker though the broadcasters will continue virtuously to proclaim their belief in balance. They know they could face increasingly bitter squabbles over coverage if they try to get rid of the strait-jacket altogether. It is more than likely that editorial decisions during elections while driven by news value will disarmingly manage to stay close to a notional ratio.

There are good defences against outraged political parties when editorial decisions are made honestly. In impartiality, balance and the general concept of fairness, as also in the Representation of the People Act, there is nothing to stop radio and television providing sharper, more incisive assessments of issues, policies and personalities. The packaging damaged the content when election campaign programmes were ever so carefully balanced and timed and otherwise measured for impartiality. An excessive concern for measurable balance encouraged too much reliance on the interview at a time when experienced public figures were so skilled that even the best interviewers made no dent. Programme use of news conferences, walkabouts, photo-calls and other forms of controlled politicking were the easy, balanceable options. Television graphics, the product of magical technology, at first provided new glosses and little substance.

For a long time, the sharpest broadcasting challenges to the politicians at election time came from ordinary voters during phone-ins and studio confrontations. Mrs Thatcher was given the most difficult time she ever had in front of the camera when she fell victim in a BBC Television *Nationwide* studio in the early 1980s to a Mrs Gould. She disconcerted the prime minister in a well-informed and persistent challenge over the sinking of the Argentine ship the *Belgrano* during the Falklands War. On local radio, independent as well as BBC, and on regional television, there were many unsung successes by voters who deflated politicians. The BBC's *Election Call*, a national phone-in which started on radio and was later extended to a simultaneous broadcast on television, was a star in the 1970s and through the 1980s because of its callers from around the country. Each weekday during the campaign, in a carefully worked out schedule of balanced party appearances, prominent politicians submitted themselves for almost an hour to calls from the public. Some of the callers seriously discomforted the politicians because they were more difficult to deal with than professional interviewers. This was partly because a caller with a passion about a single subject might know more on that one issue than the politician, and partly because politicians, ever ready to rough up a difficult professional interviewer, do not normally like to be seen and heard giving a member of the public a hard time. A tendency in the programme during the 1992 election campaign for the presenter to interrogate on behalf of callers at times let the politicians off the hook.

The way radio and television have felt

obliged to behave and the way newspapers freely choose to behave, backed by the first-past-the-post electoral system, favour the big political parties at election time, as at other times. Political forces, like the Greens, and revived forces, like the Scottish nationalists, have a difficult time being heard. The Scottish National party, though well heard in Scotland as one of four equals, is always in danger of qualifying for only marginal appearances in programmes to all of the UK unless the broadcasters go out of their way to make special features about the electoral battle-ground in Scotland – and even then, in programmes and in newspapers, these specials cannot sensibly be given the prominence accorded to the front page battles of the traditional giants. This is of particular importance in broadcasting because about 70 per cent of the election coverage available to voters in Scotland is in programmes for all of the UK. As a result, in spite of its main party status in Scotland, the SNP is demoted well below the other three in nearly three-quarters of broadcast coverage seen and heard in Scotland. The problem is not so serious in newspapers. Scottish editions compensate and newspaper readers can easily buy a Scottish newspaper to counter the imbalance in the London-based papers.

It is impossibly hard to draw a line between unfair discrimination against regional political parties or small national movements and proper recognition of political realities. How to be fair to the SNP says little, for instance, about how to be fair to the Welsh nationalists so long as Plaid Cymru is less significant in Wales than the SNP in Scotland. And whatever weight the Scot Nats could conceivably have in balance-of-power circumstances in the Westminster parliament, they are, in these UK-wide terms, less weighty than the Liberal Democrats so long as they trail markedly in seats won. In turn, the Lib Dem argument for equality with Conservative and Labour, which rises loudly in the run-up to elections, is unconvincing until a political sea-change washes away what everyone knows: that Conservative and Labour are much more likely to form or to lead government.

Representation of The People Act

One of the differences in the regimes for newspapers and for broadcasting is that the Representation of the People Act (RPA) applies significantly to programmes, barely to newspapers. It limits programmes while having hardly any editorial impact on newspapers. Its influence on programmes is a side effect, during political elections, of an intention to limit the ability of candidates to gain unfair advantage. Significant as the effect is on some kinds of programmes, it is nothing like as forbidding as some programme makers say it is. Nor is it as important as some politicians believe it to be when they say it helps them control the agenda of elections. It can however be used by politicians as a veto.

The Act affects programmes only during election campaigns. Its terms apply to elections for parliament at Westminster, for British seats in the European parliament and for local authority councils. It prevents certain kinds of programme appearances by candidates. It has more effect on local and regional programmes than on national programmes. The restriction can be stated in this way: when an election is pending (a stated number of weeks before polling day) no candidate can take part (the term 'taking part' provides a loophole) in a broadcast about an electoral area (the constituency or ward) before nomination day (the day papers have to be deposited by all candidates) and, after nomination day, a candidate can only take part (the loophole again) in a broadcast about an electoral area (another loophole) if all other candidates also take part or if those who do not take part agree to it going ahead without them.

The legalistic rigmarole sounds worse than it really is. But it does stop some kinds of programmes. If a local radio station wants to broadcast a discussion in a studio with all the candidates from a constituency talking about their campaign, it cannot do so before nomination day and then, after nomination day, if one candidate refuses and will not agree to the programme going ahead with the others, the programme cannot be broadcast. In effect, the refusing candidate vetoes the discussion. It does not matter in law whether the refusing candidate is from a major party certain to receive thousands of votes, from the serious fringe with hope of a few hundred votes or a 'loony' who will get only a handful. The same effective veto applies if after nomination day a station wishes to carry separate interviews with all the candidates in a constituency.

The veto is used in a calculated way from time to time by candidates from the major parties. Conservatives in very safe, usually rural area seats have in the past refused to take part in round table broadcast discussions on the grounds that they do not need the publicity and, speaking softly to themselves, why should they co-operate with a programme that would give publicity to opponents who badly need it. Labour candidates have used the veto in constituencies with a candidate from the extreme right-wing National Front. As a professed and probably genuine conscientious objection, Labour would not appear on any platform with an NF candidate. The law was not intended to accord such powers but, as often, well-intended legal restriction has uncalculated effects in the hands of inventive manipulators.

The Representation of the People Act adds greatly to the stresses of broadcasting during election times. All programmes have to make sure they do not fall foul of it knowingly or inadvertently. Many things are possible in spite of it but many broadcasters do not understand it and think it stops more than it really does. Local political party offices are also liable to refer to it threateningly, especially when they believe their party is being treated unfairly, which usually means they are slipping in the opinion polls. They seem to believe the RPA has something to do with impartiality which it has not. Awkward candidates exploit the RPA to their advantage. In the 1992 general election campaign, a Labour candidate in the English Midlands refused all co-operation with a local BBC station while giving interviews to national programmes, so avoiding any broadcast confrontation with opposing candidates in the constituency. Another Labour candidate, in the North-East of England, also refused interviews in an evident attempt to determine how the campaign would be covered.

For all these problems, the onerous potential

of the Act is reduced because many kinds of appearances in programmes are not legally held to be 'taking part'. A candidate making a speech in a meeting hall which is broadcast live or recorded is not regarded as 'taking part' in the programme because the speech, though intended for publicity, is an event separate from the programme and would have occurred without the broadcast. Pictures and sound of a candidate canvassing in a street and used in a programme are not regarded as 'taking part' because they too have a separate existence. Live or recorded extracts from a news conference also escape the prohibition. In difficulty, a reporter needing an extract from a candidate for a feature may snatch a few words on the street corner and escape the clutches of the RPA so long as the extract used is not like an interview. The leeways in interpretation allow candidates to appear before nomination day when 'taking part' is forbidden, and after nomination day programmes can let serious candidates be seen and heard without having to give time to the 'no-hopers'. In any case, it is always possible to turn to someone else to speak for the candidate and the party. A party agent or the consitutency chairwoman speaking on behalf of the candidate is not in any way restricted by the RPA.

Because the law applies only to 'taking part' in a broadcast about 'an electoral area', the big-name politicians who are also candidates freely appear in programmes speaking on behalf of their party rather than speaking as candidates, especially as they have a national role. Politicians, big names or little known, standing in the election can appear in *This Week* on ITV or on *Panorama* on the BBC so long as they do not talk about their candidacy or about their electoral area, to explain party policy on any topic when the same politician is prevented from appearing in a constituency based programme because it is before nomination day or because not all the other candidates are in the programme. The front bench politicians who speak at the national news conferences held every day of the campaign escape the RPA on three grounds: they are not appearing as candidates but as spokespeople; they are not legally 'taking part in a broadcast' because the news conference has an independent existence from the programmes in which extracts are used; and the broadcast is not about the electoral area in which they are standing. They escape the RPA while benefiting, usually, from the personal publicity.

Local stations find other arrangements helpful. The panel of candidates at a meeting in a school hall organised by an outside body, perhaps by the school itself, may not be complete – the mad fringe is often missing and no veto is possible – but the meeting can be broadcast because it is independent of the programme. Those taking part in the meeting are not taking part in a broadcast though they do talk about the constituency. They take part in a meeting that happens to be broadcast. The same arrangement by the radio station in a studio is forbidden.

The RPA consumes great amounts of programme makers' time and energy which do not contribute in any recognisable way to the good the public derives from programmes and which producers would rather devote to policy issues in the election. It would, more aptly, be known as the Representation of the Politicians Act.

parliament

The British parliament is one of the most conservative of institutions. Centuries ago, reporters had to fight for the right to report its deliberations. For years, like an exclusive club that disliked the electoral rabble knowing too much, it resisted the idea of broadcasting its proceedings. The ordinary business of parliament was not heard on radio and television until 1975 when a month-long experiment took the unique noise of the Commons into people's homes. It was almost three years before the success of the experiment led to the permanent sound broadcasting, and then more than another thirteen, October 1991, before televising the Commons was an accepted arrangement. The House of Lords had been more accommodating, the cameras admitted there some years earlier, partly in the hope of their lordships that it would increase the amount of attention the wisdom of their debates received – which, after an initial flush, it did not.

A few members of parliament are still opposed to the cameras and the microphones, and, to an extent, their fears have been confirmed. Most notably, since being broadcast from 1978, Prime Minister's Questions on Tuesdays and Thursdays have become a noisy sham. The behaviour of MPs has changed to a degree because they are being watched and heard. But the undesirable tendencies of the Commons – cheap party point-scoring, disruptive interruptions, the braying of disapproval, the thin attendance most of the time and occasional displays of yobbish disorder – have all been evident in spells for a very long time, for much longer than the presence of the instruments of broadcasting. As with so many of the criticisms of the effects of television, the remedy is in the hands of those whose behaviour has changed: behave better.

Light rules govern the broadcasting of parliament. The programme makers are not allowed to do just as they wish. The camera is not allowed to roam. Shots are restricted to the person speaking and long views of the chamber generally. Reaction shots, to show how a member receives a point, are allowed only insofar as they can be shown in general views. When the Speaker intervenes that is where the camera must point. The public gallery is not shown, this to deter publicity seekers, and should there be any 'noises off', say from demonstrators, these may be heard only as background to the proper business of the House. Extracts from parliament in sound or vision cannot be used in comedy programmes, in fiction or drama, satirical programmes, nor even in party political broadcasts. They can be used only in news and other factual programmes and for educational purposes. The restrictions are not as severe as those in a number of countries. Some forbid any television shot other than head and shoulders of the person speaking. None the less, any restriction is undesirable for free journalism. There is not much doubt, though, that British viewers and listeners would still be waiting to see and hear their parliament if the broadcasters had refused any rules.

As often with unregulated and relatively unfettered newspapers, there is no special relationship between them and parliament in Britain. To a great extent they are mutually antagonistic and mutually dependent. Broadcasting is, typically, different. The politically appointed authorities – the ITC, the Radio Authority, the Welsh Authority, the BBC governors and the watchdogs, the BSC and the BCC – all report to parliament. Like the rules governing the broadcasting of parliament, the connections are light and relatively free from party political pressure. But they are a connection: broadcasting in Britain, all of it having public service pretensions, answers to parliament and parliament, directed largely by government, decides how it shall be structured. As a final witness to the parliamentary influence, the BBC is required by its Licence and Agreement to broadcast 'an impartial account day by day prepared by professional reporters of the proceedings in both Houses of the United Kingdom Parliament'. In other words, the BBC must broadcast *Today in Parliament*.

The parliamentary connection with public service broadcasting is widely copied in other countries and is being reproduced in the emerging democracies of eastern, central and southern Europe. In some cases the connection is punishing. A number of directors general, appointed by parliaments, are held on short leashes and too many politicians imagine they have arbitrary powers over programmes. Where arrangements are well considered and not driven by party political needs, they work well, a natural route of accountability for broadcasting organisations that have no shareholders and no owners and which owe their responsibilities to the general public.

politicians

Politicians – like 'the press' – suffer from being lumped together as though they had outstanding common characteristics that deservedly cause them to be treated with the disdain that greets an undesirable necessity. In surveys of public opinion, politicians and journalists are near the bottom in the approval ratings. Neither group is trusted.

The reputations of both are crude generalities. True, some politicians are rude, pompous, arrogant or otherwise not likeable. Producers of current affairs programmes trying to agree an interview know that a few politicians are impossibly difficult, always trying to lay down special conditions, often disagreeably. It is not the norm. Bearing in mind the pressure many politicians are under, they are generally co-operative and agreeable. Self-interest is a strong motivating factor but a sense of public duty impels them also. They trust journalists who are trustworthy. Treated fairly, they generally accept the disadvantages of exposure and criticism. They respond best when confronted squarely by the journalists who depend on them as surely as they depend on the journalists.

political parties

The word 'assiduous' is too mild to describe the zeal with which political parties pursue their interests in the media. They are fanatically concerned about a fair show in programmes and in the papers. They are hardly ever satisfied. Between rare and short-lived honeymoons, Labour despairs of the predominantly right-leaning newspapers and all parties badger programme makers for more appearances or for more prominent appearances or for coverage more directed to the way the party sees its own policies.

The parties depend too much on the media for relaxed relationships. Exposure by traditional means – the handshake, the doorstepping, the chats with shoppers, the speeches in village halls and other assembly rooms – still matters but it comes a long way behind exposure on the media, and the continuing value of so many of the traditional activities depends heavily on their being featured in print and in broadcasts. The unphotographed handshake does a little good; the display of bonhomie shown in the television news is highly prized.

It is in any case a two-way process. The media's dependence on the political parties is just as great. The parties make news, in discussions and interviews their stars perform much better than most other individuals, they excite ready passions in audiences and readers. Antagonisms in the relationship between political parties and the media testify to their mutual dependence. They rub along warily and at times badly because they need each other so much. Neither side can comfortably take it or leave it.

In many ways, the British media have a very easy time because the political scene is stable and predictable. A handful of parties in historic positions and little prospect of other than dire-emergency coalitions are much easier to reflect than the murky deals of, say, Italian politics. The media in the emerging democracies of eastern and central Europe have, by comparison with Britain, an impossible job, contending as they do with ten or fifteen, maybe twenty or fifty political groups, all vying for attention, most shifting ground for political advantage, many of them not at all sure what they really stand for, and some small enough to fit on a sofa, as the Russians say.

Conservative party

The relationship between newspapers and the political parties is very different from the relationship the broadcasters have with the parties. Newspapers, entitled to take political stands, almost invariably do so. Broadcasters, not allowed to, are often accused of it.

National newspapers in Britain seem intent on increasing their intervention in politics. Always close to centres of political power, they are active players, not content only to comment, eager more and more to influence policies and, where they can, to determine who is in government. They work through their alliance with the Conservative party, an argumentative alliance that breaks out into the most bitter disputes. They quarrel like inseparable friends who have grown disillusioned, as in the dispute in 1993–4 that debilitated John Major's government over 'Back to Basics', over the dubious personal morality of some of his government and some of his backbenchers, and over the government's sense of direction. These political disputes are usually initiated by the papers, not by the party and they frequently have an air of journalistic guilt in them, as though the papers were ashamed of the support they had given the Conservatives in the previous general election. The passions aroused when the friends fall out are much worse than when the party has a row with the broadcasters, however bad they seem at the time. In the longer term, newspaper relations with the Tories have always been repaired, often in time for a general election.

Broadcasters are not allowed to be like that. Their legally stated commitment to impartiality rules it out. Political neutrality is regarded as the single most obvious attribute of impartiality, so they must not take sides, on any issue or generally. Disputes between broadcasters and political parties usually centre on whether coverage has been up to public service, detached standard. In the nature of it, the dispute is initiated by the political party, which may be the party in the guise of government. Notorious examples include the disputes between the BBC and the Conservatives over coverage of the bombing of Libya by American aircraft with British connivance in 1986, and later, over coverage of government plans for the National Health Service. Thames Television, later ousted from its franchise under the government's policy of highest bidder auction, was also lashed by the Conservative government in 1988 over *Death On The Rock*, an investigation of the killing of suspected IRA terrorists in Gibraltar by British security forces.

In spite of these examples, broadcasters have much the same relationship with the Conservative party as they have with other main parties. Unless the long years of Conservative rule through the 1980s and into the mid-1990s prove to have wrought fundamental change, which is unlikely, there are no abiding differences of great significance. They need each other and they rub along as best they can.

Until the 1980s, radio and television, BBC stations in particular, tended to have rather more trouble with the Labour party, especially when it was in power, than with the Conservative party. This changed during the Thatcher years when government hostility to programmes it did not like reached a pitch never sustained before. It reflected the spirit of those times, indicating Thatcherite impatience, not deep Conservative party conviction. The two were not the same in this or any other matter. It was an example of radical government expressing its frustration and anger at centres of power and influence it believed were given over to the old ways. The broadcasters, however fair they tried to be, were not regarded as 'one of us'. They allowed revanchist voices to be heard as, in the interests of balance, they were bound to do. But, worse, editorial assumptions made, especially in questions in interviews in popular news programmes, were condemned by Thatcherite forces as favouring the previous corporatist orthodoxy. There was justice in the charge. Popular, topical programmes were slow to recognise the meaning and the significance of Thatcherism, and correspondingly slow to adapt. They were not expected to adopt the cause, as that would have been partial, but Thatcherism was almost dead by the time they learned to reflect it to a fair extent in their editorial approach.

Programme makers were not entirely to blame for the failure. A number of prominent figures in the early Thatcher governments, traditionalist patricians from the shires so disliked by their leader, did not themselves recognise what was going on, or when they did recognise it, did not care to give it their help. As a result, they failed to imbue their appearances in programmes with radical enthusiasm. Sympathetic Thatcherites too failed to exploit opportunities to evangelise, partly because the 'movement' did not know clearly where it was headed.

Besides editorial antipathy, those years saw also the start of the destabilisation, leading to shake-up, of the BBC and of drastic changes to the ITV system. It was, then, no surprise when John Major succeeded Margaret Thatcher that a great sigh of relief could be heard through the corridors of broadcasting. Programmes were able, once again, to concentrate on their traditional relationship with the party in power – uneasy exercise of mutual benefit with occasional dog fights. An outbreak of hostilities against the BBC was declared by the chief secretary to the Treasury, Jonathan Aitken, in 1995 when he complained about biased interviewers and dubbed the country's main broadcaster the 'Blair Broadcasting Corporation' for favouring, so he said, the Labour party leader, Tony Blair. At the time, Aitken was himself the target of media allegations about his business connections and his attack lacked the venom of earlier years though it was picked up by a few other members of the government. Commentators expected it to continue intermittently in the long run up to the general election which had to be held by the summer of 1997, but even right-wing newspapers who had supported earlier Thatcherite attacks on the BBC savaged the government for 'whingeing'.

An illuminating spat between Conservatives and the broadcasters arose out of the collapse of Soviet Communism. When Mikhail Gorbachev and later Boris Yeltsin had trouble with people who continued to favour old ways of state control, programmes sometimes referred to these hard-liners as 'conservatives'. In the context of Soviet and Russian politics, it was reasonable: the hard-liners conservatively favoured the way things had been done for decades. But it narked enthusiastic, free-market Conservative party supporters in Britain to be labelled the same as detested and failed economic planners of the communist left. Understandable as this was, they had to put up with it because even a repeatedly re-elected Conservative party could not hijack sensible meaning by controlling usage of a word in its name.

Labour party

The Labour party in Britain gets a much better deal from broadcasting than it does from the newspapers. The reason is that under public service precepts programmes do not take sides on political issues. At the same time, those precepts, notably impartiality and balance, leave much room for judgement and in the early to late 1980s the Labour party probably received a better deal from radio and television, compared to the alliance parties, that is, the Social Democrats and the Liberals, than it should have done. By virtue of the number of seats it held, Labour was unquestionably the main party of opposition in the House of Commons, officially Her Majesty's Opposition, but because of the bias of the first-past-the-post electoral system, its support in the country was, for some years, proportionately much less than the difference in seats. Labour's presence in programmes as the voice of opposition suffered, as it should have, *vis-à-vis* the alliance, after the 1983 election in which

194

there was a difference of only 2 per cent in their share of the vote. Although the vote gap widened in favour of Labour in the 1987 election, the case for a continued programme demotion of the party might have been irresistible had not the alliance parties gravely weakened themselves by the protracted campaign, started almost immediately the 1987 result became known, to create one party which eventually became the Liberal Democrats. In terms of publicity in programmes, which politicians value so highly, the debilitating dispute between the allies of the centre, a distraction from the substance of politics, provided space for Labour to pose convincingly as a united opposition and to regain its reputation as the electable alternative to the Conservatives. While the centre parties scrapped with each other, the new centre left began to emerge, an important part of this emergence being the daily appearance of Labour spokespeople in news and current affairs programmes, inveighing against government policies.

In separate, unconnected developments, Labour condemned government upheavals to ITV and warmed towards the BBC. Before this period, Labour in government struck a typically hostile attitude towards broadcasting, especially towards the BBC, hostile because, it said, policies were misrepresented and successes under-represented, splits exaggerated and the news misleadingly dominated by bad news, especially reports of industrial strife. During Labour's period of power from 1964 to 1970, Harold Wilson's government fretted for a long time over the future of the BBC before confirming the licence fee. The Wilson cabinet contained a significant group who argued for a modicum of advertising on the BBC to ease what they regarded as the unpopularity of licence fee rises. Years later in the late 1970s, the government of James Callaghan was so concerned about the licence fee it awarded the BBC a derisory increase of £1 to last a year, a way of putting off a proper decision.

In opposition before the 1980s, Labour was often aggrieved by what it saw as bias against the left, a grievance reflected in and, to some extent, fed by the work of the Glasgow Media Group which produced influential analyses highly critical of broadcast news and its claims to impartiality.

195

Important Labour voices spoke against the BBC, believing it to be arrogant, biased and too big. They talked about splitting BBC Radio from BBC Television and about other ways of reducing the corporation to size. They sometimes made unflattering comparisons with ITV. They said dealing with ITN was much more straightforward than dealing with BBC programmes. Richard Crossman, one of Labour's best brains, commented that ITN allowed you to say what you had to say, asked a few sensible questions, gave you a drink and let you go home. But at the BBC, before you knew what was happening, you were in the middle of a terrible row.

The Crossman attitude lived on after he died and the Labour party concentrated on broadcasting rather than newspapers because that was where it should expect to be treated fairly. The party had to put up with hostile newspapers, grossly inclined as they were to the right, but it believed it deserved much better from broadcasting, especially the BBC, which was, as it still is, the purveyor of most of the news and topical programmes. The criticisms were perverse. By any objective standard, balance-driven programmes allowed Labour many more opportunities to project itself effectively than most newspapers ever did.

Labour and the free-to-say-as-they-please newspapers have a combative relationship of a different kind. Labour gets some support from local and regional papers though nearly all are Conservative. The national daily papers produced in London traditionally have a heavy bias to the Conservatives, a bias that peaked during the Thatcher years and which declined in the Major years. The *Daily Mirror*, as an exception, gave Labour strong support over many years, the only national daily paper to do so after the steadfast *Daily Herald* transmogrified into the hostile *Sun*. The *Guardian* provided half a cheer much of the time. *Today*, a struggling Murdoch acquisition, developed a politically pink tinge before it closed.

Labour party leaders were alarmed at the prospect of the loss of support from the *Mirror* as a result of the changes brought about by the death of its owner, Robert Maxwell. But the Maxwell connection had a downside for Labour because of his disreputable dealings, and by that time the *Mirror* was not the dominant tabloid it used to be.

Labour and the Tory papers have a honeymoon now and again. None lasts. Harold Wilson, as party leader and prime minister, was lionised in the mid-1960s before he was vilified in the late 1960s. Other Labour party leaders – James Callaghan, Michael Foot, Neil Kinnock and John Smith – were not so lucky. They were either instantly unpopular with most of the newspapers or were allowed the briefest intervals of admiration.

Labour talks about restrictions on newspaper ownership, ostensibly to stop any individual having too much influence. There is no good reason, though, to believe that a greater spread of national newspaper ownership would increase the spread of newspaper support for the variety of political ideas parties adhere to. Labour opinion swings about on this issue and Tony Blair's Labour party showed strong signs early on of a very relaxed attitude towards cross-media ownership.

In any case, how much it matters is much disputed. In the past, Labour has won power with newspaper opinion heavily against it, and newspaper support alone does not determine election results. But it may critically influence them at the margin. Newspapers like to believe it does, with the *Sun* taking confidence to the extreme after the Conservatives' 1992 election win when it declared that it was its coverage 'Wot Won It'. That extravagant claim has to be set against the results of reputable surveys of viewing, listening and reading habits which invariably suggest that television is far and away the most important source of election news for the great majority of people. Even before television coverage started to become very important in the 1960s, newspapers probably had only a small influence on political conviction. They follow their readers at least as much as leading them.

In supporting conservatism, newspapers may, like other businesses, believe it provides better conditions for commercial enterprise of which newspapers are part. More importantly, having cultivated a readership, they generally appeal to it in terms of style, type of coverage and opinion. That is not always the case. The *Sun*'s excited support of the Conservatives in the early 1990s went against the voting habits of nearly three-quarters of its readership while its brashness suited them very well.

The balance of newspaper opinion is not likely to change greatly over a span of years, unless the Labour party persuades people it is permanently transformed from the socialist force Conservative newspapers like to label it into a force that will allow business and the middle classes to flourish, a milder form of conservatism, just a bit left of centre.

Liberal Democrats

The Liberal Democrats, more so than the Liberal party before them, are disgruntled by the way the media treat them. They base a claim for a better deal on a number of political strengths. One is their presence in local government where they have controlled councils and shared power in others. They are also, they say, a bountiful source of new policies and radical political ideas. They claim a substantial and fairly consistent level of support in the opinion polls. They achieve dramatic swings in parliamentary by-elections. An additional argument, the strongest they use, is based on the total number of votes they win across the country at general elections: just under six million in 1992. It means, they say, that each of their MPs represents vastly more voters than do MPs of any other party. Yet they are reduced to a few lines of copy or a token sound-bite, too often a token interview, an occasional headline, and during general elections, when they fight all seats, they are treated as less than Labour and the Conservatives.

As often in matters of editorial fairness, the biggest complaint is against the public service broadcasters who are supposed to be fair to everybody. The Liberal Democrats say that in failing the party, the broadcasters are, by implication, unfair to the millions who vote for it.

Working against them are a number of political weaknesses the Liberal Democrats do not like to acknowledge but which influence editorial decisions. One is that national programmes and national newspapers are concerned more than 90 per cent of the time with national politics, not with the politics of local government. Westminster and Whitehall are

198

the headquarters of national politics. Town halls are not. The strength of the Liberal Democrats in local government is therefore of limited editorial value. A variation of the weakness is that the willingness of British voters to let Liberal Democrats into power locally is not matched by a willingness to let them into power nationally.

An important Liberal Democrat weakness influencing newspapers and programmes is that the party has so few seats in the House of Commons, twenty as a result of the 1992 election, a number increased slightly by occasional by-election victories. The small number reflects the bias of the one member, one constituency winner-takes-all system of electing a parliament, a bias programmes and newspapers do not recognise as part of their job to correct. With so few in the Commons, the Liberal Democrats are a small political presence at national level. They are a much smaller presence than Labour and the Conservatives. They do not make as much news and they do not have as much impact on newsworthy issues.

The best Liberal Democrat response is that a great deal of political news consists of comment and that their MPs are as ready as any others with relevant comment. The argument has registered to some extent with television and radio news, with a consequent increase in sound-bites of dubious value. The faces of the small band of Liberal Democrat MPs appear on the small screen and the few words they are allowed to speak after editing are quickly overtaken by the impact of the story that follows.

For contributions more substantial than the well-edited sound-bite, for programmes like *Newsnight*, *Channel 4 News* and *The World At One*, the small band has another weakness which the Liberal Democrats reject indignantly and which broadcasters do not normally express publicly, nor admit outside their own circles, but which influences editorial decisions. It is that in terms of talent, research and spread of responsibilities, a team of twenty-odd MPs cannot be as effective as bigger, better briefed teams. The figures speak clearly: John Major's government after the 1992 election was able to call on more than eighty spokespeople in the Commons while Labour had a matching number, four times the total of all Liberal Democrats in the House. No amount of hard work overcomes such imbalance. As a result, with a few exceptions, Liberal Democrat spokespeople are not as pertinent in front of the camera and the microphone as people from the Conservative and Labour benches where, with a bigger choice, subject and speaker are likely to be better matched and better informed. These things matter to programme makers because the quality of contributors is one of the differences between good programmes and mediocre programmes.

The problem of available ability becomes more marked during general elections, in contrast to parliamentary by-elections where scarce Liberal Democrat resources can be deployed most effectively. In general elections, the few nationally experienced Liberal Democrats are badly stretched. Inexperienced candidates are more exposed when the big names of the party spread themselves thinly all over the country and try at the same time to meet a multitude of media demands. The problem contributes to the party's tendency to lose, at general elections, seats won on breathtaking swings in by-elections.

The loss of such seats indicates another harsh political reality which the media absorb into their judgements: by-election voters choose a Liberal Democrat as a protest they are often not prepared to continue when it comes to choosing a government.

Whatever arguments the Liberal Democrats use and however passionately they use them, they confront convinced media scepticism. Editorial judgements are legitimately coloured by the knowledge that the Liberal Democrats are not going to gain power in their own right. Events may make them a 'balance-of-power' party in a hung parliament but they are not what is normally meant by 'a party of government'. They have not broken the two party mould of British politics as the alliance parties convincingly threatened to do before and during the 1983 general election, which was still a good possibility in the 1987 election but which was damaged, probably for a long time, very soon after the election when they launched the campaign to merge the Liberal party and the Social Democrats. This had a profound effect on the electorate and on the media. The move to merge may have been one of the great mistakes in modern British politics, a mistake seen as a betrayal. In the

1983 election, the alliance was less than a million votes behind the floored and flawed Labour party. In the 1987 election, though the alliance parties slipped further behind Labour, over seven million people voted for them. They voted for the idea of alliance and coalition, two parties working together to force political change. They did not vote for merger. The move to merge told these people, in effect, they were wrong-headed. Just as importantly, the arguments about merger also distracted attention from the alliance as an alternative source of political solutions. Labour regained the initiative as the voice of opposition and the party created by the merger, the Liberal Democrats, was gradually given a lower profile by the media and the public. The profile, rewarded by a slide to 18 per cent of the vote in the 1992 election, fits the realities of political choice in Britain in the 1990s.

nationalists

Nationalists in the countries of the United Kingdom struggle to be heard nationally. For years, only those in Northern Ireland were seriously attended to outside their own territory because their cause was associated with political violence. The passionate debate about independence or self-government for Scotland and for Wales, well heard as it is in those countries, was not really held at all, let alone heard, across Britain until the Conservative and Labour parties clashed on the issue. The dominant country of the Union, poly-racial England, with no political nationalism of its own, assumed its nationalism to be British, except when its teams were playing international cricket, soccer and rugby. As the controlling political force, English interests made sure the Union was not seriously questioned. The question was resisted rather than answered. The media, also largely controlled by and serving English interests, in effect connived in this, largely because they believed it would not sell as an interest in England, to some extent because they believed it should not be promoted. Newspapers and broadcasting outside Scotland and Wales were reluctant to recognise the argument for the break-up of the Union as a major issue. The case for changing it fundamentally, short of break up, was also not seen as an issue demanding continuous editorial attention in the way that the state of the economy gets continuous attention. Just as the argument against interference from Brussels was allowed a one-sided dominance of the European debate as though there was no case to answer, so the assumption in favour of centralised power at Westminster for years over-rode the nationalists' case. From a Scottish nationalist perspective, it looked very much like editorial suppression. It was more an outstanding case of editorial neglect.

The Scottish nationalists, with help from the less significant Welsh nationalists, press the national broadcasting organisations on the point. They look not for support for their case but for exposure of the issues. Their pressure does not make much impression on coverage outside their own countries except at general elections. There is a spurt of broadcast reports, features and discussions in UK-wide programmes during election campaigns, then a dearth. This acknowledges the importance of broadcasting in the pursuit of parliamentary power. It means, also, that the massed voters of England who are not faced with the Scottish choice get to know most about it when they least need it.

The nationalist issue is well aired most of the time by newspapers and programmes made in Scotland and Wales for Scotland and Wales. As Scottish newspapers are a strong presence in Scotland, newspaper coverage of the nationalist question is not as great an issue as broadcasting coverage. And in broadcasting, television coverage is a greater issue than coverage on radio which has exclusive, totally Scottish services. The difference is that television in Scotland, to a lesser extent in Wales, is dominated by the networks transmitting from London, particularly the ITV network and BBC1. Whatever spaces are allowed for Scottish news and other topical programmes, news viewing in Scotland depends largely on coverage from London. Because the debate over Scotland's future has only a minor place in the UK-wide media, it has a minor place in the greater part of news and current affairs television seen in Scotland, that is, in programmes like *The Nine O'Clock News*, *News At Ten* and *Newsnight*. In that way, British television transmitting programmes to all of the Union fails a vital Scottish interest, and, as a corollary, does not make the majority of non-Scots in the United Kingdom fully aware of the passions of the Scottish debate. Much the same is true also of the Welsh debate.

political labels

Condemnation by label is a favourite tactic of political antagonism. In the belief that socialism is unpopular with the conservative British, especially after the sorry collapse of European communism, Labour party policies are dismissed by their free market opponents, without the need for argument, as 'socialist'. In the belief that to be Tory denotes snobby, class-ridden, patrician attitudes, left-wing critics scoff at 'Tories', no argument needed. To evoke echoes of the political party that had no hope of success after Lloyd George split them into the wilderness, opponents of the Liberal Democrats sometimes refer to them, in spurious forgetfulness, as 'the Liberals'. Descriptions like 'hard left', 'far left', 'extreme left' and 'extreme right' all have extra connotations, political under-meanings to damage the people they describe. In the same way, 'Euro-phobe' is adversely loaded in a way that 'Euro-sceptic' is not. To improve their reputation with the sceptic or phobic doubters, 'Euro-enthusiasts' became 'Euro-realists'. In the raging years of deregulation, free-market economics, monetarism and privatisation in the 1980s, the 'wets' in British Conservative politics were dismissed by description. Labour dominated local councils in depressed, over-crowded, graffiti-ridden areas were run by the 'looney left'. 'Moderates' are always preferred to 'extremists', and 'militants' are instantly suspect without anything else being known about them.

spin doctors

The first thing to be said about spin doctors is that in the British context they are over-rated – by themselves, by political leaders who employ them and mostly by journalists who write about them. They are advisers. Their job is to help political leaders present themselves and their policies to best advantage and to underplay problems. They aim to put a spin on the news story, like the spin on a tennis ball or a cricket ball intended to make it go in the direction they desire. They have some success with advance publicity when, for instance, they influence stories about an important ministerial speech to be made or about a new policy to be announced a few days hence. When their spin works, it creates an atmosphere in which the speech or policy is favourably received or helps to concentrate the subsequent debate on the points the party wishes to emphasise.

The term 'spin doctor', like the term 'political correctness', crossed the Atlantic from America and the practice of spin doctoring is more influential in America than in Britain and Europe. United States politicians, especially those running for the highest office, have long been shaped, polished, encouraged and restrained by image makers to an extent greater than in European politics. The result is that the debate between American politicians is more controlled, less free-flowing, dedicated more to the calculated sound-bite, exceptionally careful not to provide political hostages through careless words.

In Britain, as in America, spin doctors are much written about at election times when their acclaimed powers are in greatest demand. They are supposed to protect their over-exposed clients from damage or to limit it by manipulating publicity, by encouraging favourable images and by enticing journalists into story angles advantageous to the party. They recommend 'photo-opportunities' that entice photographers and camera crews into soft shots of the leader cuddling a calf or patting a toddler and at which hard-bitten sceptics who do the reporting have no chance to throw awkward questions. They are upset when reporters at the daily election news conferences in London insist on lines of questioning the party wants to leave behind, yesterday's story which the party could not properly cope with but which, to its chagrin, is still running today. The story that will not die exposes the spin doctors' limitations. For all their supposed magic and their alleged ability to make the news go the way they want, rough reporting wins through. At the 1992 general election in Britain, no amount of spin could make Labour's punishing tax plans palatable to a decisive part of the electorate. The spinners at Conservative Central Office could not overcome the dull flatness, almost a depression, that was all too obvious in the demeanour of front bench figures when they appeared in studios for election interviews. Programmes like *Election Call*, the phone-in on BBC radio and television in which the public harasses leading politicians, are practically impervious to the efforts of the image manipulators. In the intensity of three weeks or a month of campaigning in Britain, people hear enough plain truth to overcome the gloss the parties prefer.

stop-watch editing

If it existed in newspapers, the equivalent of stop-watch editing would be counting the words, an extract of fifty words for the prime minister and much the same for the leader of the opposition. It does not happen like that in newspapers but it happens to a degree in broadcasting as a result of the notions of impartiality and balance. The raw version of stop-watch editing says that if Labour has had forty seconds of actuality, the Conservatives should be allowed much the same. But editing was never as crude as that. What is more likely is that if over a period the opposition leader is given more time in radio and television reports of the exchanges at Question Time in the House of Commons, programme editors have questions to answer. They may be able to say it was justified because the opposition leader spoke persistently at greater length while the government leader was subdued. Such an explanation is unlikely because Commons fisticuffs are rarely one-sided and to give more time consistently to the opposition leader would be a likely sign of bias.

Programme editors and producers know they have to be guided by a sense of equality but precisely calculated clips of thirty seconds each have always been rare. Programme makers' use of the stop-watch is mainly to ensure the feature is not longer than the programme wants and that the programme will end on time. In normal times, a rule of thumb is more use and more used than a stop-watch. At election times when the political parties pay fevered attention to the coverage they are given in programmes, the stop-watch is used to make a few editing decisions and editorial merit decides the vast majority. The significance of an extract from a speech or interview prevails over its length. Concessions to balance are to be found more in extracts included because 'We haven't had anything much from them for a day or two' than in allocations timed by the stop-watch.

chapter nine – state interests

censorship

Censorship as an issue suffers from much heady comment. Someone somewhere will cry censorship whenever anything is known to have been deleted. Yet all newspapers, magazines, other publications and programmes have to make decisions about what to include and what to leave out. It is part of their normal processes. When a television news editor or a newspaper editor rejects pictures of mutilated bodies, victims of, say, a bomb attack, because they are too gruesome, it is not censorship. To describe it so goes beyond reasonable meaning, losing value from the word. If however a government official had the power to order a television programme or a newspaper not to use such pictures and in fact used the power, that would be censorship. A sensible definition might be that censorship is restriction on editorial content for reasons outside the normal processes of independent editing. This allows that censorship does not have to be imposed from outside. It may result from processes inside the broadcasting or publishing organisation.

Censorship from the outside using the 'blue pencil' can be designated formal censorship. Not much of it exists these days. Restrictive regimes prefer stealthier methods. Under the blue pencil, programme scripts and newspaper copy, including simple news reports, are submitted to officials who decide whether anything is to be deleted, as happens in a few countries. It happens especially in times of war or other national emergency.

The stealthier regimes may not require to see scripts but will make sure that journalists are not able to move freely about the country, nor to talk freely to people. Such censorship prevents journalists from learning things in the first place. The Soviet Union worked that way during the communist regime, China likewise. Sometimes no restrictions are imposed but journalists are under ever present threat of being thrown out of a country should they report what the authorities do not like. As a form of control, it restricts editorial content as surely as the blue pencil. Some countries prevent all but compliant journalists from entering or ration visits and insist that 'interpreters' are always present.

British government tends to say there is no formal censorship in the United Kingdom for television, radio, newspapers, magazines, books, plays or any other form of general communication. This is true in that there is no individual official or body of officials to whom scripts or other material have to be submitted as a matter of routine or even in prescribed special circumstances. And the word 'formal' is significant. The government view is not to be trusted. There was actual censorship of an unusual kind on British radio and television in what was known as the Northern Ireland ban; there is direct theatre of war censorship when fighting is going on or is imminent; and there are plenty of restrictions on all of the media which have the same effect as censorship. Some would be widely regarded as justified as when legitimate interests of national security are being protected. All countries have some things they are entitled to keep from the public gaze, even in times of peace. The Official Secrets Act acts as a form of censorship, however justified, insofar as it causes newspapers and programmes to leave out true information of genuine interest which would be made public if nothing other than the normal editorial processes applied.

Some British restrictions are highly questionable, most notably the Northern Ireland Notice, 'the ban' imposed by the government in October 1988 which, for the six years it applied, prevented radio and television from allowing the public to hear the voices of Northern Ireland terrorists and those associated with them. It did not prevent information being given but it restricted editorial content by preventing it being given in a certain way. It banned particular voices. It denied broadcasters part of their right to choose how they would convey the views of particular kinds of people. The ban was undeniably an act of censorship. The government was able to impose it because of powers of intervention granted by parliament, in the case of independent radio and television in the Broadcasting Act and in the case of the BBC in its Licence and Agreement. Those powers allow the government to stop programmes or parts of programmes. In the legal language, they 'require' the broadcasters 'to refrain from including in the programmes . . . any matter or classes of matter specified'. In plainer words, the broadcasters must not do what the government decides they should not. These are powers of censorship. For purposes of meaning, it does not matter that they are approved by parliament, nor that the broadcasters can announce they have been restricted.

Britain does not have freedom of information – a public right of access to most officially held information – as exists in the United States and other advanced countries. As a result, a vast amount of information of legitimate interest to the public is kept confidential in the files of the civil service. Though not normally regarded as censorship, its effect is the same. It restricts editorial content less dramatically than in those countries where journalists are not allowed to move freely but journalists in Britain cannot move freely among information held by official-dom. It is akin to censorship, censorship by prevention.

No journalist likes censorship but some accept that not all censorship is bad. They wish to make their own editorial decisions within reasonable law and within reasonable bounds of taste, decency and concern for genuine national security. They recognise that censorship exists and that sometimes they have no choice but to operate under it. There are certainly situations in other countries where news correspondents submit in preference to being able to report nothing at all, believing that as good reporters they will defeat restriction, eventually.

When censorship has a significant effect newspapers and programmes can keep faith with their public by saying so. Although it does not tell people what has been left out, they then know at least that content has been interfered with. When the Northern Ireland ban significantly affected a programme, the audience was usually told it was because of 'government restrictions'. During the Gulf War in 1991 after the Iraqi occupation of Kuwait reports were often described as having been censored or restricted or subjected to supervision. There was censorship on the American, British, French and Arab side as determinedly as on the Iraqi side. From their different perspectives, both sides were equally justified. The allied censorship, though patchy and sometimes risible, was for the most part to protect military operational information. This meant not making public facts about the armed forces – their positions and strength, for instance – which would help the enemy. In featureless desert it led to reporters doing tightly shot pieces to camera that could have been recorded in a confined studio mock-up for fear that the real background might show something revealing by way of the horizon.

On a few occasions in the Gulf desert, the allied 'minders', as the censors were mildly called, deleted facts for other than direct military reasons. A BBC reporter with the British army had on one occasion to refer to the chaplain as a 'welfare officer'. The censors thought the truth might cause religious offence to the Saudis. Wariness of Saudi susceptibilities also led to removal of the observation that British soldiers had enjoyed a meal of bacon and sausages. Preparations for treating wounded soldiers and for dealing with bodies were rigorously excluded from reports.

Though they tend not to admit it, most British newspapers and broadcasting organisations accept, by their actions, that some censorship is reasonable. Furthermore, even when it is not reasonable, it is accepted as inevitable. And though the television networks in America and some of the US newspapers made a considerable noise against restrictions at the start of the Gulf War, they accepted them. Also, when they sought a better deal for the future in discussions after the war, the agreement they came to left the American military with significant powers over news. Journalism frequently takes the view that to have some facts fed to it is better than starving for a principle.

In their internal processes, news organisations often delete things for legal reasons: something may be insupportably defamatory or in contempt of court. Broadcasters remove or change scenes in plays because they would needlessly offend the taste of reasonable people. Such deletions are not what would normally be regarded as censorship. They are part of the proper process of editing.

If however a newspaper or a programme, of its own accord, deletes content for political reasons it is reasonably described as self-censorship. It is equally self-censorship when an uncomfortable meaning is softened, re-expressed in a kinder way for the sake of the feelings of political friends. There is much of this in the politically partial reporting of British newspapers, especially in the agitated run up to elections.

The early days of the BBC saw significant editorial omissions and trimmings under political pressure or for political reasons without pressure. The BBC's well meant editorial rules, heavily weighted, like British society, in favour of authority, were then so severe as to be a framework of restraint tantamount to censorship. Only approved speakers were allowed and then carefully scripted. It chimed with the times. A discordant case, out of its time, widely regarded as politically infirm, occurred in more recent times, in 1985, when the BBC governors stopped the showing of a documentary programme, *Real Lives: At the Edge of the Union*, about two characters at opposite ends of the political and sectarian divide in Northern Ireland. The governors of the time would hotly deny that their decision was censorship. They would say they were exercising their appointed function. Many of the staff believed, however, they made an improper decision. The programme was later shown after efforts by the director general of the BBC who had been absent for the original decision – and who was subsequently sacked.

DA-Notices (formerly D-Notices)

The system of Defence Advisory Notices, known for decades as D-Notices, is not well understood, nor well liked, is liable to be misrepresented by journalists on the few occasions it makes news and was creatively exaggerated by early television dramatists when characters they created declared 'Slap a D-Notice on it.'

In real life, the system is an arrangement whereby the media can be given advice, leaned on if necessary, in a gentle 'old-boyish' sort of way, when information the security services believe would help enemies of the state might be made public. It is a voluntary system with no legal force. To defy it is not an offence, though defiance would probably weaken a journalist's defence in the face of a prosecution under the Official Secrets Act. It is overseen by a committee of civil servants and media executives, the Defence, Press and Broadcasting Advisory Committee. The number of media people on the committee significantly exceeds the number of civil servants – eleven to four.

The committee does not operate the system. The principal agent in its working is the secretary to the committee, always a former high ranking member of the armed services. It is to the secretary, not to the committee, that a newspaper, a radio programme or a television programme will turn for advice. The secretary may press advice without being invited, as happened when sensitive documents and a lap-top word processor containing sensitive military information were stolen from an RAF officer's car in London in the run up to the Gulf War. Such unsolicited advice will be given, as appropriate, to all branches of the news media – newspapers, radio, television and magazines, as in the Gulf War case. All the British news media agreed not to mention the lap-top in their stories of the theft. The security concern was that hostile interests might offer very large sums of money for the lap-top if it became known that it was missing.

Publishers and authors of books tend to resist suggestions by the secretary. Journalists, including programme makers, do not always accept advice they are given, are generally not friendly to the system and some dismiss it out of hand. The advice tends to be predictable and resistant to logic: when the lap-top computer was stolen, the argument that publicity might cause information to come forward was dismissed, but when news of that part of the theft was made public after a foreign newspaper broke the silence, the lap-top reappeared. Equally, until the political will changed, the civil service side of the system resisted calls publicly to name heads of the secret services.

An important shift in the scope of the D-Notices, as they then were, occurred in 1993 when the system was extended to cover terrorism. Previously, it had referred only to matters of national security, understood on the media side to be concerned traditionally and almost exclusively with external enemies, such as the largely unfriendly, communist-ruled countries of eastern Europe during the Cold War. As communism collapsed, the national security interest was reassessed and, at the same time, Whitehall officials pressed a concern they had developed over a number of years – the need to keep helpful information from terrorists, in particular from the 'enemy within', the bombers and gunmen of the terrorist groups in Northern Ireland. Civil servants on the committee suggested that terrorism was implicitly covered by the terms of the long-standing D-Notices, that to draw this out was not an extension of the system. They argued that Northern Irish republican terrorism worked against the state, that it was, therefore, a danger to national security and, as such, was covered by the notices.

The argument did not go down well on the media side of the committee. While it was accepted that terrorism might, in some situations, be a threat to national security, a number of the media members did not accept that the terrorists of Northern Ireland sought to overthrow the state. Threats to prominent individuals in government and other official bodies, menacing as they were, were not seen as a threat to national security. They were not like the threats for so long posed by the armies, the nuclear weapons and the spies of the Warsaw Pact countries.

There was no doubt, though, that terrorism might be helped by information. A detailed newspaper story, on how a piece of anti-terrorist military equipment worked, clinched the argument, and terrorism was absorbed into the system.

Some months later, a review of the notices was completed. The word 'Advisory' was added to their title; the number of notices was reduced; their tone was made a little less formal; and their meaning remained as before. The system became yet more relaxed than it had been and was retained in the face of questions about its usefulness – just in case.

official secrets

Although the British system of governance is very secretive, true clashes with the media over official secrets are rare. The theory has long been worse than the reality. Until the Official Secrets Act was substantially amended in 1989, many trivial bits of officially held information in Whitehall were officially secret. But civil servants, politicians and journalists knew that old section two of the Act, the part most likely to catch journalism, was a discredited nonsense under which prosecutions were unlikely and, if launched, had every chance of failing. The changes of 1989 introduced a sense of reality and, in so doing, made the Act more of a threat to journalism. The areas of restriction, being much narrowed, have been strengthened. Even so and although there are real issues here about the ability of journalists to investigate matters of concern, reporters and editors do not often fall foul of official secrets.

The law is illuminating as an example of how in Britain these matters are determined by the interests of government. The perspective favours authority. It assumes that the national interest is as government sees it. Government decides what should be protected. Government then decides through a whipped parliament how it should be protected. No independent mechanism is provided by which the national interest can be tested or proved. No mechanism decides whether the motives of government in any particular instance are genuine, truly in the national interest, or self-serving, to save the government from embarrassment. The wider concept of the public interest is absent, deliberately, not by oversight. Official secrets law in its amended form in Britain, as in its old form, quite simply protects what the processes of government find it desirable to be protected. It is still a long way from protecting only that small, hard core of secrets national governments are entitled to protect at all costs.

The first important point for journalists who receive official information is whether it has been officially released. They have to know whether its disclosure is authorised. Press handouts and other generally available news releases are clearly all right. Stealthy disclosures are suspect. A document in a brown envelope delivered discreetly will not be officially released. Nor will a tip confidentially given. The shadowy rules about who has the power to do what also mean that official information from a middling civil servant may well not be authorised. Regardless of how high the civil servant is, information would not be authorised if it is information the civil servant should not have given. It is difficult to imagine circumstances in which written or spoken information from a government minister would be unauthorised but it is possible. In short, a leak is a leak unless it is not.

Risk does not attach to all official information, however disclosed. A great deal, though protected by confidentiality, is not covered by the law on official secrets. The areas to be concerned about are the obvious ones of security, intelligence and defence, official telephone tapping and the official opening of people's mail, along with the less obvious ones of crime and special investigation, official, confidential exchanges between governments, and exchanges between governments and international agencies. If the journalist receives official information about what is being done in any of those areas, leaked by someone who is not allowed to, there could be a problem.

It will not, however, be a problem for the journalist unless harm is done by the information being made public. And then, even when harm is done, the journalist would in most cases have to have known or should have known that it would be so. Unauthorised official information about crime is treated exceptionally in that if, for instance, it helps someone commit an offence or prevents an arrest then harm does not have to be proved because it is obvious.

The government set itself against calls for a | 215

public interest defence when the changes of 1989 were debated. No satisfactory answer was given at the time or since to the argument that if a person is prosecuted in the public interest it should be possible to be defended in the public interest. The effect is that a court trying a journalist is not supposed to take into account any plea that a story did good as well as harm. Some lawyers do, however, believe they could successfully argue that the public was greatly helped by the story – perhaps a story that a grave danger to public health had been kept secret, that the harm done was not great and that the journalist should be acquitted.

national security

Journalism confronts national security occasionally – and national security usually prevails. It is one of the areas in which journalists are not expected to 'publish and be damned'. It is also an ill-defined concept, one in which government expects to have the final say, frequently the only say. When the country is at war or engaged, as against continuing terrorism, in other armed conflict, the expectations of national security can become strident, driven on by an easily inflamed public fervour. Matters like the morale of the fighting forces can become a security issue. It also becomes mixed with other related generalised concepts, notably the 'national interest', for instance when publicity for the initial and subdued opposition to the Falklands War in 1982 was held to be against the national interest.

In more relaxed times than war, journalists do not lightly offend serious warnings that interesting and sensitive information would damage national security. In the operation of the system of DA-Notices (Defence Advisory Notices) to tell journalists when national security might be harmed there are many more instances of specific advice being heeded than of it being ignored. Journalists loudly object and co-operate quietly.

Reporting on Northern Ireland was at times curbed because aspects of security were at stake though there were no powers to command it.

216

Special operations were sometimes known about and not written about. A journalistic investigation into a company in Scotland with suspect financial arrangements stopped when the company was discovered to be involved in secret work for the security forces in Northern Ireland. Most cases of self-censorship on national security occurred over 'Cold War' considerations when the communist Soviet Union was a feared enemy. New weapons, their capabilities and their deployment were known to journalists and if written about at all were written about in circumspect ways that kept details from the public. Given the propensity of the British secret services to develop leaking spyholes to the enemy, the British public often knew less than the Kremlin about British devices and British precautions. In the years of international tension and the threat of nuclear holocaust, officialdom in London and at stations like the government communications headquarters at Cheltenham erred well to the safe side of caution. Better to keep quiet in case it might help the enemy.

Excessive caution often harms the notion of national security. Many journalists accept that a few things, a small core of the most important sensitive facts, deserve to be kept secret. They become sceptical when they have kept a secret only to find someone else later disclosing it without any evident harm.

war

Coverage of war between nations has become a conspiracy of authority intent on managing the news and journalism with no other realistic choice. There are plenty of journalists to deny it indignantly, female and male alike eager to declare a macho independence. The reality is otherwise. At the same time, wars bring out the best of journalism, moving descriptions of bravery and suffering, and an honest sense of responsibility to people waiting anxiously at home. International wars bring out also jingoism and other crude nationalistic sentiments of the kind that prompted the *Sun* newspaper in Britain to greet the sinking of the Argentine ship, *Belgrano*, during the Falklands

217

War with the notorious and unforgettable headline 'Gotcha'. Other people's civil wars, as distinct from wars between nations, are notable too for journalism of the highest quality, and with civil wars the journalism relies much less on facilities and favours from the warring authorities.

An important change occurred after the Americans had to retreat from Vietnam in south-east Asia in 1975, their awesome military might overcome by an intelligent and dedicated guerrilla army. The change rode on the back of a continuing belief that the war was lost because television, to a lesser extent newspapers and radio, sapped the American will to fight. Strong as that belief is, the change could not have occurred had the next war been on the scale of Vietnam. Opportunity worked to the benefit of military and political authorities determined, after Vietnam, to manage news to reduce the risk of failure. The two most notable wars involving the western countries were both in severely confined theatres – the Falklands in 1982 and the Gulf in 1991. Both were eminently suitable for news management and the news of both was heavily managed.

When the British sailed to war over the Argentine occupation of the Falklands, the only sure way for journalists from western countries to reach the islands in the south Atlantic was with the British task force, the ships, aircraft and soldiers sent to evict the invader. British journalists went with the force. All others were excluded. None was allowed from the best of allies, the United States, none from European partners France and Germany, none from the Commonwealth kin in Canada and none from anywhere else. The ostensible reason was there was too little room, the few who could be allowed must therefore be British.

On the way to the Falklands as preparations for war mounted and as overtures for peace failed, the sole channel of communications for journalists assigned to the task force was through the task force. They filed stories for their newspapers and their programmes using the electronic links and the goodwill of the military. Once in the area of the Falklands when hostilities broke out at sea and in the air, journalists depended on the task force in the same way. So it was after the landings, in the push to the capital Port Stanley. They had no other means of sending their reports to their news desks.

The dependence of the journalists was greater even than that. They were controlled in three ways, including direct double vetting of copy. In the first place, the journalists depended on the task force for information as for transport, rations, accomodation and communications. They were not in a position to learn a great deal more than the commanders allowed. But, as a precaution, a second mechanism of control applied. As the reporters lived so intimately with the people of the task force, they were bound to observe more than the military wanted them to report, to overhear more than was good for the success of the operation if reported, and at times to wheedle an insight or two from officers and lower ranks. So, the task force included people from the Ministry of Defence and from the military, known as 'minders', sometimes referred to as 'advisers', intended as censors. Their job was to examine journalists' stories – scripts for radio and television, copy for newspapers – before they were relayed to London. Their aim was to make sure the stories included nothing that would damage the military operation. News of plans, tactics, strategy, equipment, weapons, fighting numbers and dispositions was scrutinised carefully to make sure it did not tell the enemy anything new of importance that would help them. One of the neatest and most striking news comments of the campaign was the result of intervention by a minder. When the BBC reporter Brian Hanrahan wrote a piece about fighter aircraft from ships at sea attacking Argentine positions, his original script gave the actual number of aircraft that took off and returned, as all did. Before his report was sent to London, the minder said he should not give the number. It would tell the Argentines more about the air capability of the force than was good for the British operation. As a result, Hanrahan memorably told listeners and viewers 'I counted them all out, and I counted them all back.'

Had the number of aircraft not been removed at source in the south Atlantic, the third part of the vetting could have cut it. Hanrahan's report along with all other news reports from the task force was relayed to Broadcasting House, headquarters of the BBC, in London where it was recorded for use while simultaneously being listened to and recorded by the Ministry of Defence in London. The process applied to all pieces for radio, for television and for newspapers. All were pooled – that is, were available for use by all British news organisations regardless of whose reporters wrote them – and all were vetted by the Ministry, again to make sure they gave away nothing that should be kept from the Argentines.

The news reporters had no acceptable alternative but to submit. Had they refused, their reports would not have reached London until they themselves returned weeks later like weary Victorian messengers slowly bringing the news on foot from battles far away. And their output was managed, almost as effectively, very nearly nine years later when they reported from the Gulf in 1991 on 'Operation Desert Storm', the military strikes by America, Britain, France and Arab allies against Iraq to end the occupation of Kuwait. Reporters were not so tightly confined as with the Falklands fighting. But the control was as tight as it could be. The western allies or Saudi Arabia, base for the entire military operation, or both, accredited the news reporters. A number were attached to and lived with fighting units in forward positions in the desert. Their reporting was carefully scrutinised by the minders. Others covered the news conferences and briefings back at headquarters in Dhahran. And they depended heavily on them. The ready availability of satellite technology meant that the military did not have the same exclusive grip on communications as in the Falklands. As there were so many journalists from so many countries, there was no point even in trying to route all reports through a vetting channel.

Other factors, though, were to the advantage of the western allies. The Iraqis allowed only a few foreign reporters to stay in Baghdad. They were closely confined with few opportunities to go beyond their hotel, fewer to talk to ordinary Iraqis and fewer to see war damage anywhere than in the immediate vicinity of their accomodation. No western reporters were in Kuwait. In addition, the main part of the war turned out to be air strikes – on Iraq and on Iraqi positions in Kuwait. Reports of their success or failure were almost entirely in the hands of the military to be passed on to reporters as they saw fit. Not that the military was justified in being too confident in what it knew. First reports of bridges destroyed, roads blown up, installations and military positions blasted, came from the aircrews who carried out the attacks. Their cameras and their eye-witness accounts told some of the story. As it turned out, they and their commanders had a greater faith in their smart weapons than was warranted by subsequent evidence. But, again, reporters had no options. There were no other available sources, just as there were none earlier, in the weeks of build up to the war when the western media relied on the US Pentagon, the British Ministry of Defence and the French authorities for estimates of how many and what quality of forces from Iraq had dug in in Kuwait.

A further factor helped the allies with the flow of news. After the air strikes, most people expected a slow, bloody slog in the desert. The reporting of heavy land battles would have been less confined and better informed than of air strikes on distant targets unobserved. Instead and predicted by few, the allied forces raced through the desert unopposed to recapture a Kuwait abandoned by its occupiers.

For all the limitations, television viewers, radio listeners and newspaper readers all over the world learned a great deal about the fighting in the Gulf. It was not reported as independent journalism would want. But it was reported at great length and the weight of public opinion would side with the military in controlling the flow. No sensible leader, military or political, could approve the publication of information that would clearly jeopardise an operation, nor can the commanders leave it to journalists to decide what is so operationally sensitive it should be left out. Many journalists accept that – while knowing that control allows the military also to hide what it is ashamed of and persuades politicians to control bad news 'in the interests of public morale'. Elaborate guidance, as issued to news organisations by the defence ministry in London, does not resolve the differences. At the same time, political and military leaders know that bad news, whether scandalous or not, will leak out, that in the modern world rumour seeps into the public domain to be taken up as half-truth or worse by reporters.

The military was more honest in the Gulf than sceptical journalists may care to admit. But the concern of journalists is that, not knowing what is withheld, they cannot begin to pass a judgement on whether it should be. A few reporters tried to escape the confines of approved areas to see what they could for themselves – and were arrested by the Saudi authorities. For the most part though, they co-operated and came to accomodations. When British 'Tornado' aircraft on low flying missions were shot down, as they were because the risk was high, broadcasters agreed to withhold the news for a few hours so that wives and children or other next-of-kin could be told. The point of concern was that with so relatively few 'Tornado families' back at base at home it was an anguish for all when an aircraft was downed until they knew the pilot's family had been told. The British authorities themselves could not successfully stop the information getting to newspapers and broadcasting before families were told because international news agencies carried announcements from the Iraqis. So a deal was done. There was no great loss to the public interest in news of a downed aircraft being given at four in the afternoon instead of two in the afternoon. News organisations also agreed to limit personal information they published about captured RAF pilots. The concern was that the Iraqis might use it to put psychological pressure on the pilots.

Serious gaps existed in the Gulf War news given to the public, a state of affairs for which Iraq was as much responsible as the allies. How many Iraqi troops really occupied Kuwait was not convincingly known at the time and numbers given by the allies were, for the most part, unsceptically recycled. How many Iraqi casualties there were, in Iraq and in Kuwait, was not convincingly known either – and the allies could not or would not say. They refused to contribute to 'a body count'. Just how much damage was caused by the allied raids no one really knew at the time. How smart were the smart weapons, supposedly guided with great electronic accuracy, was a matter of speculation more than of reliable fact. All this will occur again if the next war between nations involving the western allies is in a place, on a scale and of a kind that makes news management possible. A widespread war on several national fronts and continuing for longer than in the Gulf or the Falklands would see a return to the stark honesty of the reporting of the later years of the war in Vietnam.

Northern Ireland ban

A clear case of censorship by government on broadcasting was imposed in Britain on 19 October 1988. It prevented the voices of Northern Ireland terrorists and their supporters from being heard on radio and television, a gag that lasted until after the IRA declared peace very nearly six years later. It became known as 'The Northern Ireland Ban', 'The Broadcasting Ban', sometimes 'The Sinn Fein Ban', in Northern Ireland simply 'The Ban'. The government said it had to be done because interviews with terrorists and their apologists caused deep offence and spread fear, especially after acts of violence. Broadcasters protested at this 'damaging precedent'. Foreign interests, notably the Soviet Union, scoffed that it proved BBC claims to independence to be hollow, and proved bias because British broadcasters continued to interview terrorists elsewhere.

The ban came in the form of a legally enforceable notice signed by the home secretary of the time, Douglas Hurd, the cabinet minister then responsible for broadcasting, and delivered to the two broadcasting authorities, the BBC and the IBA. The notice was drawn up under powers given to the home secretary in the BBC's constitution and in the Broadcasting Act governing independent television and radio.

The notice listed, initially, eleven organisations to be restricted in broadcasting, the number later increased to thirteen. They included Sinn Fein and the Protestant Ulster Defence Association (UDA), along with organisations already declared illegal, among them the Provisional IRA and the Official IRA on the republican side, and the loyalist terror groups, the Ulster Freedom Fighters (UFF) and the Ulster Volunteer Force (UVF). Some of the organisations, such as the women's movement, Cumann na mBann, were little known and some, it was suspected, had ceased to exist.

Except at election times and in reports of parliament at Westminster, people in these organisations were not allowed to be heard in radio or television programmes if they spoke for the organisations. Anyone else, high or low, important or ordinary, British or foreign, who spoke words of support for

223

them was not allowed to be heard either. Restricted people could be quoted, in paraphrase or in full, word for word, by reporters or newsreaders or by using the voices of actors or putting their words into captions. Viewers and listeners could be told exactly what they were saying but were not allowed to hear them saying it.

The ban was similar to, though less severe than a restriction imposed by the Irish government in Dublin on the national broadcaster, Radio Telefis Eireann (RTE), in 1971, and which continued in existence. The British ban was less severe, and more ridiculous, in that people of listed groups could be interviewed and could appear so long as their voices were not heard. In Ireland south of the partition line, they could not be quoted, let alone heard. One Irish journalist was sacked for interviewing a Sinn Fein official.

The chairmen of the IBA and of the BBC had been alerted by the home secretary the evening before the notice was delivered. It came as a shock to the journalists. Few knew much of the power of government to do what was being done, fewer had given thought to it and no one had imagined it would be used for such nakedly political purposes. In typically British fashion, the powers in law were briefly stated in a very generalised way, without qualification and without any indication of the kind of circumstances they were meant to cover. They allowed the relevant secretary of state 'to require', in other words, to order, the broadcasters 'to refrain at any specified time or at all times from sending any matter or matters of any class specified' in the notice. There were no guidelines or principles governing their use. In effect, they allowed government to interfere. All it needed was the will to do so.

The powers had been used on few previous occasions. One was the much ridiculed 'fourteen-day rule' in the 1950s which had prevented programmes from discussing any topic to be debated in parliament within fourteen days, a rule eventually rescinded because it was recognised to be preposterous. On another occasion the powers were used to ban subliminal messages, that is images and sounds of such short duration that people were not aware they were receiving them but which might influ-

ence them. That restriction is now fixed in law.

Dreadful atrocities over a number of months had preceded the Northern Ireland ban, all part of a long trail of violence stemming from the killing of three terrorists by British forces in Gibraltar. The trail included the killing of three people, with many more injured, by a loyalist extremist at the Milltown Cemetery in Belfast. It included, in the same close sequence of horrors, the brutal savaging of two soldiers who ran into a funeral procession in the Andersonstown Road, also in Belfast. Six soldiers were killed by a bomb in their van at Lisburn in County Antrim in June. Another eight were murdered in August when their coach was blown up on the way to barracks at Omagh. Further bombings, shootings and hijacks killed and injured dozens of other people during weeks of violence that evoked fears of the indiscriminate brutality in the streets of Northern Ireland of the early 1970s. Politicians and ordinary people began to talk again of internment and of capital punishment for terrorists.

In the desperate atmosphere, the prime minister, Mrs Thatcher, demanded action. The violence could not be allowed to go on. Something had to be done. Suggested measures were drawn up for consideration, few enthusiastically offered and most rejected. They included internment, increased numbers of troops, more patrols, and powers to seize assets that funded terrorist organisations. They included also restrictions on the right to silence in terrorist court cases and action against Sinn Fein appearances in news programmes.

The ban was a recognition that little could be done, a substitute for policy. It would do nothing practical for the beleaguered people of Northern Ireland. It would, though, please Unionist politicians because it would mainly hit their opponent, Sinn Fein, and damage its electoral prospects. It would appease opinion in England where middle-class supporters of Mrs Thatcher were exasperated by Northern Ireland, about the cost of keeping it in the United Kingdom and would prefer to hear less about the inability of the Irish to behave themselves. But it could be made to look more important than that. And so it was.

When the home secretary explained to parliament and the country why he had interfered in the editorial process, he made it sound an

225

honourable necessity. It was, he said, to deny an 'easy platform' to the terrorists and their supporters. Occasional appearances in programmes gave them an opportunity to justify their violence. They drew support and sustenance from this access. Their appearances caused the 'gravest offence', 'the deepest outrage'. Mr Hurd told the Commons:

> When there is a terrorist attack and television screens carry to mourning people pictures of tears and bloodshed, it is hard for us on this side of the water to understand the outrage that is felt when, soon afterwards, there can appear on the same screens, particularly in Northern Ireland, people who, just keeping on the right side of the law, justify and glory in what has been done and threaten more of it.

That 'kind of triumphalism' was not acceptable. And there was more:

> That direct access gives those who use it an air and appearance of authority which spreads further outwards the ripple of fear that terrorist acts create in the community. The terrorist act creates the fear and the direct broadcast spreads it.

Mr Hurd's powerful argument persuaded the Commons with little difficulty. There were a few tangles, one over whether the ban compromised the broadcasters' duty to report impartially. The home secretary implied that it did because the exemptions for coverage of parliament and at election times were, he said, to avoid problems over impartiality. But his junior minister, Tim Renton, said the restrictions did not affect impartiality.

The home secretary gave no sign of doubt on charges of censorship. He said it was not censorship because the broadcasters were still able to report what was being said and done. Reporting was not restricted. It was not even discrimination against broadcasting because it simply put programmes on 'the same level as the writing press'. Mr Hurd's narrow view of censorship did not satisfy programme journalists who continued to protest against the ban. A group under the auspices of the National Union of Journalists launched a legal challenge. It failed heavily in the Appeal Court and in the House of Lords.

Though they were urged to, the broadcasting authorities did not join the challenge, a source of resentment among some of their journalists. Expert constitutional advice to the BBC had said the chances of a legal challenge being successful were almost nil. There were also feelings at higher levels, among BBC governors and elsewhere, that a challenge in the courts would involve very large amounts of public money seeming to be spent in aid of the right to freedom of expression of a disreputable body, namely Sinn Fein.

Official arguments from the broadcasting organisations barely touched the issue of freedom of expression. They concentrated instead on the effect the ban had on the ability of programmes properly to cover events and issues in Northern Ireland. It was argued that because Sinn Fein and others could not be heard, they could not be questioned effectively. Viewers and listeners were prevented from making their own judgements because the important nuances of direct speech were missing. Sinn Fein people were able also respectably to refuse challenging interviews on the grounds that the ban discriminated against them. Sinn Fein was part of the political reality of Northern Ireland. Unionist politicians were expected to sit in the same local government councils as Sinn Fein councillors and on the same council committees, but only the Unionists could be heard in programmes, a severe limitation for local radio and television in Northern Ireland.

More profound arguments were voiced. In dealing with the republican movement which pursued its ends with a two sided policy, the bomb and the ballot box, it was crass to take action that did more damage to the ballot box side than to the bombers. Critics of the ban saw not a jot of evidence in six years that it helped the fight against terrorism. It was another miscalculation in the long line of historic British miscalculation in Ireland, another resented act of discrimination against the nationalist community, to that extent, counter-productive.

The government was impervious to the arguments. The ban became part of the familiar fabric of news and other topical programmes. Reporters and newscasters would announce of any spokesperson for Sinn Fein or other listed group that 'Because of government restrictions, their words are spoken by an actor.' A caption on screen said 'Actor's voice' and there was, nearly always, a clear hiatus between lip movement and spoken word. Occasionally, Gerry Adams, the Sinn Fein president, was heard in his own voice when he was an elected MP because he was then held to be representing his constituents, not Sinn Fein. Then he lost the seat he had never taken up and as a result completely lost his voice in programmes. Sometimes, Sinn Fein councillors were heard in local radio in Northern Ireland because they were speaking for their council or for a council committee. Now and again, evil men known for the atrocities they had committed were allowed to be heard because they spoke personally, not as representatives. They could be heard speaking about reasons for murdering if they spoke personally but could not be heard talking about trivial matters if they spoke as representatives.

In these ways, programme journalists who wanted to get on with the job of reflecting events and examining issues in a deeply divided society were required to make theological distinctions, trying to decide when someone was 'representing' an undesirable, listed organisation or when words 'supported or solicited or invited support' for such. Some inept decisions were made. The Radio Division of the IBA stopped the playing of a pop record by a group, The Pogues, when there was no good reason to regard it as covered. The BBC captioned the former MP, Bernadette McAliskey, without any real need to do so. In a few cases, also, the BBC and the IBA/ITC made different decisions on the same material, usually when the issue was whether the individual was 'representing' or was speaking personally. Generally, the notice was interpreted as liberally as possible and the broadcasters were often accused of evading the spirit of the ban.

None the less, Sinn Fein was interviewed in programmes less often than would have been the case had the ban not existed. The ban hardly affected the UDA and other of the listed organisations because they were rarely ever interviewed anyway. Programme makers were urged by senior editors to seek interviews or statements as before and then to treat them according to the terms of the notice. The aim was to try to ensure that the ban affected only the way people appeared in programmes not whether they appeared. But, inevitably, journalists decided at times that in marginal cases, the effort was not worth the effect, especially in national television news where the drop in Sinn Fein appearances was probably greatest.

The Irish government lifted its ban early in 1994 to encourage moves toward peace. The British government followed months later. Both retain the power to re-impose a ban. No serious attempt is likely to be made to remove those powers, and there is no limit to what government might be allowed to do given the permissively vague wording in which the powers are expressed.

Government in Britain has no such ability to limit newspapers. If an attempt was made, newspapers would react more aggressively than the broadcasters did.

freedom of information

The hold British officialdom has on information is still very strong in spite of genuine 'open government' changes over a few decades. The determination to keep control is manifest from the fact that improvements made so far have come, not from laws and other legally enforceable instruments where journalists and public would have rights, but in cautious memorandums and tentative guidances out of Whitehall or in flashes of liberalism from individual ministers. The British system of governance does not believe in a true, free flow of information through journalism to the mass of the people on behalf of whom government is conducted.

Government at national level and at local level sits on mountains of important information, much of which could be made public to the benefit of debate and under-standing. Much of it is, however, kept confidential until politicians and senior civil servants decide that bits be released when it is convenient for them. Frequently, the debate on public issues in

Britain is marked by a paucity of information and a surfeit of opinionated assertion.

Many justifications are advanced. Information is confidential because it is 'personal'. It cannot be made public because it is 'a commercial secret'. It is confidential because it is 'against the national interest to make it public'. To publish minutes of high level discussions would 'threaten the give and take of debate', would 'reveal too much of the cut and thrust', in other words, to publish important minutes about discussions that precede decisions affecting the lives of millions of people would mean disclosing who had made a concession and why, and who had resisted and why, a transparency that would not be in the interests of those who govern. There is no British constitutional conviction in a right to know, and there are indications from Brussels that other governments in the European Union are equally reluctant to be open about how they arrived at decisions. Some are better at giving access to the information on which decisions are based than in Britain where the gathering of vast amounts of information as part of the contract to govern is not matched by an accepted obligation to pass on, or to allow access to, as much of it as is reasonably possible.

When access is allowed in Britain, it is almost always indirect, through an agent. Journalists and public are rarely allowed to see documents. They will be told by a press or public relations officer or other public servant what is in a document. The telling will be edited, extracts or digests given, hardly ever word for word in full. This was not at all changed by the code of practice introduced in 1994 under the Citizens' Charter. In some ways, it has encouraged selective disclosure rather than full openness, a side step government spokespeople have justified by saying it is helpful to people who want the information to issue convenient digests instead of full documents. The code of 1994 gave a right of appeal to the parliamentary ombudsman, which was certainly a step forward. The ombudsman, however, has no power to enforce.

The Whitehall grip on facts works also against official inquiries and against the courts of law. They do not always get all they ask for, as happened with the Scott Inquiry into the 'Arms for Iraq' affair in 1994. Persistent questioning, as with Scott, sometimes discloses that information has been withheld but often there is no way of knowing whether anything significant has been kept secret, let alone what it is. Parliamentary answers to an MP disclosed that the financial watchdog, the National Audit Office, had been refused a total of more than 1500 files by a range of government departments. Lawyers for accused people may be denied knowledge of facts they would have used in court as significant evidence. The eventual emergence of facts not produced in trials has led to belated quashing of convictions. Higher courts have condemned the Home Office for not fully disclosing the grounds for refusal to refer cases back to appeal.

A few shafts of light penetrate the gloom, probably the most important being the decision by the chancellor of the exchequer, again in 1994, to publish minutes of his monthly meetings with the governor of the Bank of England. Although these minutes are not made public until six weeks after the meeting, they provide financial journalists and other financial commentators with very significant insights. Having been done in this highly sensitive, market-moving area of macro-economic management, it could certainly be done in other shadowy areas of government. For the most part though, real journalistic disclosures continue to depend on leaks, often by disaffected officials. This enables the system cynically to distract some of the attention from the significance of what is leaked by raising a fuss over the ethics of leaking. It has become a standard defence for government ministers to say they never comment on leaked documents. They often garnish their refusal by referring to the documents that embarrass them as having been 'stolen'. The aim is to distract attention from scandalous political decisions by drawing attention to less scandalous behaviour by journalists and their sources.

chapter ten – the public

viewers, listeners and readers

They are all counted, after a fashion. Television boasts millions of viewers, about half the population of Britain on weekdays at around eight in the evening; radio extols an impressive 'weekly reach', about 90 per cent of the population listening for a good spell at some time during the week to one or more of the radio services; and newspapers claim confidently that many more people read their pages than buy them, one paper bought being worth at least three readers. The methods of counting vary and the three varieties of consumer are not readily comparable but the counting is independent and professional, as it must be to satisfy advertisers and others with an objective interest. When the figures are released, individual stations and papers massage their message to their benefit and some degree of scepticism is warranted. The millions viewing what the industry knows as terrestrial television – that is ITV, Channel 4 and the BBC networks – plus the satellite services of BSkyB, include many not paying much attention as well as the obsessed. The millions who buy newspapers and the millions more who read them include headline scanners and light browsers who miss out the heavy pages as well as diligent readers who take in several articles at least from each page. For the majority of radio listeners, listening is a secondary activity, that is, they are nearly always doing something else at the same time, the other

232

activity being the more important. Radio survives strongly as background which means that many people attend to it only lightly and intermittently. Were it more demanding, it would have fewer listeners.

Radio is still treated as the poor relation. It is frequently left out of references to the media, commentators content to refer to 'television and newspapers'. Radio's lesser position is evident also in surveys designed to measure 'importance' of sources of information, as in the question 'From what source do you most frequently get the news of the day?' But the total of radio listening and the nature of it demonstrate the significance of radio as a presence. The growth of commercial radio has improved the profile of the medium in Britain to such an extent that it is valid to talk of a revival of the fortunes of radio since the glum days when television mesmerised most people away from the 'wireless', a revival which has not, though, added many to total numbers listening. Radio deserves better recognition, too, as a daily informant. A large number of people have their first impression of the news from the radio while only a few have their main supply of news from it.

The value of the news media to the public is seen from the different ways radio, television and the newspapers are used. The weekday peak of listening to the radio, that is, when the largest number of people is listening, is at breakfast-time, from about seven-thirty to around eight o'clock, an hour or so later on Saturdays and a little later still on Sundays. Listening across the population declines steadily during the rest of the morning and more dramatically during the afternoon while amounts of listening in the evening are minuscule. The viewing profile for television is the reverse. Audiences grow slowly during the mornings, significantly during the afternoons and explosively in the early evening. Readers treat newspapers differently again. Many people use their paper, national or local, at different times of the day because it can be read conveniently at breakfast-time, on the train or bus to work, at lunchtime and later. A newspaper, ephemeral as its appeal is, lasts longer than a news programme. As a general rule, in a business where general rules must always be heavily qualified, people receive the news from the immediate, live mediums, television and radio, and supplement it

233

in important ways from the newspapers. As television viewing and radio listening are passive activities, requiring little effort, they give all but the most attentive people impressions of the news rather than substantial accounts of it. By contrast, the positive effort of reading means that people are likely to absorb more from a newspaper. Readers concerned enough to concentrate can follow complicated written detail that was omitted on radio and television or which eluded them, possibly because it was delivered, as it must be, at someone else's pace, not at the pace preferred by the individual listener and viewer. Newspapers powerfully reinforce issues in the news by exercising them in their opinion columns. National newspapers are more targeted at sections of the population than broadcasting generally. The spread of them appeals, perhaps panders, to a wider spread of views and attitudes than does broadcasting, especially television, which in trying to be acceptable to everyone cannot afford to please any section at the expense of others.

National broadcasting in radio and television has traditionally aimed at a broad spectrum of the population, trying to serve all of the public, so that audiences to networks are mixed in terms of socio-economic groups though their age profiles vary markedly. But as independent radio expands, so those stations are becoming more targeted, especially in the big cities and conurbations where choice is possible.

Newspaper journalists like to say that broadcasting is heavily dependent on them, that stories and interviews are often 'follow-ups' of exclusives or new angles in the papers. The observation is to a degree well founded. Somewhere in the newspapers on any day there is evidence of more resourceful news journalism, a good idea effectively pursued, an angle given prominence when no one else appreciated it, or an insight by a source no one else thought of. The newspaper successes are then taken up in the news and current affairs programmes. To that extent programmes owe much to newspapers. The full story looks different. News on television and radio is certainly much 'straighter', more plainly approached than in newspapers, partly because of the duty of impartiality in broadcasting, partly because the spoken word calls for a more direct, simpler approach. It is also true that because most news is open to all available journalists, not squeezed reluctantly into the open by journalistic persistence, it is reported first by radio and television, a consequence of the immediacy of broadcasting more than a tribute to the ingenuity of radio and television journalists. Broadcasting organises itself to exploit its natural advantage. A further point is that many newspaper stories depend on broadcasting for important quotes. Day after day, serious and popular newspapers lift comments from politicians and other public figures interviewed on television and radio, quite often without attribution. Programmes have frequently to work hard for their interviews, and with an experienced, sophisticated news programme like *The World at One* at lunchtime on Radio 4, issues are drawn out and examined ahead of the national newspapers more often than behind them. Furthermore, journalists in broadcasting show more initiative than they used to but their 'exclusives' are less trumpeted than in newspapers and are more noticed by envious rival stations than by newspapers published the next day and following them up without acknowledgement.

Honours are at least even. Broadcast journalism in Britain has advanced unrecognisably since the early days when the government, listening to the pleas of an establishment fearful of the potential of the new creature and keen to soothe troubled newspaper interests, restricted the broadcasting of news to a late hour and confined it to agency reports. As importantly, in spite of closed titles, British newspapers have strongly survived the growth of broadcasting which, expected to be an onslaught, has turned out to be an ally in persuading people that news matters. The important overall point for journalists in whichever medium they work in Britain is that journalism is consumed daily by many millions of people. Suspect as journalists are, the vast majority of people, the viewers, readers and listeners, regard their work as essential.

broadcasting councils

British broadcasting has attendant bodies like boats have barnacles. The public service ethos requires it as part of the effort to know what the public is saying and to pay attention to it. The ITC has advisory bodies, committees and councils, and so does the BBC. The broadcasting councils of the BBC for Scotland, Northern Ireland and Wales are among the most worthwhile. They are a better reflection of the spread of opinion and interests in the Celtic countries of the United Kingdom than is the BBC governing board for the whole of the UK. They have a significant influence on programme policy in the BBC national regions, having to be satisfied, in fairly detailed ways, that the programme services are in the right direction. They have proved to be strong political champions of Scottish, Welsh and Northern Ireland broadcasting interests.

As with any active body of outsiders, there are stresses between the councils and the professional staff, both sides sensitive to their respective responsibilities. The existence of appointees from circles of influence, as council members are, is also bound to increase the opportunities for attempted editorial influence on the quiet, a feature of life to be coped with by independent-minded programme makers. As with the BBC board of governors, the councils do not make editorial decisions or issue editorial directives and untoward approaches are resisted.

accountability

Accountablity is flavoured with irony for the media. Newspapers, radio and television are the main means by which public figures are accountable to the public and these noisy channels of accountability resent themselves being called to account. The unresolved problem is not 'Who best judges the judges?' but whether the judges can effectively be judged without damaging their independence. Regulated broadcasting is further down the slippery slope than newspapers, and far from being satisfactory, special restraints on broadcasting encourage many people to expect it to be more accountable than it reasonably can be. Shrill newspaper comment against broadcasting adds to it, and newspapers themselves are increasingly hunted by the calls for accountability they have inflated.

Complainers against radio and television programmes are encouraged also by the public service precepts of much of British broadcasting, by the proprietorial attitude the BBC cultivated from its earliest days which has coloured all traditional, non-satellite, broadcasting in Britain, and by the intimate nature of the broadcast media. Radio and television, guests in people's homes, are expected to behave to everyone's satisfaction while few agree on what is satisfactory.

So far, market forces have not satisfied the demands for media accountability whatever right-wing ideology would wish. The worst excesses in journalism occur in the most popular newspapers and however strongly they are condemned, their readers stay with them. It is one of the favourite defences of popular journalism that 'If our readers did not enjoy what we do they would buy another paper.'

It is an exasperating problem for the media. To be accountable is usually taken to mean listening seriously to what the customer wants, doing what you reasonably can to meet it, and explaining yourself honestly and considerately even when you cannot grant all that is asked for. Lots of customers are not so reasonable as to accept this. In effect, they want all they ask for. Even reasonable resistance is received as arrogance. And when customers in their mass give inconsistent messages, especially to programmes of general appeal, less targeted than newspapers, noisy minorities easily have an influence greater than their strength and greater than the quality of their case.

Programme makers and newspapers spend more and more of their time trying to persuade people they serve society well while at the same time trying to make sure the mechanisms of accountability through bodies like the Press Complaints Commission and the broadcasting regulators do not induce editorial timidity. There is every reason to believe that in the media being more answerable means being less valuable.

access

Access allows the public to use programme time and newspaper editorial space to express views. It contributes to debate beyond the professional journalistic agenda, important in a politically and socially contentious society like Britain. For broadcasting, it can also be troublesome.

Newspapers have been passably good for a long time in providing access. It is relatively easy for them, unregulated as they are. They need only the act of will to make space available, enough editorial vigilance to make sure contributions from the public satisfy the paper's normal levels of taste and decency, and that they observe the law, most particularly on defamation. Access is provided mainly through the letters columns though, as always in the way things work, important names who need the access least make the most use of it in the 'quality' papers. Some newspapers go further than readers' letters. They allocate columns to articles of opinion, again often written by notables in politics, business or the arts. This trend, a natural growth for an active democracy, is slow to develop and, in spite of desk-top publishing which might have given it a local fillip, has a long way to go.

Its equivalent in broadcasting was slower. Broadcasting took a remarkably long time to make the elementary step of allowing programmes to encourage and regularly to broadcast letters from listeners and viewers. In the early days, when the BBC was the country's exclusive broadcaster, developments were deterred by anxieties in political circles about the potential threat from broadcasting to the established centres of authority. The concerns created an inhibiting early regime at the BBC. Stern policy included the requirement that everything to be said on air be first written down. This made sure it was not shocking and was of quality. Even interviews were scripted. Now, access broadcasting means allowing the public to make programmes. Sound-bites are not enough. Individuals or groups make substantial items or whole programmes of their choice, often to argue a special case: a protest group against the planned route of a new road, a community body complaining about police methods, a parents' association calling for better schools. The radio station or television company offers the air-time and facilities and professional programme-making advice while the individuals supply the editorial drive. It is a refreshing part of broadcasting's contribution to the exchange of ideas and argument.

Phone-ins, popular and cheap as they are, are a form of access broadcasting. They allow people to question experts and public figures, and to proclaim their own views. Phone-in polls, used sometimes by newspapers as well as by broadcasters, are another form of access. They allow people to cast a vote, often on a burning topic. Neither form of phone-in is to be relied upon as representing public opinion. The people who take part are self-selected and if a separate, reputably conducted opinion poll shows their views to be typical of the 'great British public', it is a coincidence. They are not even likely to be representative of the audience to the programme.

Politicians with enthusiasm for broadcasting regulation tend to suspect access programmes because they conflict with the simpler notions of impartiality or may give some views, in the words of the Broadcasting Act, 'undue prominence'. This attitude, though regrettable, is not surprising. Access programmes are likely to be 'personal view', not made by people with an open, balanced or impartial approach but by people who take a stand, pressing a point of view or particular perspective. If such a programme is not balanced by an equivalent programme (or programmes) from an opposing perspective or if people with different views are not given an early opportunity to speak against, the broadcasting organisation may be held not to have been impartial.

This mechanistic approach prevailed in the 1990 Broadcasting Act and, because of it, independent television and independent radio must have balancing programmes or opportunities for reply at an early date. The programme code of the regulator of commercial television, the Independent Television Commission, expresses a more relaxed view of the problem than does the code of the commercial radio regulator, the Radio Authority. Whatever the codes say, independent television and independent radio are not allowed to make truly independent judgements in this matter. Unregulated, they could justifiably choose a particular 'personal view' on the grounds that it would make an unusually illuminating programme, that public opinion would be richer for it, and that opposition would be recognised if it came along and was equally talented. Being regulated excessively, they have to make room for opponents with what may be predictable replies and unimaginative proposals – though in the face of a challenge the programme planners might successfully argue that these views have already been well aired and need not routinely be aired again.

The development of truly free-speaking community broadcasting is also held back by the same considerations and is likely to be so deterred for a very long time. In the 1980s, the home secretary, Douglas Hurd, then the secretary of state for broadcasting, spoke in favour of a 'light touch' regime for community radio. But this liberal vision faded in the face of a realisation of what agitation by unbridled radio might do to seething, discontented youth of the inner cities and the hard estates of jobless and badly housed Britain.

The BBC was able to provide more access programmes than the independent sector, partly because it was not so tightly bound, and having freed itself from some of its early, self-imposed shackles. The interpretation of impartiality as expressed in the detailed provisions of the Broadcasting Act did not at first apply to the BBC. But the new 1996 BBC constitution adds detail on impartiality and in so doing may drive the BBC to give more opportunity for 'right of reply'. In this regard, all of British broadcasting is nearly on a level editorial playing field and it amounts to increased restriction. Gone are the days when the BBC was able blithely to give access with less formal redress because its rules were more generalised, more in keeping with the precepts of free expression. Regulation has caught up with it.

phone-ins

240   Radio likes phone-ins because they are cheap and because the public can be relied upon

to provide fizz. Phone-ins are frequent and familiar. At times though they are much more than that. They become genuinely, especially on local radio, an opportunity for people to express their views and feelings in ways that satisfy them more than writing a letter to the paper. In towns overcome by disaster – after a Hillsborough where soccer fans were suffocated and trampled to death – local radio phone-ins become a collective cry of grief, part of the attempt to cope with trauma. In Northern Ireland, during the long years of terrorist violence when the gulf between loyalist and republican grew wider and wider, radio phone-ins were one of the few ways in which the hostile communities continued to hear each other. During election campaigns, they are the main means by which politicians confront the electorate.

Though phone-ins provide opportunity for mischief, callers are remarkably well behaved. They do not normally swear or abuse others unacceptably. Defamation is only rarely a problem. Long-winded observations from frequent callers are more troublesome. The growth of 'angry' radio with provocative 'jocks' as hosts could change the scene.

consumer journalism

Consumer journalism is one of the great services the media provide to the public. Newspapers and programmes have exposed many commercial villains, rip-off merchants who have gulled the unsuspecting with hard-sell techniques and shoddy products.

Many traps await consumer journalists. They are particularly prone to legal action. Also, in trying to be fair to rogues, they are beset by delaying tactics. Consultants, some of whom are former programme people, gamekeepers turned poachers, sell advice to companies on what to do when a consumer programme or consumer page is in pursuit. Programmes are at times foot-faulted by the Broadcasting Complaints Commission, found guilty of minor failures that discount major successes, though the Press Complaints Commission, displaying a more worldly attitude, gives newspapers a more realistic appraisal. An additional danger for consumer programmes is that they take a stand, as they have to, and, in so doing, seem to go against the tenets of impartiality.

In siding with the victims of shoddy work and worse, it is very easy for consumerism in the media to go too far, to be carried along in an enthusiasm of complaint against products and services that lacks perspective. Some media operators favour dramatic, foot-in-the-door or chasing-with-the-camera techniques that run the risk of overshadowing the villainy being exposed. In collecting evidence, they employ other methods every bit as underhand as practices they condemn. But always the important difference, when the cause justifies it, is that their underhand method is for a public good whereas the commercial villain's is for private gain at the expense of vulnerable individuals. The exposés of consumer exploitation do great good in a society in which exploiters flourish and in which ordinary people, desperate for redress, are too often frustrated by commercial evasion.

To try to make sure they stay on the right side of the thin line that separates fair game from victimisation, consumer journalists use legal advisers well experienced in their kind of work. They follow exceptionally diligent editorial processes, more than is called for in the normal run of news. To satisfy the lawyers, allegations must be precisely stated and strictly justified by evidence held. Sound investigations are backed by very good notes and other records from the earliest stage. They make, where possible, audio and, if necessary, video recordings of important evidence because these are as near to being unchallengeable as it is possible to get. Such recordings often have to be made secretly, that is, without the knowledge of the people being recorded, and, as such, they enjoy a strong public interest justification so long as they are genuinely an important part of the attempt to expose wrong-doing. In many cases, research already carried out before secret recording will have established strong grounds for suspicion. The secret recording clinches it.

For the strongest case in law, whatever stand is taken in the end, good programmes and good articles arrive at their conclusions impartially.

They do not assume that complaints against products are justified until they have proved them so. They go about the process of proof in an unbiased way. Journalists whose purpose is to expose unfair dealing cannot expect to persuade their public if their dealings are not scrupulously fair.

Careful editorial processes have to cope with the problem of companies with like names. A surprising number, usually small firms, share the same or similar name, and those whose products or services are not being criticised may be entitled to damages if they lose trade because an article or a programme has not made it absolutely clear what firm it was criticising. This usually means giving the full address of the company at fault along with a statement that the complaint does not apply to any company of the same or similar name whether in that area or any other. On television, such clarifying statements are often given in caption as well as in sound.

Fair dealing also means that however clear the wrong, wrong-doers deserve a fair chance to speak out for themselves. Even rogues have some rights. This decency gives rise, alas, to obstruction and delay: the accused asks for more time to prepare a proper response, then for more details of the complaints, and then for details of what exactly is alleged. Further obstruction occurs when the rogue asks for details of the people who have complained – and this sometimes to put pressure on those people to withdraw. Names are usually kept from the accused unless and until they are published or broadcast. When given in advance, the individuals concerned have normally agreed to it, and then only when the journalists are satisfied they will not be pressured, and only if it is truly necessary to allow the complaint to be answered which, quite often, it is not.

The many attempted forms of delay include hefty conditions on any interview to be given, a source of protracted and, usually, unproductive haggle. The inventiveness of people intent on delay drives consumer journalism to combine fair opportunity for response with a determination to go ahead, if necessary without any response at all, when it is clear the opportunity is being abused.

----

correspondence

Newspapers and broadcasting in Britain receive gigantic piles of letters each year from the minority of people who are moved to write and very many of them expect a reply. In turn, many journalists find replying tiresome or irritating, especially as letter writing tends to turn ordinary, friendly viewers, listeners and readers into severe correspondents because few people can write in as relaxed a way as they speak. And in radio and television, the problem is made worse because factual programmes receive mostly letters of complaint.

Newspapers are in some ways better equipped to deal with the problem. Their letters columns are an appeasing outlet, and as newspapers are free to be opinionated, they can also be more trenchant in their private replies – while sensitive to their market as well. One thing to disaffect an intermittent reader, another to dismay one of your social and political core.

In broadcasting, the public service ethos, including the duty to impartiality, inhibits replies as much as it encourages complaints. It requires letters to be answered in a balanced and well-mannered way, even when, from time to time and with gritted teeth, the programme maker encounters a discouraging degree of unctuousness, often from someone who seems not to have listened properly and whose complaint is based on a political suspicion about the programme maker rather than on what the programme has said. The longer term matters more than the immediate irritation because letters are traditionally regarded as valuable, a continuing contact with the public, and because broadcasting shows few signs of developing effective mechanisms for routine right of reply.

Reluctant as well-informed journalists may be to recognise it, some letters make good points well worth absorbing and letters ignored or treated in a cavalier way are likely to encourage more to be sent instead to the watchdogs and regulators, including the Press Complaints Commission and the Broadcasting Complaints Commission. Members of parliament are often called in too. Responding to any of these is more irksome than responding to the original letter writers. A letter well answered may not, however, stop the complainer turning next to regulator or watchdog and the first response, respectable or not, is likely to be called up as relevant when the PCC, BCC or whoever, examines the issue. Replies, legally respectable or not, can also be recited in court should a case go that far.

Journalists who reach executive positions have to spend a good deal of their time devising replies. Their best are agreeable and cogent, not abrupt, dealing with points raised and no others, offering no hostages. Discursive replies encourage persistence, liable to develop into protracted exchanges, with meandering side arguments. Honesty of reply is a priority if for no better reason than the risk of evasion and deception being caught out. The chance of this is considerable: popular newspapers are ever ready to expose the malpractices of broadcasters who claim higher standards; newspapers are readier to expose each other, dog eating dog, than they used to be; and programmes snarl at the wrong-doings of the press.

complaints

People like to complain. They enjoy a shy at the media. They are keen to call or to write to say they were 'appalled', 'scandalised', 'astonished' or experienced – perhaps, enjoyed – other extreme adverse reaction to what they have seen, heard or read. News organisations, as self-appointed critics of society on behalf of the public, are critically observed by the public. The numbers who do write or call are in fact a relatively small proportion of the population but they still amount to many thousands each year. The majority of these complain; a few express satisfaction.

Many complaints are sent in the first instance to editors, columnists, producers and presenters. Some go straight to the top, to the managing director, the chief executive or the chairperson. People who believe their complaint has not been dealt with reasonably can turn formally to the regulators and possibly to the watchdogs, in the case of broadcasters the

245

ITC, the Radio Authority, the BBC governors, the Welsh Authority, the Broadcasting Standards Council and the Broadcasting Complaints Commission, and in the case of the newspapers to the Press Complaints Commission.

Newspapers have long realised that one of the best ways to deal with complaints and simultaneously to entertain other readers is to publish them. Broadcasting does not do it to anything like the same extent and it has to be a known policy otherwise a public airing might agitate the complainer. Letting people have their say does not satisfy all complaints. Very serious complaints of the kind that challenge the substance of a programme or article in a reasoned way may justify a weightier redress – the ultimate being another article or programme that puts the case urged by the complaint.

corrections

Mistakes in newspapers and programmes are more prevalent than journalists generally admit and more than the number of corrections suggests. But British newspapers, tardy as they are in correcting their mistakes, are a beacon by comparison with British broadcasting. Programme makers, programme editors, executives, board directors and governing bodies have all been slow to recognise the rights of people misrepresented in programmes. Corrections on air are still rare. The jibe against the BBC that it 'traduces publicly and apologises privately' applies just as much to other broadcasting organisations.

Programme makers tend to the view that for programmes to put things right on air is more difficult than for newspapers to put things right in print. It is not so much difficult as painfully prominent for those who have made the mistake. A correction broadcast at whatever time of day stands out at the time more than a few lines on an inside page. Damage done by errors in a programme can also stand out more than damage done in a newspaper page.

The equitable rule for broadcasting and for print is that significant factual mistakes about

246

individuals and bodies will be put right at the earliest reasonable opportunity in a placing close to where the original mistake appeared. Although broadcasting publicly admits few mistakes, it tends to accept the justice of this rule. When, for instance, *News At Ten*, the late main news on ITV, accepts that a mistake should be put right, it is put right on *News At Ten*, not necessarily with the same prominence but in the programme and not somewhere totally different. The same applies to *Newsnight* on BBC2 or any other programme. For one-off programmes or those that have ended their run, an early correction at about the time of day the mistake was made is accepted as reasonable. Newspapers, though quicker to accept the need for a correction, devalue their willingness by obscure placing. They do not accept that a mistake on page one be put right on page one. A prominent mistake is redressed by an unobtrusive correction.

There are many difficult arguments about whether an alleged mistake really is a mistake and about who was responsible for it, the individual making the complaint or the reporter. There are more difficulties about what is 'significant', some of which need an independent arbiter, watchdog or regulator to resolve. Some programmes and newspapers try to deal with as many mistakes as possible by 'fast-track' because drawn-out processes increase dissatisfaction and also the chances of the complainer turning to higher authority. Victims of a factual mistake in a programme can call in the Broadcasting Complaints Commission if the mistake gives rise to unfairness in the way an individual or a group, including organisations, has been treated. The Commission has a statutory power to order a summary of its decision to be broadcast and published, an outcome amounting to a correction if the BCC decides in favour of the person who complained.

Mistakes about events and issues not directly affecting individuals or organisations are usually dealt with by avoiding the same mistakes in subsequent stories and, if appropriate, by pointing out the difference: 'the number of people killed in the accident was six, not eight as we said yesterday'. Difficulties less easy to deal with arise when an individual complains about a judgement as distinct from a mistake of fact. The issue of right of reply takes over from right of correction.

right of reply

The right to have factual mistakes corrected is now confused with right of reply, the opportunity to put a point of view. 'Right of redress' is better as a generic term for both assumed rights. Correcting mistakes and giving people a fair say are better separated as issues though programmes and newspapers may deal with one as they deal with the other. The theoretical distinction between them is simple: whether an individual has been legally declared bankrupt is, for example, a matter of fact but whether an individual has treated creditors badly is a matter of judgement. In the first case, an individual wrongly reported to have been declared bankrupt deserves a correction, a right to have the facts put right. In the second, the individual reported to have treated creditors badly deserves an opportunity to speak against the allegation, a right of reply.

In spite of their failings and of the need for improvement, newspapers generally are better at redress than broadcasting is. Most newspapers will usually publish a correction when they accept they printed a mistake on an important fact about an individual or an organisation. Disputed facts or minor facts are more difficult. Aggrieved individuals may then be given space for a letter to put their version of the facts. Disputed views, judgements and allegations are more difficult still, but a reader's letter is again a ready way of according a right of reply. Newspapers often agree to include balancing comments in a later news report, sometimes to devote an entire report to them, although journalistic pride, scepticism and reluctance can make them grudgingly inadequate. Newspapers also allow a few people space, very occasionally, for a special article of rebuttal written by themselves. From time to time, they agree to print a reply even when they consider their original report to have been fully justified. So long as the matter complained of directly concerns the individual or organisation making the complaint and so long as it is a matter of importance, many newspapers allow some form of redress.

Broadcasters are less forthcoming. Few corrections are heard on air and it is even more rare to hear serious rebuttals at length, whether in spots for listeners' and viewers' letters, in special statements or in special redress programmes. Some airings are compelled by the summaries of adjudications issued by the Broadcasting Complaints Commission which the erring broadcaster usually has to carry. These are a long way, though, from redress for all the people who feel aggrieved by what is said about them. Programmes like *Feedback* on Radio 4, *Points of View* and *Biteback* on BBC Television and Channel 4's *Right of Reply* do a different job because they are concerned mainly with issues, less with personal grievances.

apologies

Journalistic psychology resists ready apology for serious as for small mistakes. Lawyers may be sceptical because an apology amounts to a defence thrown away. But no programme or newspaper wants to defend legally what it knows deserves an apology and a timely apology may take the sting out of a legal action. A few altruistic souls with an honest and simple approach take the view that apologies are worth it for their own sake. They make them well considered and matter-of-fact while doing justice to people who have been traduced.

chapter eleven – social values

minorities

Minorities feel neglected and, simultaneously, abused by the mass media. Organisations for people with disabilities, Asians, black people, homosexuals, single parents, Hindus, Muslims, older people and a long list of other groups say the special interests of their members are not sufficiently catered for by the broadcasting organisations and the newspapers, and they believe bitterly that journalism routinely misrepresents them. They see themselves as victims of crass images and crude generalities: black people are unreliable, noisy and given to drugs; single parents are irresponsible; the disabled are useless; Muslims are fanatical and intolerant; retired people are of marginal importance.

Apart from a range of programmes on Channel 4 television, only a handful of national programmes reflect things as the minorities see them or would like them to be seen, and they are at obscure times, broadcasting ghettos that confirm separation and difference. National newspapers are at least as bad. Few make special provision and most behave as though a problem does not exist. Local papers and local broadcasting are better but they are of limited influence. The warmly regarded Channel 4 with its special remit to serve minorities has limited effect too because it attracts audiences generally very much smaller than ITV channel 3 and BBC1.

It is a picture of resentments passionately felt. The nature
of news is partly to blame and is not going to change. People are
newsworthy when they are involved in remarkable events or are
themselves remarkable. They are not newsworthy for their
ordinary roles. A woman working is not newsworthy, a woman
mugged is. If the attacked woman is also disabled, she is more
newsworthy. The news story naturally plays up the disability. It
evokes extra interest. The process of discrimination has started.
Soon, organisations for disabled people object that the media
portray them as 'pitiable victims' and ignore the useful
contribution they make to society in the jobs they do. In the
same way, human interest stories pick out old people as victims
of violent crime, though people in other groups are more often
victims, so helping to build a perception that older people are
weak and vulnerable when many are vigorous and active.
Equally, the general reputation of black people suffered unfairly
over many years when riots in Notting Hill and Brixton in
London, St Pauls in Bristol, Toxteth in Liverpool and other
stressed areas made the headlines. Many black people were
shown setting fire to vehicles and looting, but many more, the
vast majority, remained law abiding.

Hard news journalism is not good at perspective in such
matters and when it tries to be it is unconvincing, close to giving
the impression that disturbing events are not as bad as they seem
or that they are to be excused. Feature journalism goes some
way as a corrective but it is not usually so influential. By
comparison with television, radio and newspapers are at a
disadvantage. Television is able almost effortlessly to convey
simple perspectives that help minorities. News and other factual
programmes can show minority people in ordinary roles: black
people as shoppers talking about price inflation, people in
wheelchairs working in offices, Asian children as achievers in
school. Newspapers and radio cannot do it without explicitly
drawing attention to blackness or disability or race.

Language in all of the media is significant without being
the extraordinary power for good that some
advocates of minority interests seem to believe.
Although language follows attitude rather than
leading it, prejudiced terminology feeds prejudice.
Avoiding derogatory words for homosexuals,

words like 'queer' and 'poofter', does not root out prejudice against homosexuals but helps reduce it. To say someone 'uses a wheelchair' instead of the routine reference 'confined to a wheelchair' is not a euphemism when the wheelchair enables a disabled person to work. It is regarded as just as important not to refer to the wheelchair when the wheelchair is irrelevant. A computer programmer in a wheelchair is not materially different from a computer programmer in a chair. In the same way, a black person is not materially different from a white person in most contexts but black people still have their colour remarked upon when it is of no consequence.

racism

Racism has come to refer to any discrimination on grounds of race. The British media probably feel more guilty about it than about any other discrimination and yet there are still relatively few black and Asian journalists in newspapers and in broadcasting, especially at national level. The surge of women into journalism and into significant positions in it which started in the 1970s has not been matched by an equivalent surge of people from the main ethnic minorities. The glass ceiling for them is almost at floor level.

One of the results is that national newspapers and national programmes generally neglect issues affecting the Asian and black communities, then lack confidence when they do cover them. Lopsided newsrooms have lopsided news values as much when they are white dominated as when they are male and middle class dominated. At the same time, the aim of calls to recruit and train more Asian journalists and black journalists are not to put them to work on stories from their communities as that would be a form of discrimination. The added value lies in their contribution to editorial meetings and editorial arguments, supplying perceptions otherwise missing, the difference between dominant white cultural attitudes applying unthinkingly and unawares, and being set aside when they need to be.

252   The rise of intolerance and the growing

sense of racial unease among white people in deprived racially mixed areas, combined with the scepticism towards political correctness, have been reflected in shows of exasperation in some of the right-wing British tabloids. Even so, the case against the cruder forms of racial reference are generally accepted in journalism in Britain where all the codes and guidelines caution against discrimination. Broadcasters follow the rule that race or colour should not be given in reports unless it is relevant to the story. While not followed so firmly in newspapers, racial references in print are included by no means as routinely as they used to be. Some ambivalence remains in all parts of journalism. It shows in arguments about the relevance of colour and race, especially with regard to stories about neglected, crime-ridden urban areas with high unemployment. A deprived estate that is nearly all white will be referred to simply as a deprived estate. A deprived area that has a majority of black people is likely to be referred to as a deprived black area regardless of whether its black majority is relevant. If it is a mixed area it will be referred to as racially mixed whether the racial mix matters or not. Many people, journalists included, seem to believe that when an area is poor and black, race has something to do with it.

Serious as these failings are, they are nothing to the explosive racial hatreds that show in the media of most, if not all, of the former communist countries of eastern Europe. Hostility to gypsies, anti-semitism and suspicion of minorities who came from neighbouring lands centuries ago are flourishing after the removal of the strict regimes that stifled them or stifled references to them. Racism in league with nationalism blames minorities for ills they have not caused, a prejudice exploited also by the extreme right in Britain and other parts of rich Europe.

sexism

The women's lobby has been the noisiest, the most insistent, the most intelligent and the most persuasive of the campaigns against discrimina-

253

tion. The importance of the media was recognised as two-sided – to win more places for women at all levels in broadcasting and in newspapers, and to convert male-dominated language and images to non-sexist usage. Both are a long way from fulfilment though the first has been more successful than the second.

Critics, including a few female journalists of long experience, regard it as risible that well-meaning guidelines should try to convert reporters and newscasters to 'police officers' instead of 'policemen', 'ambulance crews' instead of 'ambulancemen', to 'staffing' instead of 'manning', and 'businesspeople' instead of 'businessmen'. Part of the critics' case is that terminology matters less than images and much less than forceful equal opportunity policies. Terminology follows change rather than leads it. When society improves, its language will improve. But conversion by language proceeds, helped by the number of female presenters of programmes on television and radio and by the prevalence of trenchant female columnists in newspapers.

Progress is not hectic, at best measured, to an extent reluctant. Britain trails determinedly correct societies. America is far ahead and the advances made by middle-class white women in the United States who have benefited most from preference policies will probably survive the right-wing backlash that threatens black people and Hispanics. The British media are, by comparison, relatively unburdened by employment quotas though the British insistence on merit disguises a social bias that makes merit in women less recognised than it is in men. The British reluctance to adopt social and economic rules is matched by scepticism towards a thorough policy on 'gender inclusive' terms: 'spokeswomen' or 'spokesman' is preferred to 'spokesperson'; 'chair' competes fairly well but has not overcome 'chairman' and 'chairwomen'. The rule seems to be that where an unstrained alternative exists, as in 'customs officer' for 'customsman', it should be used but that irrelevant attention to gender, as in 'spokeswoman', is preferable to the unnatural and distracting 'spokesperson'. In this climate, the Australian 'waitperson' instead of 'waitress' in some eateries has no chance of taking root.

Among the unconcluded parts of the debate, the British media are so far not much impressed by the argument that to give a good lead in a recalcitrant society they should reflect the situation as it ought to be rather than as it is. As a result, programmes and, to a lesser extent, newspaper articles continue to mirror the facts and values of a male-dominated society.

disabilities

British journalism was, for many years, insensitive to the interests of people who have some disability. This started to change when a lobby successfully argued for 'Down's syndrome' to be used instead of 'mongol'. The term, now often reduced to 'Down's', is widely accepted as part of general speech and of journalistic expression. A concern that it too would, with time, become unacceptable, lobbied against in favour of a more fashionable term, is so far unrealised. But the favoured language of disability is now a dense thicket, exasperating even to sympathetic journalists, and contributing to the rebellion against political correctness.

The problem was highlighted after the term 'people with disabilities' began to make headway against 'the disabled' and 'disabled people'. The reasoning in favour of 'people with disabilities' was that it was less dismissive. The terms 'the disabled' and, to a lesser extent, 'disabled people' were held to suggest that people so described are incapable, useless perhaps, when none or hardly any are so limited. The change soon became disliked by some of the people it was meant to describe. They argued that 'disabled people' emphasised they were victims more of other people's attitudes than of disability, that it helped to show how society disadvantaged them more seriously than their disabilities do, a conclusion to stretch convincing explanation. Prejudice does indeed push disabled people to the margins of social activity. And prejudiced language, in ordinary speech, in news headlines and journalistic stories, plays a part in that. But to suggest that a theology of explanation is effectively encapsulated and conveyed in the phrase 'disabled people' taxes rational belief as well as explanation.

255

The argument on this point and on others, has, though, had effects, not always the effects disabled people wanted. One effect, infiltrated through impatience, is that newspapers, more so than programmes on radio and television, have become less fastidious, more matter-of-fact, more likely to be candid, in their references to disability, at its best, common sense in league with sympathy, at its worst unfeeling. Broadcasting still tends to be a bit precious in its references, some parts inclined to the view that groups of people are entitled to decide how they will be described – and then having to contend with unreasonable expectations.

Part of the concern of journalism is that it should not be used covertly to engineer social change. It has, certainly, to be a principal vehicle for the arguments for social change, but made openly as arguments, not as soft-spoken influences hidden in undeclared changes of terminology. Journalism that moves far ahead of decent common usage puts a gap between itself and the public. But it does not prevent newspapers and programmes on radio and television acknowledging that expressions like 'wheelchair bound', 'crippled', 'handicapped', 'deaf and dumb', 'defective' and others are usually unkind, unfair, unthinking and unnecessary. It is very likely that the withering away of such terms will follow social change, not the other way about. When more people in wheelchairs are seen working in offices and shops, it will become much better understood that they are not bound by the wheelchair. In this regard, words are a feeble influence by comparison with actions.

children

A clutch of laws provides for children to be protected from exploitation by the media and, in addition, the public is quick to condemn when the media take advantage of youngsters. Their innocence or gullibility, sometimes their sense of bravado, are easily manipulated. Deserved investigations have to go ahead none the less, especially into the serious juvenile delinquency in so many of the hard and hopeless council estates up and down the country, and into the many other issues involving children – drugs, drink, homelessness, abuse and neglect. Exploring them properly involves what the children themselves say, whether the children are bystanders, victims, or perpetrators.

Reporters and producers have to be very careful in their dealings. When children are witnesses, they are easily led into exaggerations or worse. When they are victims, to recall what has happened may be traumatic for them. When they talk as hooligans, joyriders, thieves, under-age smokers and drinkers or as drug pushers and drug dealers, they easily become boastful, and it may be difficult to know whether the bravura is a real quality or adopted only for the attention of the reporter, the microphone and the camera. Children may try to glamorize or to dramatise their delinquency. They may wish to appear anonymously, as when confessing to crime, and anonymity may be justified. But it can take exaggerated forms, especially on television, such as the wearing of hoods or scarves around their faces.

Interviews with children or other appearances by them may warrant parental or teacher consent against the temptation to snatch interviews outside school grounds. Clearly, though, there are occasions when interviews deserve to be done but would not get consent from the school or the family.

animal rights

Extremist action by a few violent militants distracted attention for a time from the great concern many people in Britain feel for the welfare of animals. Terrorist tactics took over from welfare as the issue. The news media fed this by representing the concern mostly through the views of extremists, and by regarding the Animal Liberation Front (ALF) as the sole militant force. Developments in recent years have shown that other organisations exist besides those that espouse violent action and that ALF is not the only extremist group. The Animal Rights Militia (ARM) is occasionally active. A group known as the Justice Department is active also in other causes to such an extent that it may be more interested in opposing authority than in protecting animals. The Poultry Liberation Organisation expects to be taken seriously. The organisation Compassion in World Farming became notable during the protests in 1994–5 against shipping calves from Britain for the veal trade in mainland Europe. Ad hoc bodies such as BALE (Brightlingsea Against Live Exports) spring up in response to events, a strong sign of the wide interest. Though protest demonstrations are often exploited by people more interested in social disruption than animal welfare, the issues have motivated law-abiding people who have never demonstrated before, elderly, middle-aged and young, professional people, teachers and ordinary workers.

The passions make unbiased, knowledgeable comment on animal welfare hard to find. The expertise of organisations committed to the commercial exploitation of animals, important as it is as part of the story, is not likely to be open minded. Some academic opinion is committed. Disinterested journalism may be as detached as one can get in this conviction issue.

names

Journalism without names is inconceivable. Popular journalism operates on the principle that names sell news, the more names the better, and bigger names better still. Gossip columns are a way of putting names into the paper without having anything much to say about them. Although ideas and policies have a life of their own, journalism puts names to them as an added interest. Names mean people and personalities, clashes of egos and personal interests. Politicians, business bosses, sports stars, show business personalities and parades of other public figures frequently depend for their reputations more on the way they are publicised than on what they do.

Critics of journalism deplore the concentration on personality. They say it does greatest harm in politics because it detracts from the importance of issues. To them, journalism that draws excessive attention to political personalities fails to convey the true nature of political problems. In dictatorships, propaganda hypes the image of the great leader to hide the failure of policies, while in democracies, free journalism hypes the role of personalities to simplify political issues to the point of falsification. In Britain in the 1980s, Thatcherism was widely understood only in terms of the politician who gave her name to it whereas the raft of ideas the term represented owed much more to the intellectual work of other, lesser names. In an earlier political generation, the names of two leading figures, the Conservative Rab Butler and Hugh Gaitskell for Labour, were appropriated to label a cross-party consensus, 'Butskellism', a shared belief in the desirability of strong social welfare and strong economic management which they were held to typify but which was the result of much more than their advocacy.

All journalism simplifies and uses labels, often derived from personalities, in the belief that they make difficult ideas more attractive to the mass of people, the majority of readers, viewers and listeners. The journalistic instinct that highlights personality encourages wider interest. But journalism concentrates on people for a more fundamental reason. News is about occurrences that interest people and affect them. It is concerned with the interaction between people, between people and events, and between people and ideas.

The implications of not naming names are illustrated by an argument heard now and again that names of accused people in court cases should not be made public unless and until they are found guilty. The argument has a decent motive. It is that to be known to be charged is a stigma which a not guilty verdict does not fully remove. Well motivated as it is, the idea would attack the essence of open justice. To have any hope of being effective, the public and the media would have to be excluded from hearings, allowed into court only if the verdict was 'guilty' and then only to witness the decision on sentence. No public scrutiny, directly or through the media, of the operation of the system of justice would be possible. The quality of justice would erode, and the secrecy would not be fully effective. Street knowledge would substitute for reliable information. Gossip and rumour would take over. Acquitted people would be pursued by whispers and innuendo.

Personalised journalism is fundamentally important for accountability. Societies cannot properly answer to themselves unless people are held responsible and, for the most part, this has to be public, not quietly done behind closed doors, not left to the discretion of confidential officials. Part of journalism's contribution to democratic accountability is to name names and to report the nuances of issues through revealing differences of known personalities.

obscenity

Protests about obscenity in the media are nearly always aimed at fictional programmes on television, sometimes against newspapers that deal in pictures of extraordinary bosoms and small ads for dubious services, and rarely against radio. It is not a big issue in journalism, and while allegations of indecency against television fiction are taken seriously, very little if anything on British television, apart from an occasional scene in a daring film on Channel 4 late at night, deserves so strong a description as 'obscenity'.

As though to vaccinate against any possibility of an infection of obscenity in British broadcasting, the Broadcasting Act of 1990 brought television and radio under the provisions of the obscenity law, a law that already applied to newspapers. Where previously programmes had been exempt, they could now be prosecuted under the Obscene Publications Act. It would have to be proved in any court case that they would tend to 'deprave or corrupt'. A public interest defence, a rarely sighted creature in British law, is allowed. It would be possible to argue that an obscene scene in a programme was justified because it dealt genuinely with a matter of general concern, as might, for example, discreet showing of obscene pictures during a genuine exposé of the porn trade. The public interest defence also allows it to be argued that the obscenity was justified because it legitimately furthered the interests of science, literature, art or learning.

offence and outrage

Some people are easily offended, and offence is both more frequent as a problem and more difficult to deal with than the much rarer problem of obscenity. The reserved British character when offended easily becomes outraged. Though sex, violence and bad language brought into the home in television films are much the most likely sources of offence-cum-outrage, there is a high risk of the problem arising in journalism. Journalists often feel obliged to feature characters – terrorists and other criminals, for example – that large numbers of people find very objectionable. Offence may be caused by an interview with an undesirable, by a violent picture that is too explicit, by a description that seems uncaring or by crude language bad enough in the street and much worse when it is printed in a newspaper or, worse still, when spoken in a programme.

The problem is nearly impossible to deal with in the sense that when people are offended rarely will they be appeased. No amount of explanation, however genuine, changes their attitude. They seem to enjoy expressing adverse feelings. They will say they are 'deeply shocked', 'outraged' or, one of the favourite expressions of indignation, 'appalled'. These protests are often accompanied by a claim that 'everyone I know feels the same about it' or 'and in this I speak for the general public who are fed up with . . .'.

The strength of feeling in those who are offended tends to make the problem seem worse than it really is. The debate is always liable to be hijacked by people angry enough to complain. The few who protest noisily make a mark while the vast majority who remain silent make no impression. Even two hundred complaints that jam the switchboard, as the tabloids report when television comes up with a shocker, is a very small number for the mass media. The small base of actual complaints is never a good indication of what the general public thinks, so that rises and falls in the level are not much as indications either. Proper surveys of opinion tell much more but they rarely deal with particular instances. They are generalised.

Broadcasters talk about 'pushing at the

boundaries of taste'. Stated more plainly, it means calculating what you can get away with. It applies much more in matters of fiction than in factual programmes, and in fiction it has certainly changed what is generally regarded as acceptable or, at least, what is tolerated by many and enjoyed by some. Nude and sexually explicit scenes now shown frequently on television would not have been tolerated twenty or thirty years ago. Also the kind of relentlessly repetitive bad language – lots of 'fuck' and 'shit' – heard in American films even after editing for television would have caused widespread outrage a couple of decades ago when now it causes little more than embarrassment in family homes and an occasional flurry at the Broadcasting Standards Council. By comparison, broadcast journalism in Britain and probably also in America has stood still on matters of taste. In Britain, it may even have retreated: sickening scenes of carnage shown in the news in the early, shocked days of violence in Northern Ireland would now be shown less explicitly. But in many parts of the world, including countries of western Europe, France and Italy among them, factual television is so unrestrained in its portrayal of violence that the vast majority of British viewers would be deeply shocked by it.

charity appeals

Competition for donations from the public is so intense that news coverage can boost a particular charity at the expense of others. The big ones, like Oxfam and Save the Children, inevitably win so much attention through legimately newsworthy activities that the balance is already tipped heavily against the smaller, less noteworthy causes. So it is a potentially troublesome area for broadcasters. Publicity based strictly on editorial merit causes enough envy in the unmentioned that overt appeals for donations in normal coverage are often avoided. Otherwise direct publicity to one cause makes it difficult, in fairness, to reject the approaches of others. Some reported events are so likely to prompt public generosity that information about where to send donations is included.

All the broadcasting supervisors – the Independent Television Commission, the Radio Authority and the BBC governors – have rules on how to handle formal appeals for charity.

hypnosis

Hypnosis is a minor editorial issue. It holds no special problems for the editorial columns of newspapers but it would be a big problem for a programme if an hypnotist was allowed to broadcast in such a way that people at home, people listening in their cars or while operating machinery in a factory, or people watching television in the pub, became entranced in ways they did not realise and beyond the normal enjoyments of a good programme. For this reason, television and radio have traditionally controlled displays of hypnotism very carefully. The guidelines and codes are forceful on the point.

chapter twelve – regional values

Scotland

The capacity of English journalists to annoy Scots who remain in Scotland is bottomless. Scots not naturally sensitive to unfair discrimination have been made so by ill-informed references. National newspapers – which in deference to the Scottish nation really means British national – are rather less offensive than broadcasting but not because newspaper journalists are better than broadcast journalists. The reason is that newspaper readers in Scotland usually receive special Scottish editions, the work of Scots journalists who make fewer elementary mistakes of national reference, whereas programmes from London dominate Scottish screens and radios.

News programmes and English sports commentators are the worst offenders. Their offences range from omission, for instance leaving the important Scottish soccer result out of the news though that does not happen as much as it used to, through unthinking nationalistic bias, for instance referring in a commentary to the English soccer team as 'our lads' as though the Scottish team was someone else's, to crass assumptions, for instance that school holidays in Scotland start and end at the same times as those in England as in 'With the schools opening today after the holiday', or that snow in Kent is 'the first heavy snow of the winter' when parts of Scotland have been heavily snowed on for weeks. Many of the offences are sports related. They are all the more galling for Scots because their separate nationhood is most recognised in sporting competitions – in the World Cup, European soccer competitions, and rugby union internationals. Sport has helped to keep the Scottish sense of nationhood alive with the result that inept references in sport have a political sting.

Journalists well understand that the Scottish system of law is different from the system in England and Wales and when they forget, as they sometimes do over the sterner attitude to contempt of court, they are bitten by fines for their neglect. Differences in education are also known about and often neglected. Other differences in the way Scotland is politically managed give rise to journalistic failure. When the community charge, the infamous poll tax, was introduced in Scotland, well ahead of its introduction in England, mainly as a trial to see how it worked, English-based journalism in broadcasting and in newspapers paid only intermittent attention to the Scottish protests about it. The Scots were relieved of the unworkable only after it proved unworkably unpopular in England – though the more violent behaviour of the English protesters had a great deal to do with it.

There was also a strong tendency to treat the continuing Scottish debate on devolution, home rule or independence as Scottish only in spite of its implications for the rest of the United Kingdom. And regardless of the UK implications, it was arguably of greater interest to the English, Welsh and Northern Irish than the amount of coverage suggested it was. Politically connected failures combine with what Scots see as biased news judgements on natural stories – about floods, storms and accidents – to feed the belief that as they are frequently not treated as British they should become exclusively Scots.

Northern Ireland

For many years before the protracted phase of violence that started in the late 1960s and continued until the ceasefires of 1994, the national media in Britain ignored Northern Ireland, an editorial indifference to match Westminster's hands-off constitutional position with regard to the virtually autonomous Stormont regime. While Westminster and the media looked the other way, discrimination and resentment flourished in the six counties of Northern Ireland during decades of the Unionist monopoly on political power. As a result, when civil rights protests gave way to violence, politicians and journalists outside Northern Ireland did not know what it was all about. Reporters flocking to Belfast, Londonderry, Newry and other inflamed parts of the province had to learn about the subtle complications of political and religious positions, whether unionists and loyalists were the same, where nationalists stood in relation to republicans, who were the Orange marchers, why they paraded in bowler hats, why they had such a passion for the Union flag, why young Catholic men from good families became murderers, what were the B-Specials and how they related to the Royal Ulster Constabulary, and why, if this was an integral part of the non-federal United Kingdom, it had its own prime minister, government and parliament.

When violence erupted in the streets between marchers and police and between protesters and Protestants, the IRA was insignificant and had been for some years. It had virtually ceased to exist. Fearful Catholics who had been discriminated against for so many years in housing, jobs and education and who felt they had no protectors against loyalist militants ridiculed the initials as 'I Ran Away'. As though to confirm the saying 'There is no Irish problem, only a British problem', Westminster politicians, bogged down in the face of obduracy they little understood, instituted policies that enabled republican terrorism to revive and to grow into a force more menacing than it had ever been before. There was no influential body of informed journalistic opinion in the national media to give early warning against crass political action or to ventilate alternative views. Journalists from London were as mystified as were the politicians from London.

For a few years in the early 1970s, when the bombings and shootings were horrifyingly novel, civilised society in a part of the United Kingdom seemed to be about to collapse. The atmosphere was so sensitive that for the first time in the

United Kingdom reporters, particularly on instant radio and vivid television, had to be concerned that what they said and showed might quickly provoke more violence. An innocent mistake or an over-excited report could ignite a riot in the tight, nervous streets, and behind the rioters, the snipers would go to work.

Over the years though, another message became obvious. In times of trouble, especially civil disturbance, people want news they can trust. They need reliable information quickly. If they do not get it, rumour and exaggeration take over. When society is stressed by destructive dissent, to be kept in the dark makes matters much worse. In the absence of firm news, the bomb that killed two is believed to have killed five. A police raid on a house to find weapons becomes persecution. The police eventually realised this. The army learned more slowly that if they did not promptly give their version of events to reporters, local gossip would be even more powerful than it need be, determining entirely what people believed.

Government politicians were more reluctant to accept the message that facts and fears were best brought into the open. They expected broadcasters to deal with Northern Ireland in a subdued way. They created a big fuss over programmes they did not like. It did not matter that the programme had not yet been broadcast and that they had not yet seen it. Their noise unsettled the broadcasting authorities who sometimes caved in and who sometimes went ahead regardless. A huge controversy fanned by government lasted for weeks in the early 1970s over an intended BBC television programme, *A Question of Ulster*, which was to be mainly a studio debate to examine the issues. After it was shown, people wondered what all the fuss had been about. The sentiment was echoed years later in 1985 after another television programme, *Real Lives: At The Edge of the Union*, stopped by the governors of the BBC after encouragement by the home secretary, was eventually shown on the insistence of the director general, Alasdair Milne. One of the most brilliant television documentaries ever made, *Hang Up Your Brightest Colours*, an account of the life of the Irish patriot, rebel and terrorist, Michael Collins, by the Welsh actor-cum-film maker, Kenneth Griffith, was banned in 1973 by Lew Grade, boss of ATV, the independent television company for whom it had been made. There was no sign of government interference – the film simply touched too many raw nerves. It was history too painfully alive to be shown after half a century and more. It indicated sympathy for Irish republicanism at a time republican terrorists were murdering civilians, police officers and soldiers. The film was shelved. Twenty years went by before it was shown on British television, and then it was the BBC that showed it.

Tension between journalism and authority continued throughout the years of violence. A BBC reporter, Bernard Falk, went to gaol for a few days in Belfast in 1971, an early stage of the turmoil, because he refused to identify a man in court as the IRA man he had interviewed earlier. In 1992, Channel 4 was heavily fined for refusing to tell the RUC about a source for a programme, *The Committee*, in the *Dispatches* series and which alleged collusion between the police and loyalist killers. In between, in countless rows, programme journalists were bullied by government ministers and other politicians, condemned by officials, police and army, doubted by their own bosses, and eventually restricted by the Northern Ireland broadcasting ban of 1988. They had a great deal more trouble from authority than they had from terrorists.

Ireland

The British news media's ambivalence towards Ireland, an object of sentimental indulgence and political exasperation, is reflected in a reluctance to refer to 'Ireland', other than in sport and the Eurovision song contest. In news coverage of politics and terrorism, it is usually 'The Irish Republic', occasionally 'The Republic of Ireland' or less often 'Southern Ireland' when it could frequently and reasonably be plain 'Ireland' in accordance with international law and without any harm to the separate claims of 'Northern Ireland'. The distinction follows the preference of British governments and the unionists of Northern Ireland who see in a name a danger of default. It is also part of the mischief of Irish politics. For the founders of the

Irish Free State and later the Republic of Ireland it would have been treachery to have adopted 'The Republic of Southern Ireland'.

Other misnomers apply. Northern Ireland is still referred to as Ulster and the title of this historic Irish kingdom is appropriated in 'Ulster Unionists'. It is a misnomer because true Ulster consists of nine counties, three of which, to ensure a protestant majority in the North, are in the Republic, with six in Northern Ireland. Hence, the partition of Ireland was also a partition of Ulster, giving rise to yet another politically motivated variation, 'The Six Counties'. It continues to be used, always with a political flavour. It is not generally acceptable without qualification in British news reports.

The name 'Eire' is now an oddity rarely used, an out-of-date reference which, in its time, was another way of not saying Ireland while using the meaning in Erse, now usually called Gaelic.

Politically sensitive, well-meaning people in Ireland who try to avoid the distractions of name and the tangles of resentment they reflect will be heard referring to 'the South of Ireland' and 'the North of Ireland'. These labels do not appeal much to unionists, unbending as many are, partly because they are acceptable to republicans, obdurate as many are.

The North

In a British context, the term 'The North' is liable to be ill received in a way that does not apply to 'The South'. The resentment has two causes. One is that many people in 'The North' feel their economic and social interests have persistently been neglected over the years by remote governments with limited Westminster perspectives. Media references to 'The North' evoke the sense of dismissal. The other cause has to do with geographic realities. It is not clear whether 'The North' means the North of England or whether it includes Scotland as well. To a lowland Scot, 'The North' is likely to evoke Wick, Inverness and other places in northern Scotland. It means something else to a person in South Wales.

Journalists who care write about 'the North of England and Scotland' and avoid the lumpen generality 'Northerners'. Other references are as precise as possible: 'the North West of England' or 'the North East of England'. They acknowledge that 'The North' does not exist other than as a sign on the motorway.

Scilly Isles

An editorial issue from the Scilly Isles is that people there do not like the most frequent and most natural form of the name. Scillonians say it sounds as though they live on the 'Silly Isles'. Journalists who want to avoid offence to the Scillys, which form is equally objected to, use 'Isles of Scilly'.

chapter thirteen – the law

evasion and default

Journalists are not the best respecters of the law. They chafe against it when it impedes what they want to do, as it often does. Without publicly admitting it, many of them take the view by their behaviour that it is a matter of what they can get away with. In Britain, the attitude applies to official secrets and to confidentiality where, in both cases, the law is immoderate. It applies to defamation where, for some victims, the ordeal of a court hearing into painful personal matters is a worse prospect than tolerating an unjustified slur. It applies frequently to news reports of notorious criminal cases when they are at the preliminary hearing stage in court, that is, before trial. The boldest British news organisations, usually national newspapers, will go ahead with a report that clearly breaks the law on what can be made public when reporting restrictions of preliminary hearings are not lifted, a law that specifies what can be said, leaving all else forbidden. These news organisations go ahead with an offending report in the knowledge that they are very unlikely to be prosecuted for contempt.

Not all journalistic transgressions are pre-meditated. Some are the result of ignorance, the work of people new to the job, who have not had any training or who have not taken to heart the advice of lawyers and grizzled editors that they must learn what laws impinge on their work. The point of the advice is not to encourage journalists to answer difficult legal questions for themselves. They are rarely competent for that. The idea is to have them recognise areas of legal risk, to know what is allowable and what is not in the elementary areas, and to make sure editors are aware of difficult cases.

In the unspoken part of the journalist code, it is one thing to risk the law knowingly, which includes alerting a superior in good time, another to risk it ignorantly, and much worse, to do it knowingly without alerting anyone else who should know.

lawyers and legal referral

As costs rise, competition grows fiercer and income gets squeezed, legal referral is an area of economy. The price of failure to seek legal advice may be much greater than the cost saved but the reality for many news organisations, particularly for small ones like independent local radio and local newspapers on small profit margins, is that experienced journalists must make most of the decisions on legal issues, that some issues will be evaded by manipulating the words and that some important truths will be unsaid because the risk is too great. It has been the situation for a good many years.

Ideally, any legal doubt, however small, should be referred to a lawyer. Few organisations can afford it. Only the biggest – the national newspapers, the BBC and the ITV companies – can bear the cost of frequent legal advice. Legal decisions by experienced journalists have to suffice for routine matters. It is not a great difficulty much of the time, so long as the news is ordinary. It is usually clear what can safely be said about an incident, such as a road accident, that might have legal implications, whether reporting a court hearing is restricted, that privilege extends to official local council sittings and documents, and whether a critical non-privileged statement goes too far for comfort.

Beyond the routine, lawyers are necessary. Reporting does not have to be very bold to be risky. When it is tough and investigative, its best friend is a good lawyer. No one else can properly advise on any of a host of questions and the multitude of their variations – on contempt, defamation, confidentiality, the wisdom of an apology, the extent of privilege for a document, and what to say to a judge who wants an explanation for a report he did not like on a criminal trial in his court. What a good lawyer cannot protect against are naive journalists, an ever-present danger. They are the journalists who, understandably ignorant of difficult legal answers, inexcusably do not know what the potential pitfalls are. They proceed blithely, unaware that they and their paper or their programme have a problem. The adage that used to adorn newsrooms and was written on the nervous hearts of new-comers, 'If in doubt, leave it out', is defeated by the journalist who does not know enough to have a doubt.

contempt of court

The books on media law do not prepare journalists for the waywardness of the workings of contempt in English law, and the situation is worse since the Contempt Act of 1981 which was supposed to improve matters. The concept of contempt is reasonably clear but its application in the English system is unpredictable. It operates as a catch-all because it refers to anything that might seriously impede or prejudice the course of justice. As a result, journalists in England and Wales are often caught unawares. This compares badly with the Scottish system where the law of contempt is more rigorously enforced, perhaps too rigorously, but where, at least, journalists know better when they are most likely to fall foul of it.

In practice, few charges of contempt are upheld in England and Wales while many are attempted. They arise usually from current cases in the Crown and the County Courts. They are raised quite often by defence lawyers arguing that the right of the accused to a fair trial has been damaged by a report in the local paper, by comments on the local radio station or by a report in the regional television news. In such cases, much rests on the attitude of the judge in charge of the court. Sometimes, the judge initiates the complaint about coverage of a case – ominous for the journalist. Confronting the temper of the law, in the person of an offended judge, is a daunting ordeal for reporter, producer, editor or whoever is called to account, even when, in the end, it is decided they have not offended. The accusation and the process of being examined are punishing enough whatever the outcome.

The assistant editor of the *Evening Herald*, a local paper in Plymouth, experienced the ordeal in a case that illustrates how widely the net of contempt might be thrown. It was the time of the Robert Maxwell financial scandal not long after his death. His sons, concerned for their own legal well-being, had refused to answer some questions before a House of Commons committee. The *Evening Herald* in its comment column said people would draw their own conclusions, as sensible juries did when a defendant would not speak. Although the paper was commenting on a prominent public matter of national significance acted out in a political arena many miles away, a Crown Court judge in the Plymouth area was disturbed. He thought that, as a result of the *Herald*'s comment, jurors in his court, in cases in no way connected with the Maxwell affair, might draw a wrong conclusion if an accused stayed silent. He called the paper to account. Assistant editor with barrister had to appear before him. Although the judge was persuaded the paper had a right to comment as it did, his zeal in calling it to account was seriously misplaced. His concern would have been understandable had the *Herald* been commenting on a continuing case before him. But even then, a warning to the jury not to be influenced would probably have been enough.

The Plymouth and other cases of judicial anxiety suggest that juries have to be protected from the real world, that they cannot be trusted to concentrate their minds on what they have heard in court, that their good sense is liable to be subverted by irrelevant, as well as relevant, noises outside, all of which runs counter to considered legal opinion at the highest levels, expressed time and again, that ordinary people exercise very robust good sense when serving as jurors and when guided clearly as to their duties.

Concern about contempt boiled up over coverage, particularly in popular newspapers, of the infamous case of Frederick West who was charged in 1994 with multiple murders in the English West Country after bodies were found buried at his home. Lawyers and police warned repeatedly of the dangers of prejudicing West's right to a fair trial. Opinion went so far as to suggest that a fair trial would be impossible. Parts of the media certainly went further in pre-trial publicity than they had gone before, a reflection that the case, reported all over the world, was more remarkable and macabre than any for years. Concern bubbled over after West was found hanged in a prison cell before he could be tried. The concern attached to the case of West's wife, Rosemary, who was also charged with murders. Lawyers and MPs suggested that her chances of a fair trial would be seriously damaged – a fear which an independent radio station in London might have been trying to confirm when it carried a crass trail, a day or two after West's death and before any decision on it in a coroner's court, saying 'With Frederick West dead could his wife now seek the same way out of her problems?' Throughout the West controversy, those fearful for the interests of justice predicated their fears on an assumed inability of juries to detach themselves from what they have read and heard months before, a contradiction of years of experience in which the outstanding cases of miscarriage of justice were caused not by prejudices of juries but by failures of experts.

Courts other than the criminal courts are equally sensitive, and over-sensitive, to contempt. A regional BBC newsroom had a lesson in the dangers of upsetting coroners as a result of television pictures taken in the street. An inquest into a controversial death was going on in the centre of town when a cameraman used a long lens to take pictures of the outside of the court on an upper floor. Unfortunately, the long lens enabled the camera to look through the windows into the court. The pictures were innocuous, from an unrevealing angle showing a clock on a wall and a talking head and shoulders. But, as they were of the court or its precincts, they should not have been taken or shown. The matter was reported to the coroner after the pictures were shown in the news later that day. The BBC apologised readily and without reservation.

Though no harm was done, it was many weeks before the matter was dropped, and not until after one of the editorial people was interviewed by police under caution.

Pictures of people well away from the precincts of a court but included in a report of a case may be in contempt if they include and might identify a witness who was allowed to give evidence without being named openly. And other opportunities for contempt seem to multiply. They include the dangers of a report inadvertently including even a little evidence not yet given in court but passed on to reporters to help them with background coverage once the case is over: a special name for an illicit drug slipped into one news report that was subsequently upbraided as a serious contempt. Interviews with witnesses before they have given or finished evidence, and intended for 'backgrounders' after a trial is over, have also been condemned on the grounds that witnesses might stick to a questionable version of events because they have already committed themselves to it in the interview.

Another way in which reporters and news writers are liable to be in contempt, and in trouble, and which occurs chronically, is over news reports of what is said in court in the absence of the jury. A judge may, for instance, tell a jury to leave the court while counsel argue whether a particular witness can be allowed to give evidence. Fascinating and newsworthy as these exchanges often are, they are kept from the jury in the belief they might prejudice its deliberations and, accordingly, the substance cannot be reported in case jurors, reading or hearing of them, are wrongly influenced. For newspapers and news programmes one of the problems with this contempt is that the original offence may be contained in copy giving no clue that the jury was out. And when there is no clue, there is no suspicion that the story is legally dubious.

The old newspaper rule that court copy be meticulously checked is much overlooked, and the neglect of it in the haste of broadcasting is worse. Journalistic inexperience and journalistic enterprise, pressing broadcasting deadlines and legal sensitivity combine to make contempt one of the worst of all editorial pitfalls. While no precaution is infallible, well-intended programmes and papers check back with sources whenever possible, lawyers are consulted for advice, dubious content is left out until the risk is weighed, and journalistic teams are made to study media law – this last, not to encourage them to make their own legal decisions but to make them realise where problems lie.

injunctions

An injunction, in Scotland an interdict, is a court order that stops a newspaper or a programme – or anyone – from doing what they intended, sometimes from doing what they had not thought of but which someone fears might occur to them. An order may stop an entire programme or article, or only parts. Frequently, an order forbids publication of a person's name and other identifying details, that is to preserve anonymity, as did the injunction that guarded the biggest of the early winners of the national lottery in Britain in 1994 only to be cancelled the following day after newspaper challenges. In America, the process is known as 'prior restraint'. There, it is very rare, regarded as a fundamental affront to freedom of expression. In Britain, it is a familiar device, a ready legal gag for determined interests to protect themselves against prying reporters. Its effects are often little recognised because many orders are low profile, stopping people from knowing that they are being denied anything.

Occasionally a notorious case discloses the power of the gagging process. One was the interdict by a Scottish court in 1995 that stopped a BBC interview with the prime minister, John Major, in the weekly *Panorama* programme from being shown in Scotland. Opposition parties had sought the order because no equivalent interviews with other party leaders were intended in the few days before local Scottish elections. The *Spycatcher* case was also notorious. In it, in 1987 and beyond, injunctions stopped publication and sale in Britain of the book, the memoirs of a former British intelligence officer, Peter Wright, and stopped also extracts in newspapers. In a connected string of events in 1987–8, another injunction stopped *My Country, Right or Wrong*, a BBC Radio 4 series on the

277

secret services. In these cases, a significant part of public opinion was scandalised, lacking sympathy for government action that prevented people in Britain reading what the rest of the world had ready access to, and from hearing a well considered radio examination of the role of the secret services that had been cleared through the D-Notice (now DA-Notice) process whereby the media gets advice on matters of national security. In both spy cases, the injunctions were granted on grounds that Wright in his book and intelligence service people, present and former, in the Radio 4 programmes had, by writing and talking about their jobs without authorisation, breached their life-long duty of confidentiality, an eloquent demonstration of the catch-all qualities of the confidentiality concept in English law. No one really believed that the book or the programmes would damage British interests. The legal actions were government fights on matters of excited principle. The determination to stop *Spycatcher* left no option but to move against *My Country . . .* One could not be allowed to escape while the other was blocked.

Interests other than confidentiality also provide grounds for an injunction. The London stage show, *Maxwell The Musical*, about the dead and discredited tycoon, Robert Maxwell, was stopped by a court order after lawyers for Maxwell's sons, Kevin and Ian, had persuaded a judge that their right to a fair trial many months ahead might be prejudiced if people were allowed to see the stage performance. This risible decision had many precursors. Sensitivity over trials has encouraged many injunctions. An opinion programme on BBC2 television, in the series *Fifth Column* in which individuals are allowed to have their say on a topic of their choice, had an injunction granted against it about five hours before broadcast. The injunction was sought and won by the Crown Prosecution Service because the individual in the programme, an expert on prisons who was to give his views on the prisons' regime in England, was to be a witness, as an expert, not a witness of evidence, in a trial then underway on Merseyside. The CPS argued that what the expert said in *Fifth Column* might harm the conduct of the case.

The BBC2 case illustrates a number of problems connected with the injunction process.

The prosecution service had asked the BBC to see a transcript of the programme to vet its suitability in view of the trial going on. As would any worthy journalistic organisation, the BBC refused on the grounds that it could not have interested outside bodies deciding, in effect, what it might broadcast and what it might not. The CPS went to a judge on Merseyside. He heard the CPS alone. The BBC was not represented, a one-sided action that is always liable to happen when injunctions are sought urgently which they often are. As the judge knew no more than the CPS about the content of the programme, he decided that on the face of it, a prejudice might occur. He granted an order. But he told the CPS that when they reported the order to the BBC, they had to say he would reconsider if the BBC was able to appear before him. This was later arranged. A lawyer for the BBC argued that nothing in the *Fifth Column* programme could possibly jeopordise the trial, as the CPS had been assured. It did not mention the case and nothing in the script was relevant to the case. The BBC agreed to let the judge see the script, not enthusiastically but on the grounds that he was an independent arbiter to be trusted – and that if he did not see it, the programme could not go ahead. On seeing the script, the judge saw no prejudice and lifted the injunction he had granted two hours earlier.

Normally, the granting and the lifting of an injunction are not so close together. A late injunction usually means that programme or article is held up for a week or so until the broadcasting organisation or newspaper against which the order is granted can put its arguments and evidence together and arrangements be made to hear them.

An injunction may be granted very late, much less than the five hours before broadcast in the BBC2 case. A Scottish television programme on an alleged war criminal was stopped after it had been running on screen for some time because the order against it was agreed after the programme had started. There have been cases of orders granted and notified shortly before transmission. In really urgent cases, a judge may hear the argument over the telephone when there is not time to see lawyers in person. Injunctions have been granted over the phone, and then notified to programme or newspaper by phone or fax.

Sometimes, after being granted, injunctions

are not contested. They therefore remain in force or are renewed or may lapse after a while because they have achieved their purpose. When contested soon after being imposed, the judge may lift an injunction, vary it or leave it as it was. If the injunction remains in force, the judge is saying that on the face of it, there is a case to be considered fully. Programme or article should not go ahead until a full hearing can decide whether a valid interest would, in fact, be seriously damaged. Few injunction cases get to a full hearing. They are either accepted, varied by agreement or withdrawn before that stage.

A category of injunction rarely challenged relates to wards of court. There are many of these wardship injunctions. They protect children of broken homes, those who are victims of abuse and neglect or those who are involved in unusual circumstances, such as a baby born to a surrogate mother. These orders prevent publicity that directly identifies the children or might indirectly lead to their identities becoming known. They often go as far as forbidding the media from trying to find out what they cannot make public. An order of that kind was granted to protect the daughter of Sarah Keays and the former cabinet minister, Lord Parkinson. Journalists cannot approach the school she attends, nor any place where she might have medical treatment. Challenges to such orders are rare because the media generally accept that they are imposed for very good reasons.

Occasionally, news organisations suspect that, besides protecting children who need protection, a wardship injunction hides a scandal or other matter of legitimate public interest. This was the case with an order preventing publicity about youngsters treated shamefully at a children's home. The media did not want to identify the children but were concerned that the terms of the order effectively prevented the public being told of the disgraceful things that had gone on at the home. The concern of the court was that even if children from the home were not named in media reports, but the home was, some people would know of children who had lived there and would in their gossip assume they had been abused.

Journalists confronted by injunctions may find themselves in a position where they have no acceptable options. When the Treasury Solicitor's

Office, acting for government in the Radio 4 *My Country, Right or Wrong* affair, asked to see a script of the programmes, the BBC refused to have its journalism overseen by a government department. Government lawyers accordingly went to a High Court judge, as they said they would. In arguing for an injunction, they produced, as grounds for suspecting breach of confidentiality, a few lines of publicity, a puff for the programme in the *Daily Telegraph*, which said 'spies were queuing up' to appear, a producer's tongue-in-cheek exaggeration. An order so wide-ranging was granted that had certain spy matters been raised in the House of Commons the BBC would not have been able to report them because Commons privilege for reporters does not extend to reports that would breach a court order. The terms of the injunction were eventually lessened so that they did not stop parliamentary reports but the programmes remained blocked. The BBC continued to refuse to let the government see scripts. So the case proceeded towards a full hearing.

The BBC seemed to have three options: to let the treasury solicitor vet the script; to refuse and to fight the case at a full hearing in the knowledge that the programme would do no harm; or to abandon the programmes unbroadcast. In effect, the first two merged into one option. The BBC chose to fight the order. As a result, documents had to be exchanged between the BBC and the government's lawyers, as in any legal action. And the documents included the scripts of the injuncted programmes. In other words, as part of the legal process, the government was able to do what the BBC had been resisting: to vet the scripts. When it did so, it found no objection and the injunction was lifted, allowing the programmes to be broadcast about five months late.

defamation

British law on defamation is a forbidding obstacle to honest criticism. It protects big reputations against big truths that cannot be proved as well as against big lies. It does very little for ordinary people, other than to keep them ignorant of plausible but unprovable allegations against public figures who solicit their support or who presume their respect. It encourages publication of trivial truth and discourages difficult disclosure by its emphasis on what damage is or is not done to personal reputation. Harmless untruth in bad journalism escapes while damaging disclosure in good journalism risks severe redress, punishment in effect, when meaning exceeds evidence provable in court.

Defamation law conspires with the law on confidentiality to make legally acceptable proof more difficult than is reasonable. Journalistic proof and court proof are often far apart. Many programmes and articles have never appeared, and some which have appeared have been apologised for and damages paid, not because they were wrong but because allegations in them could not be proved to the law's satisfaction. Journalists have known some, at least, of them to be right, as soundly based as many critical though non-personal stories that were published. But hard documentary evidence was lacking, or essential witnesses backed off when legal action started. Knowledgeable sources frequently talk willingly without consenting to be identified. Very occasionally, a key witness who was 'on the record' retracts and 'confesses' a mistake when the lawyers' letters fly. This can happen – and has happened – after publication or broadcast, as well as before. When it happens after, the newspaper or programme has to choose between paying damages to avert action in court on an allegation it knows to be true or going to court and paying out probably even more because a witness with much to lose will renege and lie. The chances of successfully exposing a renegade witness without other evidence are poor.

American journalism serves its public better partly because it is not so hindered. The law under which it operates recognises the special position of public figures, that they must be held to account and that, to achieve this, the tests on defaming them must be looser. To win a defamation case in America, a public figure has to prove that the allegation was false, that the publisher or broadcaster knew it to be false at the time, and that it was made public maliciously. This serves the American public better than it serves American public figures, an imperfection preferable to those in British defamation law. A High Court decision in Australia in 1994 moved their law in the same direction when an action by a member of parliament was dismissed on the grounds that the needs of freedom of speech denied politicians the full protection accorded to other citizens. The Australian decision stopped short of applying the ruling to all public figures. A similar court decision took India along the same route, and a body of legal opinion in Britain believes the British higher courts will eventually move that way. That possibility, whether or not it is likely, is stronger than the possibility of a change being legislated by parliament, especially at a time when many politicians are incensed by media invasions of the privacy of political and other public figures.

confidentiality

The concept of confidentiality is as legally strong as it is uncertain. Like the notion of property to which it is allied, it is dear to the heart of British law. Journalists run up against it because facts and documents in which they are interested have owners and the owners have rights to protect their belongings against unwanted disclosure. Newspapers or programmes using confidential information directly or indirectly depend heavily on legal advice. If the confidential facts have only a titillating value a court is not likely to support the breaking of the confidentiality. To persuade a judge that the confidential information should be made public against the wishes of the owners, journalists need to be able to argue that a significant public good would be served. The best case for this is when the information exposes an iniquity. It is not enough to argue that it is interesting, or even very interesting.

The need to persuade a judge arises when the owners of confidential information learn in advance that it is to be made public and object. They are able to seek an injunction, if necessary at the very last moment, even after a programme has started or after a newspaper story has been set. Court orders of this kind have been sought, obtained and served over

283

the telephone and by fax. Because of the threat of prior restraint by injunction, journalists who intend to use confidential information try to protect their intentions against leaks. And even then, if they avoid an order to stop the information being made public, they might still have to deal with a claim for damages if using the information did harm.

court reporting

The concept of open justice implies that trials are able to be reported and that many of them will be. But the law hesitates to accord a formal place to the media, and a strong body of experienced journalistic opinion, particularly in newspapers, agrees with it. This view says the best position, overall, for journalism is to have only the same rights as the citizen, no privileges, no special constitutional protection, adding darkly that once granted, special rights can be used as a pressure by the threat to remove them. Accordingly, news reporters in British courts have the citizen's access. It is a bit of a fiction. Besides extra facilities granted to reporters, like the press bench and, for big cases, the setting aside of even more space taken from the public gallery, the right, the desirability and the importance of the media interest is attested in many high judicial judgments. When it chooses, the legal system recognises the media interest as special.

Media organisations are not charged with special duties in return. Reporters from newspapers, radio and television can turn up in court or not turn up. They can decide not to report as they see fit, and unless special conditions apply, what they do report is for them to decide. The nearest thing to a rule of reporting relates to the protection they get from court privilege. It says they cannot be sued for what is in their reports so long as reports published within a reasonable time of the case, that is contemporaneously, are 'fair and accurate'. To satisfy this thin condition, programmes and newspapers are supposed, strictly speaking, to avoid the temptation to report only the juicy opening allegations in long trials, then no more until verdicts and sentences. To be 'fair' they are expected also to report the defence though it may be nothing like as newsworthy, and may be hollow. However much space they have, newspapers and programmes are often so squeezed by other, more news-grabbing events that duller parts of cases are neglected regardless of how important they are. If pressed, the law would not accept this as good reason for seriously unfair omission, and decent journalism would not. Many long-run cases are, however, treated in a cavalier way without legal complaint.

Court reporting at local level is not as routine as it used to be, mainly because reporters are expensive, and when it is not done at local level, it does not reach national level when it deserves to. The trend is further encouraged by charges increasingly imposed on the news media for court lists and other information about cases coming up or already dealt with. These can be especially forbidding for small newsrooms, particularly in small local radio stations and small papers, operating on very small newsgathering budgets. The Lord Chancellor's Department, in line with the spirit that everything must be paid for, dismissed a plea against charges with the argument 'The function of the magistrates' courts is not to act as a news-gathering service for the media, and it would seem quite wrong for the taxpayer . . . to subsidise what are, after all, the commercial requirements of commercial organisations.' This says, in effect, that news organisations have to bear extra cost to extract from a public service information for the public about activities the public has already paid for.

court reporting: court orders

The perils of court reporting include restriction orders that are not always as well known as they need to be. Journalists know well enough of the standard, statutory restrictions on reporting, particularly those on coverage of preliminary hearings, like committals, which severely limit what can be in the news – and which are sometimes partly ignored by brash national tabloids, usually without penalty. But, since the early 1980s, an infection of ad hoc restriction has hit the English courts, notably at Crown Court and magistrate level. This is what the master of the rolls seemed to be referring to when in 1993 he cautioned against a 'creeping veil of anonymity over court proceedings'. The prevalence of these restrictions is not well known and particular orders are often not known about. They stop the reporting of all manner of facts: an entire trial because reports might prejudice a later, connected trial, the name of a witness, the identity of a victim, one or more of the charges, the connection between an accused and a witness.

The date, the early 1980s, is significant. The outbreak of restriction stems from the Contempt Act of 1981, a law the lord chancellor of the time assured newspeople would improve things for them. His blithe assurance was quickly damned by events. Judges, with large powers in regard to the conduct of any case in their court, as they all have, began to make orders restricting newspaper and broadcast reports of cases before them. The orders are made mostly at the behest of defence counsel and, whatever the stated legal reason, they limit the damage to accused clients, and in the tight world of the law where news of successful ploys travels fast, the tendency to seek orders spreads enthusiastically.

Some of the restrictions make sense. Some are unjustified, a few ridiculous. Though at heart they are meant to protect an individual's right to fair trial, they often stray beyond that vital and narrow consideration. In the early days of the Contempt Act, a judge made an order preventing the naming of a witness, a young woman, daughter of a notable father, on the grounds pressed by her lawyer who told the court she had recently been unwell and publicity arising from the case might make her ill again. The restriction had no conceivable connection with the accused's right to a fair trial or to the proper conduct of the case. Years later, magistrates banned the naming of a child victim, who was dead, for no other reason than they thought the memory of the child should be untroubled. A few restrictions, especially in the lowest courts, are so absurd they may be ignored without fear of serious reprisal – provided a lawyer with good experience advises that the order is clearly beyond the powers of the person who made it.

Many orders, though contentious, are decently motivated. They may aim to prevent any publicity outside the court that a particular witness will be a defendant in a later hearing. Here the grounds for restriction are likely to be that the jury in the case going on should have the information to take into account or to dismiss as it sees fit under the careful direction of the judge, but that the facts should not be known in advance to the people as yet unchosen who will be on the jury at the later trial. Another, overlapping area for frequent restriction and great difficulty comes with what are known as 'severed trials'. These are trials, usually of complex cases, like large company fraud, where lawyers ask for some of the charges against the same defendants to be detached and taken at a later trial. It makes juridical sense in areas of corporate malpractice that are forbiddingly complicated and, correspondingly, have highly complicated law to be applied to them. It also tends to work to the advantage of the public image of the accused, encouraging the impression that company criminals are a better class of thieves. When it is done for the sake of juries, it also underestimates their ability to weigh what is relevant and to dismiss what is not.

Decently motivated as they often are or improperly motivated as they may be, restriction orders during trials are increasingly frequent – and frequently not fully justified. The contentious element is often that they go too far, stopping news more thoroughly than it need be stopped. The good general rule that restrictions should be rare and then as narrow as possible is not best observed by hard pressed judges whose decisions will be attacked by alert lawyers if they possibly can be.

When restrictions are imposed in high profile cases, they are, at least, widely known. They are often made also in relation to cases that are not immediately interesting and therefore ignored by the news media but which may later become newsworthy. There lies the danger of not knowing about them. A restriction order made the week before, perhaps even before the trial proper has begun, may not have been written down as the law requires and may be known only to court officials, and then vaguely, until a reporter innocently transgresses.

Orders can be overturned and to this end the

law has been changed, largely as a result of the efforts of the London court reporter, Tim Crook, to allow journalists formally to challenge them. Restrictions imposed in high profile cases, especially orders that nothing or almost nothing may be reported until the second severed trial, are often challenged by broadcasting organisations and national newspapers. And the striking aspect of these challenges is that most succeed, a strong indication that too many restriction orders are ill-considered. When a challenge succeeds, costs are often met out of public funds to the relief of news budgets.

A challenge after a case is over is occasionally thought worthwhile for the sake of precedent though it can have no effect on the reporting of the case from which it arose, as with an appeal by Central Television and the BBC against a decision by a judge in the Midlands. When, in late afternoon, a jury retired to an hotel before deliberating the next day, the judge ordered that no reports of the case should be broadcast on radio or television that night or at breakfast-time the next morning so the jury could listen and watch without hearing anything about the case they were considering. It was an outstandingly unreasonable order as the media could not legally have reported anything the jury did not already know. Central and the BBC failed in an attempt to challenge the order right away. The order was overturned some months later when the case was long dead.

Restrictions in many, low profile cases go unchallenged because challenge is time-consuming, potentially expensive and belated instead of immediate, as in the Midlands case. It remains very difficult successfully to challenge orders by magistrates if they are impatient of the media interest, not readily accepting it as representing an aspect of the public interest. Sometimes they are not even prepared to listen to the media argument. As their cases are apt to be one day wonders, the newsworthiness has evaporated by the time a challenge in a higher court can be mounted and heard.

court reporting: titles

For some years there has been a weakening of the long-time convention of news reporting from the courts that the accused lost their titles, in particular the simple prefixes 'Mr, Mrs and Miss' and their younger relative 'Ms'. The law says nothing about it, and some news organisations, encouraged by a body of committed outside opinion, have embraced the policy that 'Wilson' is 'Mr Wilson' unless and until he is found guilty. Older journalists tend to feel more comfortable when telling the public of alleged misdeed that plain 'Wilson' is accused of it. The old convention was easier in that under the better mannered policy 'Mr Wilson' none the less pointedly becomes unadorned 'Wilson' on guilty verdict although media publicity and loss of title, while part of shame, are no part of legal punishment.

Each news organisation makes its own decision, and whichever it is, finds it hard to stick to. Consistency in favour of the courteous title tends to fade when 'Mr Accused' is charged with sickening crimes that have excited public outrage before arrest. Alleged terrorists, alleged abducters, alleged brutal attackers and alleged child molesters stand a strong chance of losing their titles, fairly or unfairly, as soon as they are charged.

court reporting: wild allegations

Every now and again a notable person is maligned in court, usually by a defendant desperate for a defence or vindictively eager to spread the blame. The accused drags in the name of a public figure, claiming shady deals, corrupt payments, or other favours, perhaps sexual, or a cover-up, a favourite allegation. All this is, naturally, well reported. The same fate frequently strikes lesser people with less noise and with far less shaking of heads. When it happens to an MP, fellow members commiserate and threaten legislation to stop it. When it happens to Mr or Mrs Ordinary, reaction is negligible. Sometimes an allegation is justified and if it is an important truth no one unaffected need fret that it has come out. When the allegation is unfounded and when the individual is not in court then or later to rebut, it is grossly unfair however small or large the reputation.

Politicians stirred to talk about measures against wild allegations would ban publication of maligned names, probably on a judge's say-so. A ban on reporting a name could be accompanied by an order not to say the naming was banned. More than that, judges might be empowered to ban reporting of the entire allegation: no name and no reporting of what the name was alleged to have done. The water gets deeper and murkier. Reports would be obliged to leave out evidence, another blow to open justice, giving wings to rumour and gossip. It would encourage suspicion, the belief there was something nasty to hide, which indeed there might be and which should not be hidden. It could not possibly stay within the walls of the court. Reporters gossip outside – and so do people in the public gallery. Such a ban would encourage a whispering society.

Whatever newspapers and broadcasters can eventually do in the interests of fairness when people are implicated in court in their absence with no opportunity to rebut, they can do little during the case. The danger of reporting a denial by the 'name' outside a court while the case continues is that, in effect, it accuses a witness of falsehood, maybe perjury, an encouragement to the jury not to accept the witness as reliable, an interference from outside the court in the process of justice, a potential contempt. Very occasionally, a slim-line denial is considered acceptable on legal advice and able to be repeated when the allegation is renewed in court and reported. Once the case is over, programmes and newspapers can offer to carry a more detailed rebuttal. By this time though, the victim of an unsubstantiated allegation may wish not to revive the slur by giving it the attention of denial. When a denial is issued, it warrants legal clearance: it could, for instance, defame a witness, effectively declaring evidence to be a lie, without the protection of court privilege.

Prevention of Terrorism Act

Though not much used against journalists, the Prevention of Terrorism Act threatens them in unusual ways. As a law mainly to pursue the terrorists of Northern Ireland, it made it an offence for anyone not to volunteer significant information that would help the police in the fight against terrorism. The problem for journalists is obvious insofar as they as individuals are more likely than the general public as individuals to come across relevant information. Such information does not have to be 'hot' facts, say about where weapons may be found. It could be where, when and how the reporter met a source connected with terrorists. To that extent, the law has a special relevance for journalists. Adding to it, journalists are specially threatened by the power the Act gives the police to require information and material to be handed over. The police are able, in some circumstances and if necessary in conjunction with emergency powers, to demand material without any court order and to arrest anyone who refuses. The power was used against the BBC in Northern Ireland in 1988 when it was compelled to hand over television pictures of the mobbing of the two soldiers who ran into a funeral procession in Belfast. Other parts of the Act were used against Channel 4 and the independent producer, Box Productions, when the Northern Ireland police, the RUC, won a court order for material to be handed over after a 1991 *Dispatches* programme, *The Committee*, alleged a conspiracy between the police and loyalist paramilitaries. Police again used the Prevention of Terrorism Act against Channel 4 and another independent producer, Just Television, after a programme on unofficial justice, including knee-cappings and beatings, meted out in Northern Ireland by the IRA. In that case, they were refused a court order. In a rare success for the media and when the overtures of peace were strong, the judge said the police had failed to prove the material they wanted would be of substantial value in a terrorist investigation.

paying witnesses

The prospect of another legal curb on the reckless British media emerged noisily after the trial in 1995 of Rosemary West, a Gloucester woman found guilty of the murder of ten children and young women, joint charges evaded by her husband Fred when he killed himself before trial. Journalists from all over the world went to the town in the English West Country as more and more bodies were found beneath the Wests' house. It was one of the most horrific series of murders and the media thirsted for the full, macabre personal stories of witnesses in the trial.

Some of the witnesses might easily have become murder victims had events years before been a little different. Others, not potential victims, knew a great deal about the murderous, sex-obsessed couple. Their stories were worth big money. The media interviewed many witnesses before they gave evidence in court. Reporters talked to them at length to write detailed accounts ready for publication as soon as the trial was over. Fees reportedly paid or promised included hundreds of pounds for lesser witnesses, thousands for more important witnesses, and £100,000 for one.

It was a tarnished triumph for cheque-book journalism because very soon there were powerful calls for the practice to be banned. Lawyers, politicians and social commentators complained in outrage. The grounds of complaint were at times that no one should profit from events so disgusting, from the violence and sexual abuse inflicted on the victims by the Wests. Personal profit from pain and grief is immoral, so the argument ran, a line of logic intended to condemn and down which journalists escape as its validity is suspect unless we are also to condemn handsome professional fees for anyone involved in the administration of criminal justice and other civilised services made necessary by personal suffering. The weakness of the argument is typical of the weakness of the value judgements used by indignant critics of the media.

Lawyers were concerned about another aspect: that payments could pervert the course of justice. They might threaten fair trial. The argument is that money for stories in advance of evidence might cause witnesses questioned in court to stick to challengeable versions they have already given to reporters. They have invested in their story and they have a strong interest – the money – in refusing to budge from it though it may be unreliable.

It is a familiar complaint. It has been heard for years whenever journalists wave their newspapers' generous cheque books. It has been condemned by judges. Politicians have inveighed against it and plenty of journalists think it wrong. The newspapers' code of practice, as overseen by the Press Complaints Commission, reads forbiddingly. But as with much journalistic guidance and as befits a code drawn up by newspaper editors who know their commercial interests and the way the world works, it had a clear loophole. The version of the code current at the time of the West trial said:

> Payment or offers of payment for stories, pictures or information, should not be made directly or through agents to witnesses or potential witnesses in current criminal proceedings . . . except where the material concerned ought to be published in the public interest and the payment is necessary for this to be done.

In the aftermath of the horror of what was described in court in the West case, cheque-book journalists found it easy to argue that as much as possible should be made known to the public so they might better understand what happens in the social darkness. The events in Gloucester were important; people were concerned about them; they wanted to understand; there were blameless curiosities to be satisfied; there were valid issues to be explored. The payouts were in the public interest. Ignorance is not.

Journalists have more difficulty with the claim that payments might make witnesses unreliable. But this too suffers from a considerable weakness. In this, it is like the argument that media coverage hostile to accused people before trial endangers their right of fair trial by prejudicing the views of juries, an argument equally strongly heard from time to time, much heard in the early stages of the West story and in other cases the same year. The weakness is that there is little or no evidence for either confidently asserted belief. Both are based on surmise. 'It stands to reason' is what they amount to. On excited issues, 'standing to reason' is often a substitute for reason and hard fact. One of the beliefs assumes that jurors are so impressionable they cannot be trusted to concentrate exclusively on what they hear in court. The other says, in effect, that witnesses already paid or promised payment by the media are so craven they will be dishonest in court if necessary and so determined are they for their own profit that the famed skill of cross-examining lawyers cannot penetrate their paid-for version of events.

The problem of payments by the media was taken seriously enough to be officially considered by three senior members of government – the lord chancellor, who is generally responsible for the conduct of the legal system, the attorney general, the government's chief legal adviser, and the home secretary who is responsible for policy on crime. If necessary, the law would be changed.

Prosecution is possible under the Contempt Act of 1981. It does not specifically deal with payments, so does not forbid them. But under its terms, the media could be prosecuted for contempt if a payment to a witness 'creates a substantial risk that . . . justice . . . will be seriously impeded or prejudiced'. The attorney general launches such prosecutions. The attorney does not have to prove that a case has *actually* been prejudiced or impeded. But an attack on the media, especially on truculent national newspapers who make sure their interests are shouted loudly in public, courts embarrassment when risk alone is enough to decide guilt. It is like convicting an alleged thug, without evidence that he has harmed anyone, because his existence is held to be a risk to other people. Witnesses bold enough to accept payment would hotly resist any suggestion that their evidence was tainted. Unlike routine risks of prejudice, this one does not depend on the say-so of the judge in charge of any case said to have been prejudiced.

A law specifically to make interviews and payments illegal lacks merit. It is easy to make it a criminal offence to pay or to offer payment or to promise payment to witnesses or potential witnesses in trials. The issues and variations arising are not easy. They create many reasonable objections. A comprehensive ban would stop news interviews with eye-witnesses at scenes of crime, such as bank robberies. If the law stopped interviews *after* as well as before and during trials, as with the Contempt Act ban on interviewing jurors, it would be a gross interference. It would scandalously reduce the dissemination of important knowledge. To stop *paid* interviews but not *unpaid* interviews before trials would continue the supposed risk of prejudice: you do not have to be paid to develop a commitment to views attached to your name. To stop interviews, paid or unpaid, until trials were over would encourage unseemly auctions virtually on the steps of the court. And if profit-seeking witnesses are as unscrupulous as the critics say, there is nothing to stop them dramatising their evidence to improve their future gain. Restrictive laws invite evasion or avoidance or calculated defiance – not least in the media.

index